BANFF NATIONAL PARK

ANDREW HEMPSTEAD

Contents

Although every effort was made to make sure the information in this book was accurate when going to press, research was impacted by the COVID-19 pandemic and things may have changed since the time of writing. Be sure to confirm specific details, like opening hours, closures, and travel guidelines and restrictions, when making your travel plans. For more detailed information, see p. 157.

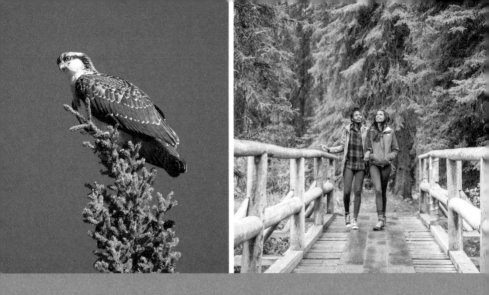

DISCOVER

Banff National Park

Banff is the crown jewel in Canada's national park system and famous for its awe-inspiring sights.

Be sure to get a photo of the colorful Lake Louise and drive the Icefields Parkway. Bike along the shoreline of Lake Minnewanka. Visit Taylor Lake when fall colors are at their height. Canoe across Bow Lake. Hike into the backcountry Mount Assiniboine Provincial Park. Get a glimpse of the park you won't see in the tourist brochures.

Clockwise from top left: osprey; Fenland Trail; Lake O'Hara; bighorn sheep; wildflowers; Bow Lake.

7 TOP
EXPERIENCES

1 **Visit Lake Louise:** Backdropped by glacially clad peaks, its famous turquoise waters are the starting point for spectacular hiking trails (page 75).

2 **See Wildlife:** You will see wildlife, including bighorn sheep, elk, and even wolves—but you'll need to have some patience (page 19).

3 **Head into the Backcountry:** Leave the crowds behind and experience true wilderness at a backcountry lodge (page 88).

4 **Fly into Mount Assiniboine Provincial Park:** Dotted with alpine lakes and laced with hiking trails, access to this park is only on foot or by helicopter (page 101).

5 **Hit the Trails:** Banff is a destination for hikers. Outings range from short strolls to all-day treks (page 15).

^^^
^^

6 **Enjoy Winter Wonders:** Although winter is low season, there's still plenty to do:, including skating, skiing, snowshoeing, and sleigh rides (page 17).

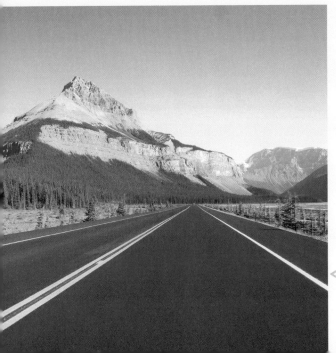

7 **Drive the Icefields Parkway:** This scenic highway will take your breath away (page 90).

<<<

Explore Banff National Park

The Best of Banff

A week in Banff will give you the opportunity to really get to know the park and its personality. You'll see all the famous attractions, as well as some lesser-known ones. For this summer itinerary, the focus should be on the outdoors, so pack your hiking boots.

Base yourself in one spot for the entire week. I've mentioned several lodging options below so you can find the place that matches your interests.

Day 1

Check into your hotel. Spend an hour or so wandering around **downtown Banff** to get a lay of the land. Stop by the visitor center, stroll along the river, explore local history at the **Whyte Museum of the Canadian Rockies** and wander the **Cascade of Time Garden.** Take the **Banff Gondola** to the top of Sulphur Mountain for magnificent views over the town to the lakes and mountains beyond.

Day 2

Spend the day hiking through the **Sunshine Meadows.** Reached by gondola, these meadows are filled with wildflowers between mid-July and mid-August. Hikes range from easy strolls like to a full day outing. Return to Banff and ride the chairlift to the **Cliffhouse Bistro** for evening drinks.

Day 3

Take a tour boat across **Lake Minnewanka,** then continue to nearby **Johnson Lake,** keeping an eye out for bighorn sheep en route. Drive the **Bow**

Banff Avenue

Top Hikes

Many visitors plan their entire vacation around hiking. Here is a list of personal favorites, each of which can easily be completed in a day by anyone with a reasonable level of fitness.

- **Tunnel Mountain** (p. 42)
- **Sunshine Meadows** (p. 44)
- **Bourgeau Lake** (p. 45)
- **Lake Agnes Trail** (p. 79)
- **Paradise Valley** (p.80)
- **Larch Valley** (p. 82)
- **Helen Lake** (p. 96)
- **Chephren Lake** (p.98)

Lake Agnes Trail

Valley Parkway, another wildlife hotspot, stopping at **Johnston Canyon,** where metal catwalks allow you to get up close and personal with numerous waterfalls. Check into **Baker Creek Mountain Resort** for two nights.

Day 4

Rise early and you'll enjoy the first rays of light hitting the Valley of the Ten Peaks at **Moraine Lake.** From the lake, take the easy one-hour hike to **Larch Valley,** a delightful place to spend the morning. Spend the afternoon exploring **Lake Louise**—hopefully you'll still have the energy to reach **Lake Agnes Teahouse,** where you can enjoy a snack.

Day 5

Head north along the famously scenic **Icefields Parkway**. The nonstop highlights include Bow Lake, Peyto Lake, and the Weeping Wall, as well as a seemingly endless panorama of snowcapped mountains. Stay at **Num-ti-jah Lodge** to be well positioned for tomorrow's hike.

Day 6

It's worth spending the full day on the adventurous hike to **Helen Lake.** This subalpine lake is perfectly placed: high above the tree line and surrounded by rugged peaks, with wildflowers and lots of marmots as a bonus. If you're reasonably fit, you can hike the trail in under three hours—and you'll be glad you did. Stay at Num-ti-jah Lodge a second night.

Day 7

Return to the town of Banff, enjoy lunch at the **Lookout Patio** at the **Fairmont Banff Springs** before heading downtown for some final souvenir shopping before heading home.

Planning Your Trip

When to Go

While Banff can be visited year-round, there are two influxes of visitors—one in the warmer months and the other in winter. Visit a month on either side of peak season—in June or September—to enjoy fewer crowds and discounted accommodations, but with the same great hiking that summer visitors enjoy. Be aware that many high alpine lakes remain frozen through June and you'll likely miss out on spring wildflowers.

SUMMER

Summer (late June-mid-Sept.) is definitely high season, especially the school holiday period of July through August and, in Calgary, the second week of July (Calgary Stampede). Simply said, the weather is unbeatable. The season is dominated by long, warm—and sometimes hot—days, everything is open, and there's plenty to do and see. Crowded parks, higher prices, and difficulty securing reservations are the downside of summer travel.

SPRING AND FALL

Late spring and early fall are excellent times to visit the Canadian Rockies for two reasons: You'll avoid the crowds, and you'll save money.

Spring (mid-Apr.-late June) is notable for long days of sunlight (in late June it stays light until after 10pm) and a sense of optimism for the upcoming warm months.

Fall (mid-Sept.-Nov.) can be delightful, especially September, with lingering warm temperatures and a noticeable decrease in crowds immediately after the long weekend (at the beginning of the month). While fall colors in general lack the intensity of those in the eastern provinces, larch turn a brilliant yellow throughout subalpine areas in mid- to late September.

WINTER

Local ski resorts begin opening for the winter (Dec.-mid-Apr.) in late November. The best powder snow conditions are January-February, although for enthusiasts looking for a combination of good snow and warmer weather, March is an excellent time of year to visit.

Before You Go

PASSPORTS AND VISAS

To enter Canada, a passport is required of citizens and permanent residents of the United States. For further information, see the website http://travel.state.gov. For current entry requirements to Canada, check the Citizenship and Immigration Canada website (www.cic.gc.ca).

All other foreign visitors must have a valid passport and may need a visa or visitors permit depending on their country of residence and the vagaries of international politics. At present, visas are not required for citizens of the United States, British Commonwealth, or Western Europe. The standard entry permit is for six months, and you may be asked to show onward tickets or proof of sufficient funds to last you through your intended stay.

Proof of Covid vaccination is currently required for visiting Canada.

PARK PASSES AND INFORMATION

Unless you're passing directly through, passes are required for entry into the park. Monies collected from these passes go directly to Parks Canada for park maintenance and improvements.

A National Parks Day Pass is adult $10, senior $8.40, up to a maximum of $20 per vehicle. It is interchangeable among parks and is valid until 4pm the day following its purchase. An annual Discovery Pass, good for entry into all of Canada's national parks and national historic

Winter Adventures

If you enjoy winter sports, you'll love traveling to Banff National Park between December and April. Instead of hiking and canoeing, you'll be skiing and snowshoeing in a magical mountain setting purified by snow. Many summer hiking trails are perfect for cross-country skiing in winter. After a long day of winter sports, there's no better way to soothe sore muscles than soaking in one of the region's many hot springs. End each day relaxing around a roaring fire each evening.

- **Downhill skiing:** Banff National Park holds three major ski resorts—**Lake Louise, Sunshine Village,** and **Norquay.**

- **Cross-country skiing:** The **Canmore Nordic Centre** is laced with cross-country trails, and it hosts world-class competitions through the winter months.

- **Snowshoeing:** This a traditional form of northern transportation has become popular recreation. Many sports stores have rentals and will lead you in the right direction.

- **Dogsledding:** If you would like to try your hand at mushing, head to Canmore, where commercial operators offer trips.

- **Frozen Waterfalls:** One of the most unusual

skiing

winter activities in the Canadian Rockies is an **ice walk** to a frozen waterfall in **Johnston Canyon.**

sites for one year from purchase, is adult $70, senior $60, to a maximum of $140 per vehicle.

Both types of pass can be purchased at the park gates and tollbooths on the Icefields Parkway, at all park information centers, and at campground fee stations. For more information on passes, check the **Parks Canada** website (www.pc.gc.ca).

Banff Visitor Centre (224 Banff Ave., 403/762-1550, 8am-8pm daily mid-May-Sept., 9am-5pm daily Oct.-mid-May) is in downtown Banff. There is also an information desk at the Arrivals level of Calgary International Airport.

TRANSPORTATION
Visitors have the option of arriving by **road, rail,** or **air.** The main gateway city for flights from

North America and Europe is **Calgary,** while **Vancouver** is also a popular starting point. From these two cities, as well as points across Canada, scheduled train and bus services pass through the region year-round.

Banff and Canmore have excellent **public transit,** with buses linking the two communities as well as reaching popular tourist areas such as the campgrounds on Tunnel Mountain and the gondola base on Sulphur Mountain. However, the easiest way to get around is in your own vehicle or a rental.

Avoid the Crowds
Banff National Park can get very crowded, especially in summer. The most popular tourist

Ride public transit to avoid parking problems.

attractions are sometimes overwhelmed with visitors, parking is impossible to find, and every campsite and hotel room may be booked well in advance.

Rising early is the best way to avoid the crowds. Parking fills up at Moraine Lake before 6am (often earlier) and at Lake Louise before 7am. (Use **public transit** to avoid the parking hassle altogether). Try to arrive early whenever you can, whether you're planning on a lake cruise or hope to snag an outdoor table at a café.

Parks Canada and local municipalities have implemented many programs to deal with **traffic** and **parking problems.** Use the public transit provided through the south end of the park. Leave your vehicle at your lodge or campground and ride or catch a bus into town. Two helpful websites are www.banffparking.ca and www.pc.gc.ca/banffnow.

Most visitors will focus their time only on the most famous sights, but there are many lesser-known places that are equally as scenic. Escaping the crowds is easy if you are experienced in **backcountry hiking** (think Skoki Lodge near Lake Louise) or have the budget to include flying into **Mount Assiniboine Provincial Park.**

Banff National Park

This park encompasses some of the world's

most magnificent scenery. The snowcapped peaks of the Rocky Mountains form a spectacular backdrop for glacial lakes, fast-flowing rivers, and endless forests.

.   Deer, moose, elk, mountain goats, bighorn sheep, black and grizzly bears, wolves, and cougars inhabit the park's vast wilderness, while the human species is concentrated in the picture-postcard towns of Banff and Lake Louise—two of North America's most famous resorts. Banff is near the park's southeast gate, 128 kilometers (80 miles) west of Calgary. Lake Louise, northwest of Banff along the Trans-Canada Highway, sits astride its namesake lake, which is regarded as one of the seven natural wonders of the world. The lake is rivaled for sheer beauty

Highlights

Look for ★ to find recommended sights, activities, dining, and lodging.

★ **Whyte Museum of the Canadian Rockies:** If you visit only one museum in Banff, make it this one for a snapshot of the park's human history (page 30).

★ **Fairmont Banff Springs:** You don't need to book a room here to enjoy the many wonders of one of the world's great mountain resorts—join a guided tour, enjoy a meal, or simply wander through the grandiose public areas (page 35).

★ **Lake Louise:** Famous Lake Louise has hypnotized visitors with her beauty for more than 100 years. Visitors can rent canoes from the boathouse (page 75).

★ **Moraine Lake:** If anywhere in the Canadian Rockies qualifies as a Double Must-See, it would be this deep-blue body of water surrounded by glaciated peaks (page 75).

★ **Lake O'Hara:** Quite simply, magical. Access is limited by a quota system, so take heed of the reservation information and be prepared for a day of hiking you will always remember (page 76).

★ **Lake Agnes Trail:** You won't completely escape the crowds by hiking this trail from Lake Louise, but you will leave many of them behind (page 79).

★ **Larch Valley Trail:** This walk is a good introduction to hiking in the Canadian Rockies, especially in fall when the larch trees have turned a brilliant gold (page 82).

★ **Peyto Lake:** Another one of Banff's famous lakes. The main difference is the perspective from which it is viewed—a lookout high above its shoreline (page 91).

★ **Columbia Icefield:** Don't miss this glacial area at the southern end of Jasper National Park. Take the Ice Explorer tour to get a close-up view of this natural wonder (page 94).

★ **Helen Lake Trail:** A moderately steep hiking trail leads through glorious wildflower meadows to this beautiful lake, whose shores are populated by noisy marmots (page 96).

★ **Mount Assiniboine Provincial Park:** Accessible only on foot or by helicopter, this roadless park is filled with glacier-capped peaks and turquoise lakes (page 101).

Park Entry

only by Moraine Lake, down the road. Just north of Lake Louise, the Icefields Parkway begins its spectacular course alongside the Continental Divide to Jasper National Park.

One of the greatest draws of this 6,641-square-kilometer (2,564-square-mile) park is the accessibility of its natural wonders. Most highlights are close to the road system, but adventurous visitors can follow an excellent network of hiking trails to alpine lakes, along glacial valleys, and to spectacular viewpoints where crowds are scarce and human impact has been minimal. Summer in the park is busy. In fact, the park receives nearly half of its four million annual visitors in just two months (July and August). The rest of the year, crowds outside the town of Banff are negligible. In winter, three world-class ski resorts—Ski Norquay, Sunshine Village, and Lake Louise (Canada's second-largest ski resort)—crank up their lifts. During this low season, hotel rates are reasonable. If you tire of downhill skiing and snowboarding, you can try cross-country skiing, ice-skating, or snowshoeing; take a sleigh ride; soak in a hot spring; or go heli-skiing nearby.

The park is open year-round, although occasional road closures occur on mountain passes along its western boundary in winter due to avalanche-control work and snowstorms.

PLANNING YOUR TIME

If you are planning to visit the Canadian Rockies, it is almost inevitable that your itinerary will include Banff National Park, both for its many and varied outdoor attractions and for its central location. The park can be anything you want it to be, depending on the time of year you visit and what your interests are. The main population center is Banff, which has all the services of a large town, as well as attractions such as the landmark **Fairmont Banff Springs** hotel and the **Whyte Museum of the Canadian Rockies.** The park holds three lakes that you won't want to miss for their scenic beauty: **Lake Louise, Moraine Lake,** and **Peyto Lake.** All three are easily accessible by road but also offer surrounding hiking, and the first two have canoe rentals. Hiking is the park's biggest attraction, and many visitors plan their itinerary around it. I'd suggest mixing it up—choosing from the hikes that reflect your fitness level and combining them with visits to the major natural attractions. For example, when in the vicinity of Lake Louise, walk the **Lake Agnes Trail,** and while at Moraine Lake, plan on visiting **Larch Valley.** For the more adventurous, **Helen Lake** is a stunning day-hike destination. Keen hikers with more time should also consider including **Mount Assiniboine Provincial Park,** which is renowned for its network of trails and backcountry lodging and camping.

You can book one accommodation for your entire stay or spend an equal number of nights in Banff and Lake Louise. If you have a family or like the convenience of staying put for your

Banff National Park

5 mi

5 km

To Rocky
Mountain House

Abraham
Lake

Coral Creek

Obstruction
Mountain

White Goat
Wilderness
Area

ALBERTA

Mt Cline

Jasper

National

Park

Cirrus
Mountain

Mt Wilson

THE CROSSING

Nigel Peak

Sunwapta
Pass

North Saskatchewan River

SASKATCHEWAN
RIVER CROSSING

To
Jasper

ICEFIELD
CENTRE

Parker's Ridge

RAMPART
CREEK

GLACIER
SKYWALK

Mt
Andromeda

Mt
Athabasca

Saskatchewan
Glacier

Mt Saskatchewan

Mt Amery

Banff
National
Park

Mt Eramus

Alexandra

River

Glacier
Lake

Snow Dome

Castleguard
Mountain

Watchman
Peak

Mt Lyell

Mt Outram

Columbia
Icefield

Mt Forbes

Mt Columbia

Lyell
Glacier

Rostrum
Peak

Banff National Park (continued)

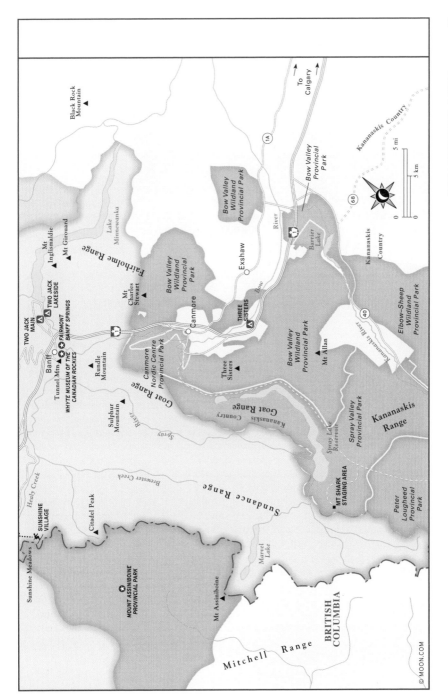

© MOON.COM

Banff in One Day

- Rise before dawn and head northwest from Banff to **Moraine Lake.** It's about an hour's drive northwest on the Trans-Canada Highway; plan on arriving before 6am to ensure a parking spot. Watch the first rays of light hit the surrounding mountains.

- Drive 35 minutes along Moraine Lake Road and head up to **Lake Louise.** Lace up for a three-hour round-trip **hike** to **Lake Agnes,** where you can enjoy a snack at the delightful teahouse.

- Take a one-hour **scenic drive** north up the Icefields Parkway, stopping at Bow Lake to enjoy a **picnic lunch** before continuing to the viewpoint at **Peyto Lake.**

- Return to Banff and wander through the shops of **Banff Avenue** and explore local history at the **Whyte Museum of the Canadian Rockies.**

- Enjoy **dinner** at the iconic **Fairmont Banff Springs hotel.** Dine at the **Lookout Patio** for wonderful valley views, or splurge at **1888 Chop House.**

- After dinner, take advantage of the long days of summer to enjoy a late **evening stroll** or drive along **Vermilion Lakes.**

entire vacation, it is practical to book a room in either Banff or Lake Louise and use it as a base—spending your days in the park but also venturing farther afield.

Unless you're a die-hard skier or snow-boarder, summer is definitely the best time of year to visit. The months of July and August are the busiest, with crowds decreasing exponentially in the weeks before and after these two months. June and September are wonderful times to visit the park. Aside from the crowd factor, in June, wildflowers start blooming and wildlife is abundant. September sees temperatures ideal for hiking, and the turning colors are at their peak. In either month, discounted accommodations are a welcome bonus. In May and October-November, the park is at its quietest. Temperatures in any of these three months are generally too cool for hiking (although welcome warm spells are common). The park's three alpine resorts begin opening in November and remain in operation until April or May. While skiing and boarding are the big wintertime draws, plan on expanding your experience by joining a sleigh ride, learning to snowshoe, or heading out for some ice fishing.

THE LANDSCAPE

The park lies within the main and front ranges of the Rocky Mountains, a mountain range that extends the length of the North American continent. Although the mountains are composed of bedrock laid down up to one billion years ago, it wasn't until 100 million years ago that forces below the earth's surface transformed the lowland plain of what is now western Canada into the varied, mountainous topography we see today.

The front ranges lie to the east, bordering the foothills. These geologically complex mountains are made up of younger bedrock that has been folded, faulted, and uplifted. The main ranges are older and higher, with the bedrock lying mainly horizontal and not as severely disturbed as the front ranges. Here the pressures have been most powerful; these mountains are characterized by castle-like buttresses and pinnacles and warped waves of stratified rock. Most glaciers are found among these lofty peaks. The spine of the main range is the **Continental Divide.** In Canadian longitudes to the east of the divide, all waters flow to the Atlantic Ocean; those to the west flow into the Pacific.

The Elk of Banff National Park

Few visitors leave Banff without having seen elk—a large member of the deer family easily distinguished by its white rump. Though the animals have been reported passing through the park for a century, they've never been indigenous. In 1917, 57 elk were moved to Banff from Yellowstone National Park. Two years later, 20 more were transplanted, and the new herd multiplied rapidly. At that time, coyotes, cougars, and wolves were being slaughtered under a predator-control program, leaving the elk unfettered by nature's population-control mechanisms. The elk proliferated and soon became a problem as they took to wintering in the range of bighorn sheep, deer, moose, and beaver. Between 1941 and 1969, controlled slaughters of elk were conducted in an attempt to reduce the population.

Today, with wolf packs returning to the park, the elk population has stabilized at about 2,000. In summer, look for them in open meadows along the Bow Valley Parkway, along the road to Two Jack Lake, or at Vermilion Lakes.

Each fall, traditionally, hundreds of elk moved into the town itself, but starting in recent years, Parks Canada has been making a concerted effort to keep them away from areas such as the golf course and recreation grounds. The main reason for this is that fall is rutting season, and the libidinal bull elk become dangerous as they gather their harems.

You may still see the odd elk feeding in downtown Central Park or walking proudly down a fairway at the Fairmont Banff Springs Golf Course, but it's more likely you'll spot one while driving along park highways.

Since rising above the surrounding plains, these mountains have been eroding. At least four times in the last million years, sheets of ice have covered much of the land. Advancing and retreating back and forth like steel wool across the landscape, they rounded off lower peaks and carved formerly V-shaped valleys into broad U-shaped ones; **Bow Valley** is the most distinctive. Meanwhile, glacial meltwater continued carving ever-deeper channels into the valleys, and rivers changed course many times.

This long history of powerful and even violent natural events over the eons has left behind the dramatic landscape visitors marvel over today. Now forming the exposed sides of many a mountain peak, layers of drastically altered sediment are visible from miles away, especially when accentuated by a particular angle of sunlight or a light fall of snow. **Cirques,** gouged into the mountains by glacial action, fill with glacial meltwater each spring, creating trademark translucent green lakes that will take your breath away. The wide, sweeping U-shaped valleys scoured out by glaciers past now create magnificent panoramas that will draw you to pull off the road and gasp in awe; open views are easy to come by here, thanks to a climate that keeps the tree line low.

HISTORY

Although the valleys of the Canadian Rockies became ice-free nearly 8,000 years ago and humans periodically hunted in the area since that time, the story of Banff National Park really began with the arrival of the railroad to the area.

The Coming of the Railway

In 1871, Canadian prime minister John A. MacDonald promised to build a rail line linking British Columbia to the rest of the country as a condition of the new province joining the confederation. It wasn't until early 1883 that the line reached Calgary, pushing through to **Laggan,** now known as Lake Louise, that fall. The rail line was one of the largest and costliest engineering jobs ever undertaken in Canada.

Discovery of the Cave and Basin

On November 8, 1883, three young railway workers—Franklin McCabe and William and Thomas McCardell—went prospecting for gold on their day off. After crossing the Bow River by raft, they came across a warm stream and traced it to its source at a small, log-choked basin of warm water that had a distinct smell of sulfur. Nearby they detected the source of the foul smell coming from a hole in the ground. Nervously, one of the three men lowered himself into the hole and came across a subterranean pool of aqua-green warm water. The three men had found not gold, but something just as precious—a hot mineral spring that in time would attract wealthy customers from around the world. Word of the discovery soon got out, and the government encouraged visitors to the Cave and Basin as an ongoing source of revenue to support the new railway.

A 2,500-hectare (6,177-acre) reserve was established around the springs on November 25, 1885, and two years later the reserve was expanded and renamed **Rocky Mountains Park.** It was primarily a business enterprise centered on the unique springs and catering to wealthy patrons of the railway. At the turn of the 20th century, Canada had an abundance of wilderness; it certainly didn't need a park to preserve it. The only goal of Rocky Mountains Park was to generate income for the government and the Canadian Pacific Railway (CPR).

A Town Grows

After the discovery of the Cave and Basin across the Bow River from the railway station (then known as Siding 29), many commercial facilities sprang up along what is now Banff Avenue. The general manager of the CPR (later to become its vice president), William Cornelius Van Horne, was instrumental in creating a hotel business along the rail line. His most recognized achievement was the Banff Springs Hotel, which opened in 1888. It was the world's largest hotel at the time.

Enterprising locals soon realized the area's potential and began opening restaurants, offering guided hunting and boating trips, and developing manicured gardens. Banff soon became Canada's best-known tourist resort, attracting visitors from around the world. It was named after Banffshire, the Scottish birthplace of George Stephen, the CPR's first president.

In 1902, the park boundary was again expanded to include 11,440 square kilometers (4,417 square miles) of the Canadian Rockies. This dramatic expansion meant that the park became not just a tourist resort but also home to existing coal-mining and logging operations and hydroelectric dams. Government officials saw no conflict of interest, actually stating that the coal mine and township at Bankhead added to the park's many attractions. Many of the forests were logged, providing wood for construction, while other areas were burned to allow clear sightings for surveyors' instruments.

After a restriction on automobiles in the park was lifted in 1916, Canada's best-known tourist resort also became its busiest. More and more commercial facilities sprang up, offering luxury and opulence amid the wilderness of the Canadian Rockies. Calgarians built summer cottages, and the town began advertising itself as a year-round destination. As attitudes began to change, the government set up the Dominion Parks Branch, whose first commissioner, J. B. Harkin, believed that land set aside for parks should be used for recreation and education. Gradually, resource industries were phased out. Harkin's work culminated in the National Parks Act of 1930, which in turn led Rocky Mountains Park to be renamed Banff National Park. The park's present boundaries, encompassing 6,641 square kilometers (2,564 square miles), were established in 1964.

Icefields Parkway

Indigenous peoples and early explorers found the swampy nature of the Bow Valley north of

Wild Bill Peyto

These words from a friend sum up Bill Peyto, one of Banff's earliest characters and one of the Canadian Rockies' greatest guides: "rarely speaking—his forte was doing things, not talking about them." In 1886, at the tender age of 18, Ebenezer William Peyto left England for Canada. After traveling extensively, he settled in Banff and was hired as an apprentice guide for legendary outfitter Tom Wilson. Wearing a tilted sombrero, fringed buckskin coat, cartridge belt, hunting knife, and six-shooter, he looked more like a gunslinger than a mountain man.

As his reputation as a competent guide grew, so did the stories. While guiding clients on one occasion, he led them to his cabin. Before entering, Peyto threw stones in the front door until a loud snap was heard. It was a bear trap that he'd set up to catch a certain trapper who'd been stealing his food. One of the guests commented that if caught, the trapper would surely have died. "You're damned right he would have," Bill replied. "Then I'd have known for sure it was him."

In 1900, Peyto left Banff to fight in the Boer War and was promoted to corporal for bravery. This title was revoked before it became official after army officials learned he'd "borrowed" an officer's jacket and several bottles of booze for the celebration. Returning to a hero's welcome in Banff, Peyto established an outfitting business and continued prospecting for copper in Simpson Pass. Although his outfitting business thrived, the death of his wife left him despondent. He built a house on Banff Avenue; its name, "Ain't it Hell," summed up his view of life.

In his later years, he became a warden in the Healy Creek-Sunshine district, where his exploits during the 1920s added to his already legendary name. After 20 years of service he retired, and in 1943, at the age of 75, he passed away. One of the park's most beautiful lakes is named after him, as are a glacier and a popular Banff watering hole (Wild Bill's—a designation he would have appreciated).

Lake Louise difficult for foot and horse travel. When heading north, they used instead the Pipestone River Valley to the east. In 1896, Banff guide Bill Peyto led American explorer Walter Wilcox up the Bow Valley to the high peaks along the Continental Divide northeast of Lake Louise. The first complete journey along this route was made by Jim Brewster in 1904. Soon after, A. P. Coleman made the arduous journey, becoming a strong supporter of the route aptly known as The Wonder Trail. During the Great Depression of the 1930s, as part of a relief-work project, construction began on what was to become the Icefields Parkway. The road was completed in 1939, and the first car traveled the route in 1940. In tribute to the excellence of the road's early construction, the original roadbed, when upgraded to its present standard in 1961, was followed nearly the entire way.

Town of Banff

For most of its existence, the town of Banff was run as a service center for park visitors by the Canadian Parks Service in Ottawa, a government department with plenty of economic resources but little idea about how to handle the day-to-day running of a midsized town. Any inconvenience this arrangement caused park residents was offset by cheap rent and subsidized services. In June 1988, Banff's residents voted to sever this tie, and on January 1, 1990, Banff officially became an incorporated town, no different from any other in Alberta (except that Parks Canada controls environmental protection within the town of Banff).

Town of Banff

Many visitors planning a trip to the national park don't realize that the town of Banff is a bustling commercial center. The town's location is magnificent. It is spread out along the Bow River, extending to the lower slopes of Sulphur Mountain to the south and Tunnel Mountain to the east. In one direction is the towering face of Mount Rundle, and in the other, framed by the buildings along Banff Avenue, is Cascade Mountain. Hotels and motels line the north end of Banff Avenue, while a profusion of shops, boutiques, cafés, and restaurants hugs the south end. Also at the south end, just over the Bow River, is the Park Administration Building. Here the road forks—to the right is the historic Cave and Basin Hot Springs, to the left the Fairmont Banff Springs and Banff Gondola. Some people are happy walking along the crowded streets or shopping in a unique setting; those more interested in some peace and quiet can easily slip into pristine wilderness just a five-minute walk from town.

SIGHTS AND DRIVES
Banff Park Museum

Although displays of stuffed animals are not usually associated with national parks, the downtown **Banff Park Museum** (93 Banff Ave., 403/762-1558, 10am-5pm Wed.-Sun. mid-May-June, 10am-5pm daily July-Aug., 10am-5pm Wed.-Sun. Sept.-early Oct., closed the rest of the year, adult $4, senior $3.50, child $3) provides insight into the park's early history. Visitors during the Victorian era were eager to see the park's animals without actually having to venture into the bush. A lack of roads and the scarcity of large game (a result of hunting) meant that the best places to see animals, stuffed or otherwise, were the game paddock, the zoo, and this museum, which was built in 1903. In its early years, the Banff Zoo and Aviary occupied the grounds behind the museum. The zoo kept more than

60 species of animals, including a polar bear. The museum itself was built before the park had electricity, hence the railroad pagoda design using skylights on all levels.

As times changed, the museum was considered outdated; plans for its demolition were put forward in the 1950s. Fortunately, the museum was spared and later restored for the park's 100th anniversary in 1985. While the exhibits still provide visitors with an insight into the intricate workings of various park ecosystems, they are also an interesting link to the park's past. The museum has a Discovery Room, too, where touching the displays is encouraged, and a reading room that is stocked with natural history books.

★ Whyte Museum of the Canadian Rockies

The Whyte Foundation was established in the mid-1950s by local artists Peter and Catharine Whyte to help preserve artistic and historical material relating to the Canadian Rockies. Their **Whyte Museum of the Canadian Rockies** (111 Bear St., 403/762-2291, 10am-5pm Thurs.-Mon., adult $10, senior $9, child $5) opened in 1968 and grown ever since. It now houses the world's largest collection of Canadian Rockies literature and art. Included in the archives are more than 4,000 volumes, oral tapes of early pioneers and outfitters, antique postcards, old cameras, manuscripts, and a large photography collection. The highlight is the photography of Byron Harmon, whose black-and-white studies of mountain geography have shown people around the world the beauty of the Canadian Rockies. The downstairs gallery features changing art exhibitions. The museum also houses the library and archives of the Alpine Club of Canada. On the grounds are several heritage homes and cabins formerly occupied by local pioneers.

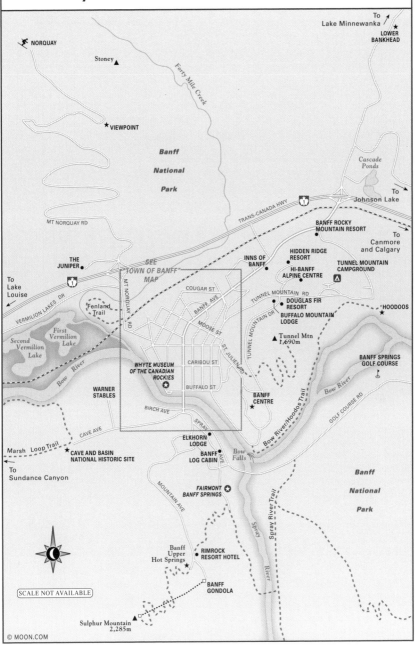

Vicinity of Banff

NORQUAY

Stoney ▲

To Lake Minnewanka

LOWER BANKHEAD

VIEWPOINT

Banff

National

Park

Forty Mile Creek

Cascade Ponds

To Johnson Lake

MT NORQUAY RD

TRANS-CANADA HWY

BANFF ROCKY MOUNTAIN RESORT

To Canmore and Calgary

THE JUNIPER

SEE "TOWN OF BANFF" MAP

INNS OF BANFF

HIDDEN RIDGE RESORT

HI-BANFF ALPINE CENTRE

TUNNEL MOUNTAIN CAMPGROUND

To Lake Louise

VERMILION LAKES DR

Fenland Trail

MT NORQUAY RD

COUGAR ST

BANFF AVE

MOOSE ST

TUNNEL MOUNTAIN RD

DOUGLAS FIR RESORT

BUFFALO MOUNTAIN LODGE

HOODOOS

Second Vermilion Lake

First Vermilion Lake

Bow River

ST JULIEN RD

CARIBOU ST

TUNNEL MOUNTAIN DR

Tunnel Mtn 1,690m

BANFF SPRINGS GOLF COURSE

WHYTE MUSEUM OF THE CANADIAN ROCKIES

BUFFALO ST

BANFF CENTRE

Bow River/Hoodoos Trail

Bow River

GOLF COURSE RD

WARNER STABLES

BIRCH AVE

CAVE AVE

Marsh Loop Trail

CAVE AND BASIN NATIONAL HISTORIC SITE

To Sundance Canyon

SPRAY AVE

ELKHORN LODGE

BANFF LOG CABIN

Bow Falls

Banff

National

Park

MOUNTAIN AVE

FAIRMONT BANFF SPRINGS

Spray River Trail

Spray River

Banff Upper Hot Springs

RIMROCK RESORT HOTEL

BANFF GONDOLA

SCALE NOT AVAILABLE

Sulphur Mountain 2,285m

© MOON.COM

Town of Banff

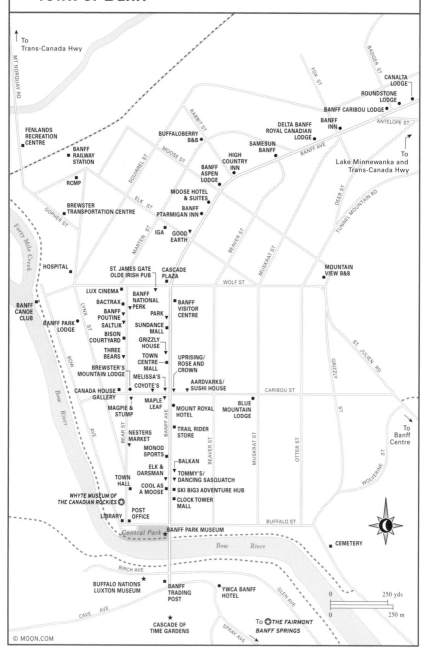

To Trans-Canada Hwy

MT NORQUAY RD

FOX ST

BADGER ST

CANALTA LODGE

ROUNDSTONE LODGE

BANFF CARIBOU LODGE

BANFF INN

ANTELOPE ST

DELTA BANFF ROYAL CANADIAN LODGE

RABBIT ST

BANFF AVE

To Lake Minnewanka and Trans-Canada Hwy

FENLANDS RECREATION CENTRE

BUFFALOBERRY B&B

SAMESUN BANFF

DEER ST

BANFF RAILWAY STATION

MOOSE ST

HIGH COUNTRY INN

TUNNEL MOUNTAIN RD

SQUIRREL ST

BANFF ASPEN LODGE

RCMP

ELK ST

MOOSE HOTEL & SUITES

BREWSTER TRANSPORTATION CENTRE

BANFF PTARMIGAN INN

GOPHER ST

MARTEN ST

IGA

GOOD EARTH

BEAVER ST

MUSKRAT ST

Forty Mile Creek

HOSPITAL

ST. JAMES GATE OLDE IRISH PUB

CASCADE PLAZA

MOUNTAIN VIEW B&B

WOLF ST

LUX CINEMA

BACTRAX

BANFF NATIONAL PERK

BANFF VISITOR CENTRE

BANFF CANOE CLUB

LYNX ST

BANFF POUTINE

PARK

SALTLIK

SUNDANCE MALL

ST JULIEN RD

BANFF PARK LODGE

BISON COURTYARD

GRIZZLY HOUSE

THREE BEARS

TOWN CENTRE MALL

UPRISING/ ROSE AND CROWN

GRIZZLY ST

BOW

BREWSTER'S MOUNTAIN LODGE

MELISSA'S

CANADA HOUSE GALLERY

COYOTE'S

AARDVARKS/ SUSHI HOUSE

CARIBOU ST

Bow River

MAGPIE & STUMP

MAPLE LEAF

MOUNT ROYAL HOTEL

BLUE MOUNTAIN LODGE

To Banff Centre

BEAR ST

AVE

NESTERS MARKET

BANFF AVE

TRAIL RIDER STORE

BEAVER ST

MUSKRAT ST

OTTER ST

MONOD SPORTS

BALKAN

WOLVERINE ST

TOWN HALL

ELK & OARSMAN

TOMMY'S/ DANCING SASQUATCH

COOL AS A MOOSE

SKI BIG3 ADVENTURE HUB

WHYTE MUSEUM OF THE CANADIAN ROCKIES

CLOCK TOWER MALL

POST OFFICE

LIBRARY

BUFFALO ST

Central Park

BANFF PARK MUSEUM

CEMETERY

Bow River

BIRCH AVE

BUFFALO NATIONS LUXTON MUSEUM

BANFF TRADING POST

YWCA BANFF HOTEL

GLEN AVE

CAVE AVE

0   250 yds

0   250 m

CASCADE OF TIME GARDENS

To THE FAIRMONT BANFF SPRINGS

SPRAY AVE

© MOON.COM

MUSEUM TOURS

The Whyte Museum hosts interesting walking tours during the summer. The most popular of these is the **Heritage Homes Tour,** which allows an opportunity for visitors to take a closer look at the historic residences located among the trees behind the museum, including that of Peter and Catharine Whyte. Details can be found at www.whyte.org.

Cascade of Time Garden

Across the river from downtown, Cascade of Time Garden offers a commanding view of Banff Avenue and Cascade Mountain. The gardens are immaculately manicured, making for enjoyable strolling on a sunny day. The stone edifice in the center of the garden is the **Park Administration Building** (101 Mountain Ave., free), which dates to 1936. It replaced a private spa and hospital operated by one of the park's earliest entrepreneurs, Dr. R. G. Brett. Known as Brett's Sanatorium, the original 1886 structure was built to accommodate guests drawn to Banff by the purported healing qualities of the hot springs' water.

Buffalo Nations Luxton Museum

Looking like a stockade, the **Buffalo Nations Luxton Museum** (1 Birch Ave., 403/762-2388, 10am-7pm daily in summer, 11am-5pm daily the rest of the year, adult $10, senior $9, child $5) overlooks the Bow River across from Central Park. It is dedicated to the heritage of the First Nations who once inhabited the Canadian Rockies and adjacent prairies. The museum was developed by prominent local resident Norman Luxton in the early 1900s. At that time it was within the Indian Trading Post, an adjacent gift shop that still stands. The museum contains memorabilia from Luxton's lifelong relationship with the Stoney people, including an elaborately decorated tepee, hunting equipment, arrowheads dating back 4,000 years, stuffed animals, original artwork, peace pipes, and traditional clothing. Various aspects of First Nations culture—such as ceremonial gatherings, living in a tepee, and weaving—are also displayed. The Indian Trading Post is one of Banff's more distinctive gift shops and is definitely worth a browse.

Cave and Basin National Historic Site

At the end of Cave Avenue, the **Cave and Basin National Historic Site** (403/762-1566, 10am-5pm daily in summer, noon-4pm Wed.-Sun. the rest of the year, adult $7.80, senior $7, child $4.80) is the birthplace of Banff National Park and of the Canadian National Parks system. Here, in 1883, three men employed by the Canadian Pacific Railway (CPR) stumbled upon the hot springs now known as the Cave and Basin and were soon lounging in the hot water—a real luxury in the Wild West. They built a fence around the springs, constructed a crude cabin, and began the long process of establishing a claim to the site. But the government beat them to it, settling their claims for a few thousand dollars and acquiring the hot springs.

Bathhouses were installed in 1887, and bathers paid $0.10 for a swim. The pools were eventually lined with concrete, and additions were built onto the original structures. Ironically, the soothing minerals in the water that had attracted millions of people to bathe here eventually caused the pools' demise. The minerals, combined with chlorine, produced sediments that ate away at the concrete structure until the pools were deemed unsuitable for swimming in 1993.

Although the pools are now closed to swimming, the site is still one of Banff's most popular attractions. Interpretive displays describe the hows and whys of the springs. A narrow tunnel winds into the dimly lit cave, and short trails lead to the cave entrance and through a unique environment created by the hot water from the springs.

Banff Upper Hot Springs

The **Banff Upper Hot Springs** (Mountain Ave., 403/762-1515, 9am-11pm daily mid-May-mid-Oct., 10am-10pm Sun.-Thurs. and 10am-11pm Fri.-Sat. mid-Oct.-mid-May), toward

the Banff Gondola, were first developed in 1901. The present building was completed in 1935, with extensive renovations made in 1996. Water flows out of the bedrock at 47°C (116.6°F) and is cooled to 40°C (104°F) in the main pool. Swimming is $8.50 adults, $7.20 seniors and children; lockers and towel rental are a couple of dollars extra.

Banff Gondola

The easiest way to get high above town without breaking a sweat is on the **Banff Gondola** (403/762-2523, 8:30am-9pm daily in summer, shorter hours the rest of the year, closed for two weeks in January, adult $70, child $35, less outside summer). The modern four-person cars rise 700 meters (2,300 feet) in eight minutes to the summit of 2,285-meter (7,500-foot) **Sulphur Mountain.** From the observation deck at the upper terminal, the breathtaking 360-degree view includes the town, the Bow Valley, Cascade Mountain, Lake Minnewanka, and the Fairholme Range. Inside the upper terminal are interactive displays, a theater, and three eateries. Bighorn sheep often hang around below the upper terminal. The short **Sulphur Mountain Boardwalk** leads along a ridge to a restored weather observatory. Between 1903 and 1931, long before the gondola was built, Norman Sanson was the meteorological observer who collected data at the station. During this period he made more than 1,000 ascents of Sulphur Mountain, all in the line of duty.

From downtown, the gondola is three kilometers (1.9 miles) along Mountain Avenue. May-October, **Pursuit** (403/762-6700 or 866/606-6700, www.banffjaspercollection.com) provides free shuttle service to the gondola from downtown hotels.

A 5.5-kilometer (3.4-mile) hiking trail to the summit begins from the Upper Hot Springs parking lot. Although it's a long slog, you have the option of a gondola ride down ($35 one-way).

1: Banff Upper Hot Springs 2: Fairmont Banff Springs 3: Lake Minnewanka 4: Vermilion Lakes

★ Fairmont Banff Springs

On a terrace above a bend in the Bow River is one of the largest, grandest, and most opulent mountain-resort hotels in the world. What better way to spend a rainy afternoon than to explore the turreted 20th-century castle that is the **Fairmont Banff Springs** (405 Spray Ave., 403/762-2211, www.fairmont.com), seeking out a writing desk overlooking one of the world's most photographed scenes and penning a long letter to the folks back home?

"The Springs" has grown with the town and is an integral part of local history. William Cornelius Van Horne, vice president of the CPR, decided that the best way to encourage customers to travel on his newly completed rail line across the Rockies was to build a series of luxurious mountain accommodations. The largest of these was begun in 1886, as close as possible to Banff's newly discovered hot springs. The location chosen had magnificent views and was only a short carriage ride from the train station. Money was no object, and architect Bruce Price began designing a mountain resort the likes of which the world had never seen. At some stage of construction his plans were misinterpreted, and much to Van Horne's shock, the building was built back to front: The best guest rooms faced the forested slopes of Sulphur Mountain while the kitchen had panoramic views of the Bow Valley.

On June 1, 1888, it opened, the largest hotel in the world, with 250 rooms beginning at $3.50 per night including meals. Water from the nearby hot springs was piped into the hotel's steam baths. Rumor has it that when the pipes blocked, water from the Bow River was used, secretly supplemented by bags of sulfur-smelling chemicals. Overnight, the quiet community of Banff became a destination resort for wealthy guests from around the world, and the hotel soon became one of North America's most popular accommodations. Every room was booked every day during the short summer seasons. In 1903 a wing was added, doubling the hotel's capacity. The following year a tower was added to each wing. Guest numbers reached 22,000 in 1911, and construction of a new hotel, designed by Walter Painter, began that year. The original design—an 11-story tower joining two wings in a baronial style—was reminiscent of a Scottish castle mixed with a French country château. This concrete-and-rock-faced, green-roofed building stood as it did at its completion in 1928 until 1999, when an ambitious multiyear program of renovations commenced. The most obvious change was a new lobby, moved to a more accessible location; in addition, all rooms were refurbished and many of the restaurants changed or upgraded. The Canadian Pacific moniker remained part of the Banff Springs's official name until 2000, when the hotel, and all other Canadian Pacific hotels, became part of the Fairmont Hotels and Resorts chain.

Don't let the hotel's opulence keep you from spending time here. Wander through, admiring the 5,000 pieces of furniture and antiques (most of those in public areas are reproductions), paintings, prints, tapestries, and rugs. Take in the medieval atmosphere of Mount Stephen Hall, with its lime flagstone floor, enormous windows, and large oak beams; take advantage of the luxurious spa facility; or relax in one of 12 eateries or four lounges.

The hotel is a 15-minute walk southeast of town, either along Spray Avenue or via the trail along the south bank of the Bow River. **Roam** buses leave Banff Avenue for the Springs twice an hour; $2. Alternatively, horse-drawn buggies take passengers from the Trail Rider Store (132 Banff Ave., 403/762-4551) to the Springs for about $237 for up to six passengers.

Bow Falls

Small but spectacular Bow Falls is below the Fairmont Banff Springs, only a short walk from downtown. The waterfall is the result of a dramatic change in the course of the Bow River brought about by glaciation. At one time the river flowed north of Tunnel Mountain and out of the mountains via the valley of Lake Minnewanka. As the glaciers retreated, they left terminal moraines, forming natural dams and changing the course of the river. Eventually the backed-up water found an outlet here between Tunnel Mountain and the northwest ridge of Mount Rundle. The falls are most spectacular in late spring when run-off from the winter snows fills every river and stream in the Bow Valley watershed.

To get there from town, cross the bridge at the south end of Banff Avenue, scramble down the grassy embankment to the left, and follow a pleasant trail along the Bow River to a point above the falls. This easy walk is one kilometer (0.6 mile), taking 20 minutes each way. By car, cross the bridge and follow the Golf Course signs. From the falls, a paved road crosses the Spray River and passes through the golf course.

Banff Centre

On the lower slopes of Tunnel Mountain is Banff Centre, whose surroundings provide inspiration for one of Canada's leading centers for postgraduate students in a variety of disciplines, including mountain culture, arts, and leadership development. The Banff Centre opened in the summer of 1933 as a theater school. Since then it has grown to become a prestigious institution attracting artists of many disciplines from throughout Canada. The Centre's **Walter Phillips Gallery** (107 Tunnel Mountain Dr., 403/762-6281, 12:30pm-5pm Wed.-Sun., free) presents changing exhibits of visual arts from throughout the world.

Activities are held on the grounds of the Banff Centre year-round. Highlights include a summer educational program, concerts, displays, live performances, and the Banff Mountain Festivals. Visit www.banffcentre.ca for a schedule.

Vermilion Lakes

This series of three shallow lakes forms an expansive montane wetland supporting a variety of mammals and more than 200 species of birds. Vermilion Lakes Drive, paralleling the Trans-Canada Highway immediately west of

Banff, provides the easiest access to the area. The level of **First Vermilion Lake** was once controlled by a dam. Since its removal, the level of the lake has dropped. This is the beginning of a long process that will eventually see the area evolve into a floodplain forest such as is found along the Fenland Trail. The entire area is excellent for wildlife viewing, especially in winter when it provides habitat for elk, coyotes, and the occasional wolf.

Mount Norquay Road

One of the best views of town accessible by vehicle is on this road, which switchbacks steeply to the base of Mount Norquay, the local winter hangout for skiers and boarders. On the way up are several lookouts, including one near the top where **bighorn sheep** often graze.

Want even better views? Where the road ends, the North American chairlift at the **Norquay** ski resort (2 Mt. Norquay Rd., 403/762-4421, 9am-6pm daily mid-June-mid-Oct., adult $37 child $24) lifts visitors even higher—to an elevation of 2,400 meters (8,000 feet) for unparalleled views across the town and Bow Valley. Also at the top is the Via Ferrata, a European-style climbing route in which even visitors without mountaineering experience can try their hand at climbing (from $169 for two hours). The **Cliffhouse Bistro** (11am-6pm daily mid-June-mid-Oct., lunches $15-24), ensconced in a stone building clinging to the mountain slope, has sharable snacks, salads, and burgers.

To Lake Minnewanka

Lake Minnewanka Road begins where Banff Avenue ends at the northeast end of town. An alternative to driving along Banff Avenue is to take Buffalo Street, opposite the Banff Park Museum, and follow it around Tunnel Mountain, passing the campground and several viewpoints of the north face of Mount Rundle, rising vertically from the forested valley. This road eventually rejoins Banff Avenue at the Banff Rocky Mountain Resort.

After passing under the Trans-Canada Highway, **Cascade Falls** is obvious off to the left. The base of the falls can be reached in 15 minutes, although the trail is steep and has lots of loose rock (climbing higher without the proper equipment is dangerous). In winter, these falls freeze, and you'll often see ice climbers slowly making their way up the narrow thread of frozen water. Directly opposite is a turn to **Cascade Ponds,** a popular day-use area where families gather on warmer days to picnic and barbecue.

The next turnout along this road is at **Lower Bankhead.** During the early 1900s, Bankhead was a booming mining town producing 200,000 tons of coal a year. The poor quality of the coal and bitter labor disputes led to the mine's closure in 1922. Soon after, all the buildings were moved or demolished. From the parking lot at Lower Bankhead, a 1.1-kilometer (0.7-mile) interpretive trail leads down through the industrial section of the former town and past an old mine train. The town's 1,000 residents lived on the other side of the road at what is now known as **Upper Bankhead.** Just before the Upper Bankhead turnoff, the foundation of the Holy Trinity Church can be seen on the side of the hill to the right. Not much remains of Upper Bankhead. It is now a day-use area with picnic tables, a kitchen shelter, and firewood. Through the meadow to the west are some large slag heaps, concealed mine entrances, and various stone foundations.

Lake Minnewanka

Minnewanka (Lake of the Water Spirit) is the largest body of water in Banff National Park. Mount Inglismaldie (2,964 meters/9,720 feet) and the Fairholme Range form an imposing backdrop. The reservoir was first constructed in 1912, and additional dams were built in 1922 and 1941 to supply hydroelectric power to Banff. Even if you don't feel up to an energetic hike, it's worth parking at the facility area and going for a short walk along the lakeshore. You'll pass a concession selling snacks and drinks, then the tour boat dock, before entering an area of picnic tables and covered cooking shelters—the perfect place for a picnic. Children will love exploring the rocky shoreline and stony beaches in this area, but you should continue farther around the lake, if only to escape the crowds.

Banff Lake Cruise (403/762-3473) is a 90-minute cruise to the far reaches of the lake, passing the Devil's Gap formation. It departs from the dock from late May to early October 4-8 times daily (first sailing at 10am, adult $72, child $36). An easy walking trail leads past a number of picnic spots and rocky beaches to Stewart Canyon. The lake is great for fishing (lake trout to 15 kilograms/33 pounds) and is the only one in the park where motorboats are allowed. The same company operating the tour boats rents aluminum boats with small outboard engines.

From Lake Minnewanka, the road continues along the reservoir wall, passing a lookout point. You'll often have to slow down along this stretch of road for bighorn sheep. The road then descends to **Two Jack Lake** and a lakefront day-use area. Take the turnoff to **Johnson Lake** to access a lakeside trail, Banff's busiest swimming and sunbathing spot on the warmest days of summer, and picnic facilities with views across to Mount Rundle.

Bow Valley Parkway

Two roads link Banff to Lake Louise. The Trans-Canada Highway is the quicker route and more popular with through traffic. The other is the more scenic 51-kilometer (32-mile) Bow Valley Parkway, which branches off the Trans-Canada Highway five kilometers (3.1 miles) west of Banff. Cyclists will appreciate this paved road's two long, divided sections and low speed limit (60 kph/37 mph). Along this route are several impressive viewpoints, interpretive displays, picnic areas, good hiking, great opportunities for viewing **wildlife** (including **wolves**), three lodges, campgrounds, and one of the park's best restaurants. Note: In May, June, and September, the southern end of the parkway (as far north as Johnston Canyon) is closed to

vehicles, allowing cyclists to enjoy the road at a leisurely pace. This closure has been extended in recent years throughout summer. For up-to-date information, visit www.pc.gc.ca/banffnow.

As you enter the parkway, you pass a short side road to the creek-side **Fireside** picnic area. At **Backswamp Viewpoint,** you can look upstream to the site of a former dam, now a swampy wetland filled with aquatic vegetation. Farther along the road is another wetland at **Muleshoe.** This wetland consists of oxbow lakes that were formed when the Bow River changed its course and abandoned its meanders for a more direct path. Across the parkway is a 1-kilometer (0.6-mile) trail that climbs to a viewpoint overlooking the valley. (The slope around this trail is infested with wood ticks during late spring and early summer, so be sure to check yourself carefully after hiking in this area.) To the east, **Hole-in-the-Wall** is visible. This large-mouthed cave was created by the Bow Glacier, which once filled the valley. As the glacier receded, its meltwater dissolved the soft limestone bedrock, creating what is known as a solution cave.

Beyond Muleshoe the road inexplicably divides for a few car lengths. A large white spruce stood on the island until it blew down in 1984. The story goes that while the road was being constructed, a surly supervisor was asleep in the shade of the tree, and not daring to rouse him, workers cleared the roadway around him. The road then passes through particularly hilly terrain, part of a massive rockslide that occurred approximately 8,000 years ago.

Continuing down the parkway, you'll pass the following sights.

JOHNSTON CANYON

Johnston Creek drops over a series of spectacular waterfalls here, deep within the chasm it has carved into the limestone bedrock. The canyon is not nearly as deep as Maligne Canyon in Jasper National Park—30 meters (100 feet) at its deepest, compared to 50 meters

Bow Valley Parkway

© MOON.COM

(165 feet) at Maligne—but the catwalk that leads to the lower falls has been built through the depths of the canyon rather than along its lip, making it seem just as spectacular. The lower falls are one kilometer (0.6 mile) from the Bow Valley Parkway, while the equally spectacular upper falls are a farther 1.6 kilometer (one mile) upstream. Beyond this point are the **Ink Pots,** shallow pools of spring-fed water. While in the canyon, look for fast-moving black swifts zipping through the air.

SILVER CITY

At the west end of **Moose Meadows,** a small plaque marks the site of Silver City. At its peak in the mid-1800s, this boomtown had a population of 2,000, making it bigger than Calgary at the time. The city was founded by John Healy, who also founded the notorious Fort Whoop-Up in Lethbridge. During its heyday, five mines were operating, extracting not silver but ore rich in copper and lead. The town had a half-dozen hotels, four or five stores, two real estate offices, and a station on the transcontinental rail line when its demise began. Two men, named Patton and Pettigrew, salted their mine with gold and silver ore to attract investors. After selling 2,000 shares at $5 each, they vanished, leaving investors with a useless mine. Investment in the town ceased, mines closed, and the people left. Only one man refused to leave. His name was James Smith, but he was known to everyone as Joe. In 1887, when Silver City came under the jurisdiction of the National Parks Service, Joe was allowed to remain. He did so and was friendly to everyone, including Stoney people, Father Albert Lacombe (who occasionally stopped by), well-known Banff guide Tom Wilson, and of course the animals who grazed around his cabin. By 1926, he was unable to trap or hunt due to failing eyesight, and many people tried to persuade him to leave. It wasn't until 1937 that he finally moved to a Calgary retirement home, where he died soon after.

CASTLE MOUNTAIN TO LAKE LOUISE

After you leave the former site of Silver City, the aptly named Castle Mountain comes into view. It's one of the park's most recognizable peaks and most interesting geographical features. The mountain consists of very old rock (approximately 500 million years old) sitting atop much younger rock (a mere 200 million years old). This unusual situation occurred as the mountains were forced upward by pressure below the earth's surface, thrusting the older rock up and over the younger rock in places.

The road skirts the base of the mountain, passes Castle Mountain Village (with gas, groceries, and accommodations), and climbs a small hill to Storm Mountain Viewpoint, which provides more stunning views and a picnic area. The next commercial facility is **Baker Creek Mountain Resort** (403/522-3761), where you can buy snacks and hot drinks from the deli. Then it's on to another viewpoint at Morant's Curve, from where rail line, river, and mountains combine for perfect symmetry. After passing another picnic area, the Bow Valley Parkway rejoins the Trans-Canada Highway at Lake Louise.

HIKING

After experiencing the international thrills of Banff Avenue, most people will want to see the *real* park, which is, after all, the reason that millions of visitors flock here, thousands take low-paying jobs just to stay here, and others become so severely addicted that they start families and live happily ever after here.

Although many landmarks can be seen from the roadside, to really experience the park's personality you'll need to go for a hike. One of the best things about Banff's 80-odd hiking trails is the variety. From short interpretive walks originating in town to easy hikes rewarded by spectacular vistas to myriad

1: pedestrian bridge across the Bow River **2:** lower falls in Johnston Canyon **3:** hiking in Banff **4:** Spray River

overnight backcountry opportunities, Banff's trails offer something for everyone.

Before attempting any hikes, visit the **Banff Visitor Centre** (224 Banff Ave., 403/762-1550), where staff can advise you on the condition of trails and closures. The best book on hiking in the park is the *Canadian Rockies Trail Guide,* which covers each trail in exacting detail, or you can buy a waterproof Gem Trek hiking map, both of which are available at the visitor center.

Fenland

Length: 2 kilometers/1.2 miles (30 minutes) round-trip
Elevation gain: none
Rating: easy
Trailhead: Forty Mile Creek Picnic Area, Mount Norquay Road, 300 meters (0.2 mile) north of the rail crossing

If you've just arrived in town, this short interpretive trail provides an excellent introduction to the Bow Valley ecosystem. As you walk around the loop, you'll clearly see the various stages in the transition between wetland and floodplain spruce forest. This fen environment is prime habitat for many species of birds. The work of beavers can be seen where the trail parallels the creek, and elk are here during winter. This trail is also a popular shortcut for joggers and cyclists heading out from town to Vermilion Lakes.

Tunnel Mountain

Length: 2.3 kilometers/1.4 miles (30-60 minutes) one-way
Elevation gain: 300 meters/990 feet
Rating: easy/moderate
Trailhead: St. Julien Road, 350 meters (0.2 mile) south of Wolf Street

Accessible from town, this short hike is an easy climb to one of the park's lower peaks. It ascends the western flank of Tunnel Mountain through a forest of lodgepole pine, switchbacking past some viewpoints before reaching a ridge just below the summit. Here the trail turns northward, climbing through a forest of Douglas fir to the summit (which is partially treed, preventing 360-degree views).

Bow River/Hoodoos

Length: 4.8 kilometers/3 miles (60-90 minutes) one-way
Elevation gain: minimal
Rating: easy
Trailhead: Bow River Viewpoint, Tunnel Mountain Drive

From a viewpoint famous for its Fairmont Banff Springs outlook, the trail descends to the Bow River, passing under the sheer east face of Tunnel Mountain. It then follows the river a short distance before climbing into a meadow where deer and elk often graze. From this perspective the north face of Mount Rundle is particularly imposing. As the trail climbs, you'll hear the traffic on Tunnel Mountain Road long before you see it. The trail ends at a viewpoint above the hoodoos, strange-looking limestone-and-gravel columns jutting mysteriously out of the forest. An alternative to returning the same way is to catch the Banff Transit bus from Tunnel Mountain Campground. It leaves every 30 minutes; the trip costs $2.

Sundance Canyon

Length: 8.4 kilometers/5.2 miles (three hours) roundtrip
Elevation gain: 100 meters/330 feet
Rating: easy
Trailhead: Cave and Basin National Historic Site

Sundance Canyon is a rewarding destination across the river from downtown. Unfortunately, the first 3 kilometers (1.9 miles) are along a paved road that is closed to traffic (but not bikes) and hard on your soles. Occasional glimpses of the Sawback Range are afforded by breaks in the forest. Where the paved road ends, the 2.4-kilometer (1.5-mile) Sundance Loop begins. Sundance Creek was once a larger river whose upper drainage basin was diverted by glacial action. Its powerful waters have eroded into the soft bedrock, forming a spectacular overhanging canyon whose bed is strewn with large boulders that have tumbled in.

Spray River

Length: 12 kilometers/7.4 miles (4 hours) round-trip
Elevation gain: 70 meters/230 feet
Rating: easy/moderate
Trailhead: From the Bow Falls parking lot, cross the Spray River and walk along Golf Course Road to behind the green of the first golf hole on the right-hand side of the road.

This trail follows one of the many fire roads in the park. It is not particularly interesting, but it's accessible from downtown Banff and makes a pleasant way to escape the crowds. From behind the green of the 15th hole, the trail heads uphill into the forest. It follows the Spray River closely—even when not in sight, the river can always be heard. For those so inclined, a river crossing one kilometer (0.6 mile) from the golf course allows for a shorter loop. Continuing south, the trail climbs a bluff for a good view of the Fairmont Banff Springs and Bow Valley. The return journey is straightforward with occasional views, ending at a locked gate behind the Fairmont Banff Springs, a short walk to Bow Falls.

For serious hikers, there's another interesting option involving this trail. It requires arranging a lift to the trailhead of the Goat Creek hike in Spray Valley Provincial Park in Kananaskis Country. From this trailhead, it's 19 kilometers/11.8 miles (six hours) one-way back to Banff down the Spray River watershed on a trail that drops 370 meters (1,210 feet) in elevation. The trail is most popular with mountain bikers and cross-country skiers.

Western Slope of Mount Rundle

Length: 5.4 kilometers/3.3 miles (2 hours) one-way
Elevation gain: 480 meters/1,755 feet
Rating: moderate
Trailhead: From the Bow Falls parking lot, cross the Spray River and walk along Golf Course Road to behind the green of the first golf hole on the right-hand side of the road.

At 2,950 meters (9,680 feet), Mount Rundle is one of the park's dominant peaks. Climbing to its summit is possible without ropes, but previous scrambling experience is necessary. An alternative is to ascend the mountain's western slope along an easy-to-follow trail that ends just over 1,000 vertical meters (3,280 vertical feet) before the summit. The trail follows the Spray River Trail from Golf Course Road, branching off left after 700 meters (0.4 mile). Climbing steadily, it breaks out of the enclosed forest after 2.5 kilometers (1.6 miles). The trail ends in a gully from which the undefined route to the summit begins.

Stoney Peak

Length: 2.4-kilometer/1.5-mile loop (1 hour round-trip)
Elevation gain: 180 meters/590 feet
Rating: easy
Trailhead: day lodge, top of Mount Norquay Road, 6 kilometers (3.7 miles) from town

As you look north along Banff Avenue, Stoney's 1,884-meter (6,180-foot) summit is dwarfed by Cascade Mountain, directly behind it. To get to the trailhead of a route that leads to its easily reached summit, follow Mount Norquay Road to a parking lot in front of the resort's day lodge. Immediately to the right of the entrance, a small sign marks the trail. The narrow, slightly overgrown trail passes through a thick forest of lodgepole pine and spruce before breaking out into the open near the summit. The sweeping panorama includes Vermilion Lakes, the Bow Valley, Banff, Spray River Valley, Mount Rundle, Lake Minnewanka, and the imposing face of Cascade Mountain (2,998 meters/9,840 feet). The return trail follows the northwest slope of Stoney to an old ski run at the opposite end of the parking lot.

Cascade Amphitheatre

Length: 6.6 kilometers/4.1 miles (2-3 hours) one-way
Elevation gain: 610 meters/2,000 feet
Rating: moderate/difficult
Trailhead: day lodge, top of Mount Norquay Road, 6 kilometers (3.7 miles) from town

This enormous cirque and the subalpine

Sunshine Meadows

Rock Isle Lake

Sunshine Meadows, straddling the Continental Divide, is a unique and beautiful region of the Canadian Rockies. It's best known as home to Sunshine Village, a self-contained alpine resort accessible only by gondola from the valley floor. But for a few short months each summer, the area is clear of snow and becomes a wonderland for hiking. Large amounts of precipitation create a lush cover of vegetation—over 300 species of wildflowers alone have been recorded here.

From Sunshine Village, trails radiate across the alpine meadow, which is covered in a colorful carpet of fireweed, glacier lilies, mountain avens, white mountain heather, and forget-me-nots (the meadows are in full bloom mid-July-early August). The most popular destination is **Rock Isle Lake,** an easy 2.5-kilometer (1.6-mile) jaunt from the upper village that crosses the Continental Divide while only gaining 100 meters (330 feet) of elevation. Mount Assiniboine (3,618 meters/11,870 feet), known as the "Matterhorn of the Rockies," is easily distinguished to the southeast. Various viewpoints punctuate the descent to an observation point overlooking the lake. From here, options include a loop around Larix and Grizzly Lakes and a traverse along Standish Ridge. If the weather is cooperating, it won't matter which direction you head (so long as it's along a formed trail); you'll experience the Canadian Rockies in all their glory.

It's possible to walk the 6-kilometer (3.7-mile) restricted-access road up to the meadows, but a more practical alternative is to take the **Banff Sunshine Summer Gondola** (8am-6pm daily July-mid-Sept., adult $50, senior $46, child $25). For information, call 403/705-4000 or visit www.banffsunshinemeadows.com. To get to the base of the gondola from Banff, follow the Trans-Canada Highway 9 kilometers (5.6 miles) west to Sunshine Village Road, which continues a similar distance along Healy Creek to the Sunshine Village parking lot.

meadows directly behind Cascade Mountain are one of the most rewarding destinations for hiking in the Banff area. The demanding trail begins by passing the Norquay day lodge, then skirting the base of several lifts and following an old road to the floor of Forty Mile Valley. Keep right at all trail junctions. One kilometer (0.6 mile) after crossing Forty Mile Creek, the trail begins switchbacking up the western flank of Cascade Mountain through a forest of lodgepole pine. Along the way are breathtaking views of Mount Louis's sheer east face. After the trail levels off, it enters a magnificent U-shaped valley, and the amphitheater begins to define itself. The trail becomes indistinct at the top end of the subalpine meadow, which is carpeted in colorful wildflowers during summer. Farther up the valley, vegetation thins out as boulder-strewn talus slopes cover the ground. If you sit still long enough on these rocks, marmots and pikas will slowly appear, emitting shrill whistles before disappearing again.

The most popular route to the summit of 2,998-meter (9,840-foot) Cascade Mountain is along the southern ridge of the amphitheater wall. It is a long scramble up scree slopes and is made more difficult by a false summit; it should be attempted only by experienced scramblers.

C Level Cirque

Length: 4 kilometers /2.5 miles (90 minutes) one-way
Elevation gain: 455 meters/1,500 feet
Rating: moderate
Trailhead: Upper Bankhead Picnic Area, Lake Minnewanka Road, 3.5 kilometers (2.2 miles) beyond the Trans-Canada Highway underpass

From a picnic area on the site of an abandoned mining town, the trail climbs steadily through a forest of lodgepole pine, aspen, and spruce to a pile of tailings and broken-down concrete walls. Soon after, there is a panoramic view of Lake Minnewanka, and then the trail reenters the forest before ending in a small cirque with views down the Bow Valley to Canmore and beyond. The cirque is carved into the eastern face of Cascade Mountain, where snow often lingers until July. When the snow melts, the lush soil is covered in a carpet of colorful wildflowers.

Aylmer Lookout

Length: 12 kilometers/7.5 miles (4 hours) one-way
Elevation gain: 810 meters/2,660 feet
Rating: moderate/difficult
Trailhead: Lake Minnewanka, Lake Minnewanka Road, 5.5 kilometers (3.4 miles) beyond the Trans-Canada Highway underpass

The first 8 kilometers (5 miles) of this trail follow the northern shore of Lake Minnewanka from the day-use area to a junction. The right fork leads to a campground, while the left climbs steeply to the site of an old fire tower on top of an exposed ridge. The deep-blue waters of Lake Minnewanka are visible, backed by the imposing peaks of Mount Girouard (2,995 meters/9,830 feet) and Mount Inglismaldie (2,964 meters/9,725 feet). Bighorn sheep often graze in this area. From here a trail forks left and continues climbing to the alpine tundra of Aylmer Pass. (Access along this trail is often restricted in summer due to bear activity—check at the visitors center before heading out.)

Cory Pass

Length: 5.8 kilometers/3.6 miles (2.5 hours) one-way
Elevation gain: 920 meters/3,020 feet
Rating: moderate/difficult
Trailhead: Fireside Picnic Area, Banff end of the Bow Valley Parkway

This strenuous hike has a rewarding objective—a magnificent view of dog-toothed Mount Louis. The towering slab of limestone rises more than 500 meters (1,640 feet) from the valley below. Just over one kilometer (0.6 mile) from the trailhead, the trail divides. The left fork climbs steeply across an open slope to an uneven ridge that it follows before ascending yet another steep slope to Cory Pass—a wild, windy, desolate area surrounded by jagged peaks dominated by Mount Louis. An alternative to returning along the same trail is continuing down into Gargoyle Valley, following the base of Mount Edith before ascending to Edith Pass and returning to the junction one kilometer (0.6 mile) from the picnic area. Total distance for this trip is 13 kilometers (8 miles), a long day considering the steep climbs and descents involved.

Bourgeau Lake

Length: 7.6 kilometers/4.7 miles (2.5 hours) one-way
Elevation gain: 730 meters/2,400 feet
Rating: moderate
Trailhead: signposted parking lot, Trans-Canada Highway, 3 kilometers (1.9 miles) west of Sunshine Village Junction

This trail follows Wolverine Creek to a small

subalpine lake nestled at the base of an impressive limestone amphitheater. Although the trail is moderately steep, plenty of distractions along the way are worthy of a stop (and rest). Back across the Bow Valley, the Sawback Range is easy to distinguish. As the forest of lodgepole pine turns to spruce, the trail passes under the cliffs of Mount Bourgeau and crosses Wolverine Creek (below a spot where it tumbles photogenically over exposed bedrock). After strenuous switchbacks, the trail climbs into the cirque containing Bourgeau Lake. As you explore the lake's rocky shore, you'll hear the colonies of noisy pikas, even if you don't see them.

Shadow Lake

Length: 14.3 kilometers/8.9 miles (4 hours) one-way
Elevation gain: 440 meters/1,445 feet
Rating: moderate
Trailhead: Redearth Creek Parking Area,
Trans-Canada Highway, 11 kilometers (6.8 miles) west
of Sunshine Village Junction

Shadow is one of the many impressive subalpine lakes along the Continental Divide and, for those staying at **Shadow Lake Lodge** or the backcountry campground, a popular base for day trips. The trail follows an abandoned fire road for 11 kilometers (6.8 miles) before forking right and climbing into the forest. The campground is 2 kilometers (1.2 miles) beyond this junction, and just 300 meters (0.2 mile) farther is Shadow Lake Lodge. The lake is nearly 2 kilometers (1.2 miles) long, and from its eastern shore trails lead to Ball Pass, Gibbon Pass, and Haiduk Lake.

Castle Lookout

Length: 3.7 kilometers/2.3 miles (90 minutes)
one-way
Elevation gain: 520 meters/1,700 feet
Rating: moderate
Trailhead: Bow Valley Parkway, 5 kilometers (3.1
miles) northwest of Castle Junction

However you travel through the Bow Valley, you can't help but be impressed by Castle Mountain rising proudly from the forest floor. This trail takes you above the tree line on the mountain's west face to the site of the Mount Eisenhower fire lookout, abandoned in the 1970s and burned in the 1980s. From the Bow Valley Parkway, the trail follows a wide pathway for 1.5 kilometers (0.9 mile) to an abandoned cabin in a forest of lodgepole pine and spruce. It then becomes narrower and steeper, switchbacking through a meadow before climbing through a narrow band of rock and leveling off near the lookout site. Magnificent panoramas of the Bow Valley spread out before you in both directions. Storm Mountain can be seen directly across the valley.

Rockbound Lake

Length: 8.4 kilometers/5.2 miles (2.5-3 hours)
one-way
Elevation gain: 760 meters/2,500 feet
Rating: difficult
Trailhead: Castle Junction, Bow Valley Parkway, 30
kilometers (18.6 miles) west of Banff

This strenuous hike leads to a delightful body of water tucked behind Castle Mountain. For the first 5 kilometers (3.1 miles), the trail follows an old fire road along the southern flanks of Castle Mountain. Early in the season or after heavy rain, this section can be boggy. Glimpses of surrounding peaks ease the pain of the steady climb as the trail narrows. After eight kilometers (five miles) you'll come to Tower Lake, which the trail skirts to the right before climbing up a rocky cliff line. From the top of the ridge, Rockbound Lake comes into view, and the reason for its name immediately becomes apparent. A scramble up any of the nearby slopes will reward you with even better views.

BIKING

Whether you have your own bike or you rent one from the many bicycle shops in Banff or Lake Louise, cycling in the park is for everyone. Two options present themselves for riding in the park: paved roads and unpaved hiking/biking trails. The roads along the Vermilion Lakes, to Lake Minnewanka, to Mount Norquay, through the golf course, to Sundance Canyon, along the Bow Valley Parkway, and the Legacy Trail to Canmore are all popular paved routes. Several unpaved trails radiating from Banff and passing through the backcountry have been designated as bicycle trails. These include a network of trails on the east side of Tunnel Mountain, the Rundle Riverside to Canmore, and the Spray River Loop. Before heading into the backcountry, download the *Mountain Biking and Cycling Guide* from the Brochures page of the Parks Canada website (www.pc.gc.ca/banff). Backcountry riders are particularly susceptible to sudden bear encounters. Be alert and make loud noises when passing through heavy vegetation.

Banff Cycle (327 Railway Ave., 403/985-4848, wwwbanffcycle.com, summer only) is based out front of the Banff Railway Station, making parking a breeze and access to the cycling route to Vermilion Lakes and onto the Bow Valley Parkway easy. Half-day rentals are $50 for a high-quality hybrid bike or $90 for an e-bike. This company also offers e-bike tours, including a three-hour guided ride out to Lake Minnewanka for $189 per person. Downtown, **Bactrax** (225 Bear St., 403/762-8177) and **Banff Adventures Unlimited** (211 Bear St., 403/762-4554) rent front- and full-suspension mountain bikes for $20-25 per hour and $60-100 per day. Rates include a helmet, lock, and biking map.

HORSEBACK RIDING

Jim and Bill Brewster led Banff's first paying guests into the backcountry on horseback more than 100 years ago. Today visitors are still able to enjoy the park on this traditional form of transportation.

Banff Trail Riders (403/762-4551 or 800/661-8352, www.horseback.com) offers a great variety of trips. Their main office is downtown in the **Trail Rider Store** (132 Banff Ave., 403/762-4551), although trips depart from either **Warner Stables** (Sundance Rd., 403/762-2832), behind the recreation grounds off Cave Avenue, or **Spray River Corrals** (Spray Ave., 403/762-2848), below

the Fairmont Banff Springs. From Warner Stables, a two-hour trip around the Sundance Loop ($129) departs four times daily. Other longer trips include the three-hour Cowboy Cookout, with a suitably western steak and baked bean meal along the trail (departs three times daily; $179).

In addition to day trips, Banff Trail Riders runs a variety of overnight rides that include lodgings in backcountry lodges or tent camps. The main accommodation is Sundance Lodge, an easy 18-kilometer (10-mile) ride from Warner Stables, which has 10 guest rooms, a large living area, and even hot showers. The shortest option is an overnight trip departing twice weekly through the summer for $729 per person. A three-day trip is $1,569. Five-night ($2,399) trips split their time between Sundance Lodge and Halfway Lodge, which is farther up the Spray Valley. Rates include horse rental, all meals, and accommodation.

WATER SPORTS
White-Water Rafting

Anyone looking for white-water-rafting action will want to run the **Kicking Horse River,** which flows down the western slopes of the Canadian Rockies into British Columbia. Many operators provide transportation from Banff and Lake Louise. The rafting season runs mid-May-mid-September, with river levels at their highest in late June. The Lower Canyon, immediately upstream of Golden, offers the biggest thrills, including a 3-kilometer (1.9-mile) stretch of continuous rapids. Upstream of here, the river is tamer but still makes for an exciting trip, while even farther upstream, near the western boundary of Yoho National Park, it's more of a float—a good adventure for the more cautious visitor. The river is run by several companies, most of which offer the option of half-day ($90-110) or full-day ($140-190) trips. The cost varies with inclusions such as transportation from Banff and lunch.

From Lake Louise, **Wild Water Adventures** (403/522-2211 or 888/647-6444, www.wildwater.com) leads half-day

trips down the river for $115, including a narrated bus trip to their purpose-built RiverBase put-in point 27 kilometers (17 miles) east of Golden. Departures are from Lake Louise at 8:15am and 1:30pm. The full-day ($165) trip is broken up by a riverside lunch. **Canadian Rockies Rafting** (403/678-6535 or 877/226-7625, www.rafting.ca) operates on the Kicking Horse from Banff, as does the similarly Banff-based **Hydra River Guides** (403/762-4554 or 800/644-8888, www.raftbanff.com).

Rocky Mountain Raft Tours (403/762-3632, www.banffrafttours.com) offers a one-hour (adult $70, child $30) float trip down the **Bow River,** beginning just below Bow Falls and ending along the golf course loop road. No rapids are involved, so you'll stay dry.

Canoeing

On a quiet stretch of the Bow River at the north end of Wolf Street, **Banff Canoe Club** (403/762-5005, www.banffcanoeclub.com, 9am-9pm daily mid-June-Sept., $50 one hour, $30 each additional hour) rents canoes and paddleboards. From here you can paddle upstream, or along Echo Creek to First Vermilion Lake. It's an extremely peaceful way to leave the bustle of Banff behind, especially the Echo Creek option, where beavers are often spotted at dusk.

Fishing and Boating

The finest fishing in the park is in Lake Minnewanka, where lake trout as large as 15 kilograms (33 pounds) have been caught. One way to ensure a good catch is through **Banff Lake Cruise** (866/474-4766), which offers fishing trips in a heated cabin cruiser; trolling and downrigging are the preferred methods of fishing the lake. A half-day's fishing (4 hours) is $575 for two people. The company also rents small aluminum fishing boats with outboard motors for $115 for the first hour, then $65 for each additional hour.

Before fishing anywhere in the park, you

need a national park fishing license ($10 per day, $35 per year), available from the Banff and Lake Louise Visitor Centres, Home Hardware in Banff, and sport shops throughout the park.

GOLFING

One of the world's most scenic golf courses, the **Banff Springs Golf Course** spreads out along the Bow River between Mount Rundle and Tunnel Mountain. The first course was laid out here in 1911, but in 1928 Stanley Thompson was brought in by the CPR to build what was at the time North America's most expensive course. In 1989, the Tunnel 9 opened (along with a new clubhouse), creating today's 27-hole course.

The course is typical Thompson, taking advantage of natural contours and featuring elevated tees, wide fairways, treacherous fescue grass rough, and holes aligned to distant mountains. From the back markers it is 7,087 yards and plays to a par of 71. The course is not only breathtakingly beautiful, but it's also challenging for every level of golfer. Pick up a copy of the book *The World's Greatest Golf Holes,* and you'll see a picture of the fourth hole on the Rundle 9. It's a par three, over Devil's Cauldron 70 meters (230 feet) below, to a small green backed by the sheer face of Mount Rundle rising vertically more than 1,000 meters (3,280 feet) above the putting surface. Another unique feature of the course is the abundance of wildlife: There's always the chance of seeing elk feeding on the fairways, or coyotes, deer, or bears scurrying across.

Greens fees (including cart and driving range privileges) are $289, discounted to $219 in May and late September-early October. The Tunnel 9 offers the same spectacular challenges as Thompson's original layout but lacks the history; nine holes cost $115. Free shuttle buses run from the Fairmont Banff Springs to the clubhouse. There you'll find club rentals ($70-90), putting greens, a driving range, a pro shop, two chipping greens, and a restaurant with a stunning wraparound deck.

1: rafting on the Bow River 2: Rockbound Lake
3: saddling up for a ride at Sundance Lodge
4: Banff Springs Golf Course

The Brewster Boys

Few guides in Banff were as well known as Jim and Bill Brewster. In 1892, at ages 10 and 12, respectively, they were hired by the Banff Springs Hotel to take guests to local landmarks. As their reputation as guides grew, they built a thriving business. By 1900, they had their own livery and outfitting company, and soon thereafter they expanded operations to Lake Louise. Their other early business interests included a trading post, the original Mount Royal Hotel, the first ski lodge in the Sunshine Meadows, and the hotel at the Columbia Icefield.

Today, a legacy of the boys' savvy, Pursuit, a transportation and tour company, has grown to become an integral part of many visitors' stays (although it is no longer owned by the Brewster family). The company operates some of the world's most advanced sightseeing vehicles, including a fleet of Ice Explorers on the Columbia Icefield.

Booking tee times well in advance is essential; call 403/762-2211 or visit www.banffmountaingolf.com.

TOURS

Pursuit (403/762-6700 or 866/606-6700, www.banffjaspercollection.com) is the dominant tour company in the area. The 4.5-hour Explore Banff bus tour takes in downtown Banff, Tunnel Mountain Drive, the hoodoos, the Cave and Basin, and Banff Gondola (gondola fare included). This tour runs in summer only and departs from the bus depot at 8:30am daily; call for hotel pickup times. Adult fare is $165; children are half price. A six-hour tour to Lake Louise departs select Banff hotels daily ($175). In winter this tour departs Tuesday and Friday mornings, runs five hours, and includes Banff sights ($125). During summer, the company also offers tours from Banff to the Columbia Icefield ($268, includes lunch).

Discover Banff Tours (Sundance Mall, 215 Banff Ave., 403/760-5007 or 877/565-9372, www.banfftours.com) is a smaller company, with smaller buses and more personalized service. A three-hour Discover Banff tour visits Lake Minnewanka, the Cave and Basin, the Fairmont Banff Springs, and the hoodoos for adult $95, child $45; a two-hour Evening Wildlife Safari is adult $58, child $35. This company offers a good selection of other tours throughout the

year, including a wintertime ice walk in frozen Johnston or Grotto Canyon (adult $82, child $54).

WINTER RECREATION

From November to May, the entire park transforms itself into a winter playground covered in a blanket of snow. Of Alberta's six world-class winter resorts, three are in Banff National Park. Norquay is a small but steep hill overlooking the town of Banff; Sunshine Village perches high in the mountains on the Continental Divide, catching more than its share of fluffy white powder; and Lake Louise, Canada's second-largest ski resort, spreads over four distinct mountain faces. Apart from an abundance of snow, the resorts have something else in common—spectacular views, which alone are worth the price of a lift ticket. Although the resorts operate independently, the **Ski Big3 Adventure Hub** (114 Banff Ave., 403/762-4754, www.skibig3.com, 9am-8pm daily) represents all three and is the place to get information on multiday ticketing and transportation.

Other winter activities in the park include cross-country skiing, ice-skating, snowshoeing, dogsledding, and just relaxing. Crowds are nonexistent, and hotels reduce rates by up to 70 percent (except Christmas holidays)—reason enough to venture into the mountains. Lift-and-lodging packages begin at $150 per person.

Norquay

Norquay (403/762-4421, www.banffnorquay.com) has two distinct faces—literally and figuratively. There are some great cruising runs and a well-respected ski school, but also the experts-only North American Chair (the one you can see from town), which opens up the famous double-black-diamond Lone Pine run. A magnificent post-and-beam day lodge nestled below the main runs is flanked on one side by a wide deck that catches the afternoon sun, while holding a cafeteria, restaurant, and bar inside. Lift tickets are adult $100, youth and senior $78, child $48; lift, lesson, and rental packages cost about the same. One run is lit for night skiing and boarding on Friday and Saturday evenings January-March (adult $42, senior $34, child $24). A shuttle bus makes pickups from Banff hotels for the short 6-kilometer (3.7-mile) ride up to the resort. The season at Norquay usually runs mid-November to mid-April.

Sunshine Village

Sunshine Village (403/762-6500 or 877/542-2633, www.skibanff.com) has lots going for it—more than six meters (20 feet) of snow annually (no need for snowmaking up here), wide-open bowls, a season stretching for nearly 200 days (late Nov.-late May), skiing and boarding in two provinces, North America's only heated chairlift, and the only slope-side accommodations in the park. For experts only, one of Canada's most infamous runs, Delirium Dive, drops off the northeast-facing slope of Lookout Mountain; to ski or board this up-to-50-degree run, you must be equipped with a transceiver, shovel, probe, and partner, but you'll have bragging rights that night at the bar (especially if you've descended the Bre-X line). Aside from Delirium Dive, the area is best known for its excellent beginner and intermediate terrain, which covers 60 percent of the mountain. The total vertical rise is 1,070 meters (3,510 feet), and the longest run (down to the lower parking lot) is 8 kilometers (5 miles). Day passes are adult $135, senior $115, youth $95, child $70, and those younger than six ride free. Two days of lift access and one night's lodging at slope-side Sunshine Mountain Lodge cost from $500 per person in high season. The inn has a restaurant, lounge, game room, and large outdoor hot tub.

Rentals and Sales

Each resort has ski and snowboard rental and sales facilities, but getting your gear down in

ice crystals on a frozen lake

Ski Banff

Banff National Park is busiest during summer, but for many visitors from outside North America—especially Europeans and Australians—it is the winter season for which they know Banff. Although winter (Dec.-Apr.) is considered low season, the park remains busy as powder enthusiasts from around the world gather for world-class skiing and boarding.

It hasn't always been this way. As recently as the 1960s, many lodgings—including the famous Fairmont Banff Springs—were open only for the summer season. With winter tourism nonexistent, the first skiers were Banff locals, who would climb the surrounding peaks under their own steam. Due mostly to its handy location close to town, a popular spot was **Norquay,** which was skied as early as the 1920s. In 1948, Canada's first chairlift was installed on the mountain's eastern slopes. In the ensuing years, newer and faster lifts have created a convenient getaway that fulfills the needs of locals and visitors alike, who can buzz up for an afternoon of skiing or boarding on slopes that suit all levels of proficiency.

The first people to ski the **Sunshine Meadows** were two local men, Cliff White and Cyril Paris, who became lost in the spring of 1929 and returned to Banff with stories of deep snow and ideal slopes for skiing. In the following years, a primitive cabin was used as a base for overnight ski trips in the area. In 1938 the Canadian National Ski Championships were held here, and in 1942 a portable lift was constructed. The White family was synonymous with the Sunshine area for many years, running the lodge and ski area while Brewster buses negotiated the steep, narrow road that led to the meadows. In 1980, a gondola was installed to whisk skiers and snowboarders 6 kilometers (3.7 miles) from the valley floor to the alpine village.

The best known of Banff's three resorts is **Lake Louise,** an hour's drive north of town but still within park boundaries. This part of the park also attracted early interest from local skiers, beginning in 1930 when Cliff White and Cyril Paris built a small ski chalet in the Skoki Valley (now operating as Skoki Lodge). The remoteness of this hut turned out to be impractical, so another was built, closer to the road. In 1954, a crude lift was constructed up Larch Mountain from the chalet. The lift had only just begun operation when a young Englishman, Norman Watson (known as the "Barmy Baronet"), who had inherited a fortune, saw the potential for a world-class alpine resort and made the completion of his dream a lifelong obsession. Over the years more lifts were constructed, and two runs—Olympic Men's Downhill and Olympic Ladies' Downhill—were cut in anticipation of a successful bid for the 1968 Winter Olympics (the bid failed).

town is often easier. **Abominable Ski & Sportswear** (229 Banff Ave., 403/762-2905) and **Monod Sports** (129 Banff Ave., 403/762-4571) have been synonymous with Banff and the ski industry for decades, and while the **Rude Boys** (205 Caribou St., 403/762-8211) has only been around since the 1980s, it is *the* snowboarder hangout. Other shops with sales and rentals include **Chateau Mountain Sports** (Fairmont Banff Springs, 405 Spray Ave., 403/762-2500), **Ski Hub** (114 Banff Ave., 403/762-4754), and **Snow Tips** (225 Bear St., 403/762-8177). Basic packages—skis, poles, and boots—are $40-50 per day, while high-performance packages range $70-90. Snowboards and boots rent for $40-70 per day.

Cross-Country Skiing and Snowshoeing

No better way of experiencing the park's winter delights exists than gliding through the landscape on cross-country skis. Many summer hiking trails are groomed for winter travel. The most popular areas near town are Johnson Lake, Golf Course Road, Spray River, Sundance Canyon, and upstream from the canoe docks. The booklet *Cross-Country Skiing—Nordic Trails in Banff National Park* is available from the Banff Visitor Centre. Weather forecasts (403/762-2088) are posted at both visitors centers. Rental packages are available from **Snow Tips** (225 Bear St., 403/762-8177). Expect to pay $30-40 per day. **White Mountain Adventures**

(403/678-4099, www.whitemountainadventures.com) offers a four-hour snowshoeing tour at Sunshine Meadows for $109 per person, which includes a gondola ride and transportation from Banff hotels.

Ice-Skating

The location of skating rinks changes annually, but one reliable location is on the golf course side of the **Fairmont Banff Springs**. The rink is lit after dark, and a raging fire is built beside it—the perfect place to enjoy a hot chocolate. Early in the season (check conditions first), skating is often possible on **Vermilion Lakes** and **Johnson Lake**. Rent skates from **Snow Tips** (225 Bear St., 403/762-8177) or **Chateau Mountain Sports** (Fairmont Banff Springs, 405 Spray Ave., 403/762-2500) for $12 per hour.

Sleigh Rides

Banff Trail Riders offers sleigh rides ($65 per person) on the frozen terrain around their stables on the south side of the Bow River. For reservations, call 403/762-4551 or stop by the Trail Rider Store (132 Banff Ave., www.horseback.com).

Ice Walks

Between December and late March, Johnston Canyon, a 20-minute drive from Banff along the Bow Valley Parkway, is a wonderland of frozen waterfalls. Two local companies, **Discover Banff Tours** (403/760-5007 or 877/565-9372) and **White Mountain Adventures** (403/678-4099 or 800/408-0005), offer ice walks through the canyon. Both tours reach as far as the Upper Falls and provide guests with ice cleats for their shoes and hot drinks to take the chill off this outdoor activity. Transportation from Banff is included in the rate of $82 per person.

Other Winter Activities

Beyond the skating rink below the Fairmont Banff Springs is an unofficial **toboggan** run; ask at your hotel for sleds or rent them from the sports store at the Fairmont Banff Springs ($10 per hour).

Anyone interested in **ice climbing** should register at the national park desk in the Banff Visitor Centre or call 403/762-1550. The world-famous (if you're an ice climber) Terminator is just outside the park boundary.

INDOOR RECREATION
Swimming and Fitness Facilities

Many of Banff's bigger hotels have fitness rooms, and some have indoor pools. A popular place to swim and work out is at **Sally Borden Fitness and Recreation** (Banff Centre, St. Julien Rd., 403/762-6450, 6am-11pm daily, www.banffcentre.ca), which holds a wide range of fitness facilities, a climbing gym, squash courts, a 25-meter-long heated pool, a wading pool, and a hot tub. General admission is $18, or pay $6.50 to swim only most evenings.

Willow Stream Spa

The luxurious **Willow Stream Spa** in the Fairmont Banff Springs (405 Spray Ave., 403/762-2211, 6am-10pm daily) is the place to pamper yourself. It sprawls over two levels and 3,000 square meters (0.7 acre) of a private corner of the hotel. The epicenter of the facility is a circular mineral pool capped by a high glass-topped ceiling and ringed by floor-to-ceiling windows on one side and on the other by hot tubs fed by cascading waterfalls of varying temperatures. Other features include outdoor saltwater hot tubs, private solariums, steam rooms, luxurious bathrooms, and separate male and female lounges complete with fireplaces and complimentary drinks and snacks. Numerous other services are offered, including facials, body wraps, massage therapy, salon services, and hydrotherapy. Entry to Willow Stream is included in some package rates for guests at the hotel. Admission is $80 per day, which includes the use of a locker and spa attire, with almost 100 services available at additional cost (most of these include general admission, so, for example, you can spend the day at Willow Stream and receive a one-hour massage for $230).

Other Indoor Recreation

High Rollers (110 Banff Ave., 403/762-2695, 4pm-2am daily), downstairs in the Clock Tower Mall, has six bowling lanes and hip ambience that includes an upscale menu and almost 50 craft beers on tap.

The **Lux Cinema Centre** (229 Bear St., 403/762-8595) screens new releases for $15 ($10 for midweek matinees).

Banff's only waterslide is in the **Douglas Fir Resort** (Tunnel Mountain Dr., 403/762-5591, 4pm-10pm Mon.-Fri., 9am-10pm Sat.-Sun.). The two slides are indoors, and the admission price of $20 (free for kids age five or under) includes use of a hot tub and exercise room.

NIGHTLIFE

Like resort towns around the world, Banff has a deserved reputation as a party town, especially among seasonal workers, the après-ski crowd, and young Calgarians. Crowds seem to spread out, with no particular bar being more popular than another or being a place where you can mingle with fellow travelers. Given the location and vacation vibe, drink prices are as high as you may expect, with attitude thrown in for free.

Also note that the Royal Canadian Mounted Police (RCMP) patrol Banff all night, promptly arresting anyone who even looks like trouble, including anyone drunk or drinking on the streets.

Bars and Lounges

One of Banff's most distinctive bars is **Park Distillery** (219 Banff Ave., 403/762-5114, 11am-2am daily), a beautifully designed two-story space that reflects the history of the park through the use of wood and stone and features such as a huge canvas tent that rolls over one section of the upstairs seating area. Beer choices represent many local breweries, while spirits such as gin are distilled in-house using glacial water and local Alberta grains.

Melissa's (201 Banff Ave., 403/762-5511, 8am-2am daily) is in a new location as of 2021, overlooking the town's main intersection from a second-story location, but this place remains a longtime favorite drinking hole for locals. Expect weekday drink specials and live music on the large stage two or three nights a week.

Across a side street from Melissa's, the **Maple Leaf** (137 Banff Ave., 403/760-7680, 10am-10pm daily) has a stylish space at street level set aside as a bar. A few doors down from the Maple Leaf, at the **Magpie & Stump** (203 Caribou St., 403/762-4067, 11:30am-2am daily), a casual, family-friendly vibe fills a room stuffed with eclectic furnishings. Start with free peanuts, continue with well-priced Mexican dishes, and wash them down with margaritas or Mexican beer. If the weather is warm, make your way upstairs to the fashionable rooftop patio.

The **Elk & Oarsman** (119 Banff Ave., 403/762-4616, 11am-1am daily) serves up beer and more in a clean, casual atmosphere that is as friendly as it gets in Banff. The **Rose and Crown** (202 Banff Ave., 403/762-2121, 11am-2am daily), serves local and British beers and hearty pub fare. It also features a rooftop patio and rock-and-roll bands a few nights a week, but there's not much room for dancing. Also down the main drag is **Tommy's** (120 Banff Ave., 403/762-8888, 11am-2am daily), a perennial favorite for locals of all ages.

Around the corner from Banff Avenue, the **St. James Gate Olde Irish Pub** (207 Wolf St., 403/762-9355, 11am-1am daily) is an Irish-style bar with a reputation for excellent British-style meals and occasional appearances by Celtic bands.

One block back from Banff Avenue are two excellent choices for a quiet drink. Relative to other town drinking spots, prices at the **Bear Street Tavern** (Bison Courtyard, 211 Bear St., 403/762-2021, 11:30am-10pm daily) are decent. Add funky surroundings and a courtyard to the mix, and you have an excellent choice for a drink and meal. Along the same strip, is **Three Bears** (205 Bear St., 403/985-80838, 11:30am-10pm), a two-story, open concept brewery with a wide range of beers brewed inhouse. The atmosphere buzzes most nights and the food is also noteworthy.

Hotel Hangouts

Many Banff hotels have lounges open to guests and nonguests alike. They are generally quieter than the bars in town and often offer abbreviated menus from adjacent restaurants. For old-world atmosphere, nothing in town comes close to matching the **Grapes,** in the Fairmont Banff Springs (405 Spray Ave., 403/762-2211, 5pm-9:30pm daily). Another place to enjoy a drink in the park's landmark hotel is the mezzanine-level **Rundle Bar** (Fairmont Banff Springs, 403/762-2211, 11am-1am daily), an open space with views extending down the Bow Valley, or the adjacent outdoor patio. Below the hotel is the **Waldhaus Pub** (Fairmont Banff Springs, 403/762-2211, 11am-11pm daily in summer). It has the best deck in town for sweeping mountain views, but it's mainly the haunt of locals coming off the golf course or savvy visitors (such as those who've read this book).

Nightclub

Banff's most popular nightclub is **Sasquatch** (120 Banff Ave., 403/762-4002, 9pm-2am Fri.-Wed., cover charge varies), a modern, intimate space that gets very loud, especially when a celebrity DJ is in town spinning discs.

FESTIVALS AND EVENTS
Spring

Most of the major spring events take place at local ski resorts, including a variety of snowboard competitions that make for great spectator viewing. At Lake Louise, a half-pipe and jump are constructed right in front of the day lodge for this specific purpose. One long-running spring event is the **Slush Cup,** which takes place at Sunshine Village (www.skibanff.com) in late May. Events include kamikaze skiers and boarders who attempt to skim across an almost-frozen pit of water. While winter enthusiasts are at higher

elevations, swooshing down the slopes of some of North America's latest-closing resorts, early May sees the Banff Springs Golf Course open for the season.

During the second week of June, the **Banff World Media Festival** (403/678-1216, www. banffmediafestival.com) attracts the world's best television directors, producers, writers, and even actors for meetings, workshops, and awards, with many select screenings open to the public. For many delegates, pitching their ideas is what draws them to this event. The main venue is the Fairmont Banff Springs.

Summer

Summer is a time of hiking and camping, so festivals are few and far between. On July 1, Banff kicks off **Canada Day** with Sidewalk Art in front of the Whyte Museum on Bear Street and musical performances in Central Park. An impressive parade along Banff Avenue begins at 1pm, followed by a concert in Central Park and fireworks.

Each summer the national park staff presents an extensive **Park Interpretive Program** at locations in town and throughout the park, including downstairs in the visitors center at 8:30pm daily. All programs are free and include guided hikes, nature tours, slideshows, campfire talks, and lectures. For details, drop by the Banff Visitor Centre (403/762-1550) or look for postings on campground bulletin boards.

Fall

Fall is the park's quietest season, but it's busiest in terms of festivals and events. First of the fall events, on the last Saturday in September, **Melissa's Road Race** (www.melissasroadrace.com) attracts more than 2,000 runners (the race sells out months in advance) in 5-, 10-, and 21-kilometer (3-, 6- and 14-mile) races.

One of the year's biggest events is the **Banff Centre Mountain Film and Book Festival,** held the first weekend of November. Mountain-adventure filmmakers from around the world submit films to be judged

by a select committee. Films are then shown throughout the weekend to an enthusiastic crowd of thousands. Exhibits and seminars are also presented, and top climbers and mountaineers from around the world are invited as guest speakers.

Tickets to the Banff Mountain Film Festival go on sale one year in advance and sell out quickly. Tickets for daytime shows start at $65 (for up to 10 films). Night shows are priced from $45, and all-weekend passes cost around $280. Films are shown in the two theaters of the **Banff Centre** (St. Julien Rd.). For more information, contact the festival office (403/762-6675); for tickets, contact the Banff Centre box office (403/762-6301 or 800/413-8368, www.banffcentre.ca). If you miss the actual festival, it hits the road on the Best of the Festival World Tour. Look for it in your town, or check out www.banffcentre.ca for venues and dates.

Starting in the days leading up to the film festival, then running in conjunction with it, is the book component of the festival, which showcases publishers, writers, and photographers whose work revolves around the world's great mountain ranges. Tickets can be purchased for individual events ($15-35).

Winter

By mid-December, lifts at all local ski resorts are open. **Santa Claus** makes an appearance on Banff Avenue at noon on the last Saturday in November; if you miss him there, he usually goes skiing at each of the local resorts on Christmas Day. Events at the resorts continue throughout the long winter season, among them **World Cup Downhill** skiing at Lake Louise in late November. **SnowDays** is a mid-winter celebration starting mid-January that features ice sculpting on Bear Street in downtown Banff and on the frozen lake in front of the Chateau Lake Louise, a frozen playground, and a spirits festival.

1: Canada Day parade on Banff Avenue 2: Saltlik has a patio that catches the afternoon sun.
3: Lookout Patio at the Fairmont Banff Springs

SHOPPING

Banff Avenue is renowned for its shops, but in reality has evolved into a continuous stretch of tacky tourist shops and international chains. An exception is **Cool as a Moose** (115 Banff Ave., 403/985-4612, 9am-9pm daily), which does an excellent job of creating bright and cheery Banff-themed gifts and clothing.

Canadiana and Clothing

Few companies in the world were as responsible for the development of a country as was the **Hudson's Bay Company** (HBC) in Canada. Founded in 1670, the HBC established trading posts throughout western Canada, many of which attracted settlers, forming the nucleus for towns and cities that survive today, including Alberta's capital, Edmonton. HBC stores continue their traditional role of providing a wide range of goods, in towns big and small across the country. In Banff, the HBC store is at 125 Banff Avenue (403/762-5525, 9:30am-9pm Mon.-Sat., 9:30am-7pm Sun.).

Another Canadian store, this one famous for its fleeces, sweaters, and leather goods and for its role as supplier to the Canadian Olympic teams, is **Roots** (227 Banff Ave., 403/762-9434, 10am-9pm daily). For belts, buckles, and boots, check out the **Trail Rider Store** (138 Banff Ave., 403/762-4551, 10am-7pm daily). Also check out **Rude Boys Snowboard Shop** (205 Caribou St., 403/762-8211, 10am-9pm daily), but don't expect to find anything suitable for your grandparents.

Camping and Outdoor Gear

Inexpensive camping equipment and supplies can be found in **Home Hardware** (223 Bear St., 403/762-2080, 8:30am-6pm Mon.-Sat., 10am-4pm Sun.). More specialized needs are catered to at **Monod Sports** (129 Banff Ave., 403/762-4571, 10am-8pm daily). Locally owned **Abominable Sports** (229 Banff Ave., 403/762-2905, 9am-9pm daily in summer, 8am-8pm daily the rest of the year) has a good selection of hiking boots and outdoor clothing.

Gifts and Galleries

Banff's numerous galleries display the work of mostly Canadian artists. The town's best-known shopping experience is at the **Banff Trading Post** (1 Birch Ave., 403/762-2456, 9am-8pm daily in summer, 9am-6pm daily the rest of the year), across the Bow River from downtown in a distinctive building overlooking the river. Open since 1903, walking through the historic building is like stepping back in time. **Canada House Gallery** (201 Bear St., 403/762-3757, 9:30am-6pm daily) features a wide selection of Canadian landscape and wildlife works and First Nations art. Up in the Fairmont Banff Springs, the **Quest Gallery** (405 Spray Ave., 403/762-4422, 10am-6pm daily) offers a diverse range of Canadian paintings and crafts, as well as more exotic pieces such as mammoth tusks from prehistoric times and Inuit carvings from Nunavut.

FOOD

Whether you're in search of an inexpensive snack for the family or silver service, you can find it in the town of Banff, which has more than 80 restaurants (more per capita than any other town or city across Canada). The quality of food varies greatly. Some restaurants revolve solely around the tourist trade, while others have reputations that attract diners from Calgary who have been known to stay overnight just to eat at their favorite haunt. While the quality of food is most people's number one priority when dining out, the level of service (or lack of it) also comes into play in Banff, especially if you are paying big bucks for a fine-dining meal. Getting it all right—good food, top-notch service, and a memorable ambience—in a tourism-oriented town is rare. Which leads to the restaurants I've recommended below, the best of a very varied bunch.

Groceries

Banff has two major grocery stores. In addition to a wide selection of basic groceries, **Nesters Market** (122 Bear St., 403/762-3663, 8am-11pm daily in summer, shorter hours the rest of the year) has a good deli with pre-made salads and sandwiches, as well as meats, cheeses, and rotisserie chickens. At the other end of downtown is **IGA** (318 Marten St., 403/762-5329, 8am-11pm daily). In summer, try to avoid both places between 4pm and 7pm as they get very crowded.

Coffee and Baked Goods

My favorite Banff coffee joint is **Whitebark** (Banff Aspen Lodge, 401 Banff Ave., 403/760-7298, 6:30am-7pm daily), a few blocks north of the main shopping strip but well worth searching out for the finest coffee in town, including one of the best places in Banff to pour true Americanos. The outside patio is a great place to soak up summer sun. Back toward town and overlooking a busy intersection is another great patio, this one the **Good Earth Coffeehouse** (Elk + Avenue Hotel, 333 Banff Ave., 403/985-0989, 7am-5pm daily), and if it's not so warm, there's a central outdoor gas fireplace surrounded by Adirondack chairs.

Uprising (202 Banff Ave., 403/985-0989, 8am-7pm daily) is a great place to pick up a coffee or pastry, but where this place really shines is its delicious array of gourmet breads. The breads are used in the premade sandwiches, or you can buy a loaf to go. Banff's other bakery is **Wild Flour** (Bison Courtyard, 211 Bear St., 403/760-5074, 7am-4pm daily), and it's also a good one, with organic ingredients used whenever possible. The result is an array of healthy breads, gluten-free choices, mouthwatering cakes and pastries, and delicious meat pies. Eat inside or out in the courtyard.

Modern **Evelyn's Coffee World** (Sundance Mall, 215 Banff Ave., 403/762-0352, 7am-9pm daily, sandwiches $10) has a very central location pouring good coffee sourced from around the world and serving huge sandwiches. The few outside tables—on the busiest stretch of the busiest street in town—are perfect for people-watching. **Banff National Perk** (220 Bear St., 403/762-8642, 7am-5pm daily, cakes from $5) is another local place serving decent coffee and delicious pastries, muffins, and cakes baked daily on the premises.

Cheap Eats

For something completely unique, plan on riding the chairlift at Norquay to the ★ **Cliffhouse Bistro** (Mount Norquay Rd., 6 kilometers/3.7 miles from downtown Banff, 403/762-4421, mid-June-mid-Oct. 11am-6:30pm daily, lunches $15-24). Access is by chairlift (adult $37, child $24) to a 1950s stone building that has been creatively revamped to bring back its vintage glory, complete with views across the Bow Valley and a log fireplace. You can enjoy the panorama over tea or coffee, or order lunches such as paninis, salads, and nachos to share.

A good place to begin looking for cheap eats is the food court in the lower level of Cascade Shops (317 Banff Ave.). Here you'll find a juice bar, a fried chicken outlet, a place selling pizza by the slice, and **Banff Edo,** which sells simple Japanese dishes for around $12, including a drink. Also downtown is **Banff Poutine** (223 Bear St., 403/985-3333, 11am-10pm daily, $9-16), a hole-in-the-wall eatery with a couple of indoor tables and a menu of traditional Canadian poutine (potatoes and cheese curds smothered in gravy) and smoked meat sandwiches.

The main reasons for visiting the Banff Centre include attending the many events, exercising at the fitness facility, or wandering through the grounds. Add to this list having a casual meal at **Le Cafe** (Banff Centre, Tunnel Mountain Dr., 403/762-6100, 10am-10pm daily, $8-14), overlooking the swimming pool within the Sally Borden Building. The coffee is roasted locally and the sandwiches are made to order, or try a mini-pizza or bowl of steaming soup. In the adjacent Kinnear Centre, **Maclab Bistro** (Banff Centre, Tunnel Mountain Dr., 403/762-6100, 7am-midnight daily, $14-22) is a much larger space with tables spilling outside onto a patio. The menu features flatbread pizzas, healthy sandwiches, and gourmet burgers.

Cougar Pete's Restaurant in the Banff Alpine Centre (810 Hidden Ridge Way, off Tunnel Mountain Rd., 403/762-4122, 7am-1pm and 5pm-10pm daily, $11-18) offers free wireless Internet and a great outdoor patio. The menu features all the usual café-style dishes, such as a pile of nachos for $11.

Aardvarks (304 Caribou St., 403/762-5500, noon-4am daily) is a late-night pizza hangout.

Family-Style Dining

Children will love the food and parents will love the prices at **Old Spaghetti Factory** (2nd Fl., Cascade Shops on Banff Ave., 403/760-2779, 11:30am-10pm daily, $13-28). The large room is casual-rustic, with a few tables spread along a covered balcony. Sort through a maze of combinations and specials (kids get their own color-in menu), and the most you'll pay for a meal is $25, which includes soup or salad, a side of bread, dessert, and coffee.

A town favorite that has faithfully served locals and visitors alike for many years is **Melissa's** (218 Lynx St., 403/762-5776, 7am-10pm daily, $18-40), housed upstairs overlooking the busiest intersection on Banff Avenue. It's the best place in town for classic North American cooked breakfasts in the $15-18 range. Lunch and dinner are traditional, casual affairs. Choose from a wide variety of generously sized burgers, freshly prepared salads, and Alberta beef.

Steak

Alberta beef is mostly raised on ranchland east of Banff National Park and features prominently on menus throughout town. Finely marbled AAA beef is used in most better restaurants and is unequaled in its tender, juicy qualities.

★ **Saltlik** (221 Bear St., 403/762-2467, 11am-midnight daily, $29-58) is the perfect choice for serious carnivores with cash to spare. At one of Banff's most fashionable restaurants, the dining room is big and bold, and the concrete-and-steel split-level interior is complemented by modish wood furnishings. Facing the street, glass doors in the street-level lounge fold back to a terrace for warm-weather dining. The specialty is AAA Alberta beef, finished with grain feeding to enhance the flavor, then flash-seared at 650°C (1,200°F) to seal in the juices, and served with a side platter of seasonal vegetables. Entrées are priced comparable to a city steak house, but the cost creeps up as you add side dishes.

Classically Canadian

★ **Park** (219 Banff Ave., 403/762-5114, 11am-midnight daily, $18-35) does a wonderful job of combining classic campfire cooking with modern dining trends—all within a massive space in the heart of downtown that perfectly reflects the food and the history of the park, with a massive stone fireplace and seating choices that include a balcony overlooking Banff Avenue and communal tables beside the open kitchen. Many of the dishes are cooked over a wood-fired grill or on a rotisserie, creating deliciously smoky campfire-like flavors: You could start with rotisserie chicken chowder or corn bread smothered in maple-rum butter, and then choose from mains such as pork-and-beans or AAA T-bone. Craft beers and house-distilled spirits round out this excellent choice.

The retractable roof at **T3 Bears** (205 Bear St., 403/985-80838, 11:30am-10pm, $22-30) may be the showstopper, but the food at the upscale brewpub is designed to be shared and is relatively well priced (for Banff). You can't go wrong with the crab doughnuts, roasted cauliflower, lamb ribs, or single-serve pizzas.

The Prow (Buffalo Mountain Lodge, 700 Tunnel Mountain Dr., 403/762-4484, 7am-11:30am, noon-10pm daily, $24-46) offers the perfect setting for a moderate splurge. It features a distinctive mountain-rustic setting—complete with stone fireplace and a chandelier made entirely from elk antlers—along with large windows that frame the surrounding forest. The featured cuisine is referred to as Rocky Mountain, reflecting an abundance of Canadian game meats offered both as tapas-style dishes and as full meals.

The food at ★ **Storm Mountain Lodge** (Hwy. 93, 403/762-4155, 8am-10:30am, 11:30am-3pm, and 5pm-9pm daily May-mid-Oct., 5pm-9pm Fri.-Sun. early Dec.-Apr., $29-45) is excellent, but it's the ambience you'll remember long after leaving—an intoxicating blend of historic appeal and rustic mountain charm. The chef uses mostly organic produce with seasonally available game and seafood—bison, venison, wild salmon, and the like—to create tasty and interesting dishes well suited to the I-must-be-in-the-Canadian-wilderness surroundings. Storm Mountain Lodge is a 25-minute drive northwest from Banff; take the Trans-Canada Highway toward Lake Louise and head west at the Castle Mountain interchange.

Canadian Contemporary

Occupying the prime position on one of Banff's busiest corners is the **Maple Leaf** (137 Banff Ave., 403/760-7680, 10am-10pm daily, $28-47). Take in the dramatic Canadian-themed decor—exposed river stone, polished log work, a two-story interior rock wall, and a moose head (tucked around the corner from the street-level lounge). Some tables surround a busy area by the bar, so try to talk your way into the upstairs back corner. The modern dishes use an abundance of Canadian game and produce. The lunch menu has a bison burger, along with lighter salads and gourmet sandwiches. Some of Canada's finest ingredients appear on the dinner menu; stuffed halibut and the bacon-wrapped bison tenderloin are standouts. Treat yourself to a glass of Canadian ice wine to accompany dessert.

Bison Banff (Bison Courtyard, 211 Bear St., 403/762-5550, 5pm-10pm daily, $25-66) is an upstairs eatery featuring the very best Canadian ingredients. The interesting decor sees chic-industrial blending with mountain rustic. Tables are inside or out at this upstairs dining room, and almost all have a view of the open kitchen. The food is solidly Canadian, with a menu that takes advantage of wild game, seafood, and Alberta beef.

Juniper Bistro (The Juniper, off Mt. Norquay Rd., 403/763-6219, 7am-1:30pm and 5pm-10pm daily, $17-35) is well worth searching out for both Canadian cuisine and unparalleled views across town to Mount Rundle and the Spray Valley. The stylish interior may be inviting, but in warmer weather you'll want to be outside on the patio, where the panorama is most spectacular. The menu blends traditional tastes with Canadian produce. If your taste runs toward the adventurous, there's duck wings as a starter. For those looking for something a little more local, the AAA ribeye is a good choice. Most breakfasts are in the $14-18 range, while at lunch, the Caesar salad is one of the best in town.

Southwestern

Banff's original bistro-style restaurant, which opened in the early 1990s, is **Coyote's** (206 Caribou St., 403/762-3963, 7:30am-10pm daily, $17-29). Well-priced meals are prepared in full view of diners, and the menu emphasizes fresh, health-conscious cooking, with just a hint of Southwestern/Mediterranean style. To start, it's hard to go past the sweet potato and corn chowder; then choose from mains such as barbecued flank steak marinated in Cajun spices and topped with a generous dab of corn-and-tomato salsa.

European

The **Balkan** (120 Banff Ave., 403/762-3454, 11:30am-9pm Sun.-Thurs., 11:30am-10pm Fri.-Sat., $24-37) is run by a local Greek family, but the menu blends their heritage with the cuisines of Italy, China, and Canada. Select from Greek ribs (pork ribs with a lemon sauce), the Greek chow mein (stir-fried vegetables, fried rice, and your choice of meat), or Greek spaghetti. But the most popular dishes are souvlaki and an enormous Greek platter for two.

★ **Ticino** (High Country Inn, 415 Banff Ave., 403/762-3848, 5:30pm-10pm daily, $19-38) reflects the heritage of the park's early mountain guides, with solid timber furnishings, lots of peeled and polished log work, and old wooden skis, huge cowbells, and an alpenhorn decorating the walls. It's named for the southern province of Switzerland, where the cuisine has a distinctive Italian influence. The Swiss chef is best known for a creamy wild mushroom soup, unique to the region; his beef and cheese fondues; juicy cuts of Alberta beef; and veal dishes. Save room for one of Ticino's sinfully rich desserts. Also of note is the professional service.

Fondue

Even if you've tried exotic meats, you probably haven't had them in a restaurant like the ★ **Grizzly House** (207 Banff Ave., 403/762-4055, 11:30am-midnight daily, $45-80 per person for four courses), which provides Banff's most unusual dining experience. The decor is, to say the least, eclectic (many say eccentric). Think lots of twisted woods, a motorbike hanging from the ceiling, a melted telephone on the wall. Each table has a phone for cross-table conversation, or you can put a call through to your server, the bar, a cab, diners in the private booth, or even those who spend too long in the bathroom. The food is equally unique, and the service is as professional as anywhere in town. The menu hasn't changed in decades, and this doesn't displease anyone. Most dining revolves around traditional Swiss fondues, but with nontraditional dipping meats such as rattlesnake, alligator, shark, ostrich, scallops, elk, and wild boar. Four-course table d'hôte fondue dinners are $45-80 per person, which includes soup or salad, a cheese fondue, a choice of one of six meat and seafood fondue (or hot rock) selections, and finally a fruity chocolate fondue. The Grizzly House is also open at lunch, when you can sample Canadian game at reduced prices; wild game meat loaf is $28, and an Alberta-farmed buffalo burger is $25.

Asian

At the back of the Clock Tower Mall, **Pad Thai** (110 Banff Ave., 403/762-4911, noon-9pm daily, $14-20) is a real find for those looking for inexpensive Thai cuisine. The namesake pad thai is $16, curries are all around the same price, and delicious spring rolls are $6. You can eat in or take out.

A couple of doors off Banff Avenue, **Sushi House Banff** (304 Caribou St., 403/762-2971, 11:30am-10pm daily, $16-26) is a tiny space with a dozen stools set around a moving miniature railway that has diners picking sushi and other delicacies from a train as it circles the chef, who is loading the carriages as quickly as they empty.

Fairmont Banff Springs

Whether guests or not, most visitors to Banff drop by to see one of the town's biggest tourist attractions, and a meal here might not be as expensive as you think. The hotel itself has more eateries than most small towns—from a deli serving coffee and muffins to the finest of fine dining in the 1888 Chop House.

For excellent coffee, or if you are in the mood for a snack such as soups or sandwiches, head to the lobby level and **STOCK Food & Drink** (6:30am-9:30pm daily, $8-14).

The **Rundle Bar** (11am-1am daily, $16-33) combines an area filled with comfortable sofas with an upstairs piano bar, where most tables offer views down the Bow Valley. The doors of the Rundle Lounge open to the ★ **Lookout Patio** (11:30am-sunset daily, summer only, $16-21), featuring magnificent views down the Bow Valley. The menu is Mexican-inspired, but you can also simply kick back with a cold drink and appetizer to share.

If you're looking for a more intimate experience, two in-house restaurants shine. **Grapes** (5pm-9:30pm daily, $18-26) is a cozy, casual wine bar noted for its fine cheeses, cured meats, and pâtés. More substantial meals such as fondues are also offered. Ensconced in an octagonal room of the Manor Wing, **Castello Ristorante** (6pm-9:30pm daily, $36-53) is a seductive dining room with a modern, upscale ambience. The menu is dominated by Italian favorites, with traditional pastas and specialties such as veal tenderloin.

The hotel's breakfast venue is the **Vermillion Room,** a pleasant dining room that seats over 250 diners. Each morning from 6am, an expansive buffet of hot and cold delicacies, including freshly baked bread and seasonal fruits, is laid out for the masses (adult $34, child $17). Lunch offers a wide-ranging menu featuring everything from salads to seafood. The evening menu is decidedly French, with mains in the $30-48 range. The weekend brunch (11am-3pm Sat.-Sun., adult $54, child $27) is legendary, with chefs working at numerous stations scattered around the dining area and an enormous spread not equaled for variety anywhere in the mountains.

The hotel's most acclaimed restaurant is **1888 Chop House** (6pm-9:30pm daily, $42-80), which seats just 65 guests. This fine-dining restaurant is a bastion of elegance, apparent once you arrive through a gated entrance. Inside, extravagantly rich wood furnishings, perfectly presented table settings, muted lighting, and professional staff create an atmosphere as far removed from the surrounding wilderness as is imaginable. Reservations are required.

Two restaurants lie within the grounds surrounding the hotel, and both are worthy of consideration. Originally the golf course clubhouse, the **Waldhaus Restaurant** (6pm-9pm daily, $23-34) is nestled in a forested area directly below the hotel. The big room is dominated by dark woods and is warmed by an open fireplace. The menu features German specialties, such as fondues. Below the restaurant is a pub (noon-11pm daily) of the same name, with a pub-style dinner menu offered in a casual atmosphere. Wonderful views are the main draw at **Stanley's Smokehouse** (10am-8pm daily in summer, $16-34), a seasonal restaurant on the golf course proper that serves casual meals ranging from salads to smoked beef brisket. A free shuttle bus runs every 30 minutes between the main hotel lobby and the clubhouse.

For all Fairmont Banff Springs dining reservations, call 403/762-6860.

ACCOMMODATIONS AND CAMPING

Finding a room in Banff National Park in summer is nearly as hard as trying to justify its price. By late afternoon, just about every room and campsite in the park will be occupied, and basic hotel rooms start at $400. It is also worth noting that prices vary according to demand. If hotels have rooms available, they may sell them off more cheaply at the last minute, but when demand is high, room prices at many hotels can start at $400. Fortunately, many alternatives are available. Rooms in private homes begin at around $200 d and dorm beds at local hostels run from $45. Bungalows or cabins can be rented, which can be cost-effective for families or small groups. Approximately 2,400 campsites in 13 campgrounds accommodate campers. Wherever you decide to stay, it is vital to book well ahead during summer and the Christmas holidays. The park's off-season is October-May, and hotels offer huge rate reductions during this period. Shop around, and you'll find many bargains.

All rates quoted are for a standard room in the high season (June-Sept.).

In and Around the Town of Banff

Banff has a few accommodations right downtown, but most are strung out along Banff Avenue, an easy walk from the shopping and dining precinct. Nearby Tunnel Mountain is also home to a cluster of accommodations.

UNDER $100

The only beds in town less than $100 are in dormitories, and therefore, rates given are per person.

HI-Banff Alpine Centre (801 Hidden Ridge Way, 403/762-4123 or 866/762-4122, www.hihostels.ca) is just off Tunnel Mountain Road, 3 kilometers (1.9 miles) from downtown. This large, modern hostel sleeps 216 in small two-, four-, and six-bed dormitory rooms as well as four-bed cabins. The large lounge area has a fireplace, and other facilities include a recreation room, public Internet access, a bike and ski/snowboard workshop, large kitchen, self-service café/bar, and laundry. In summer, members of Hostelling International pay $54-58 per person per night (nonmembers $60-66) for a dorm bed or from $180 s or d ($200 for nonmembers) for a private room. During July and August, reserve at least a couple of months in advance to be assured of a bed. The hostel is open all day, but check-in isn't until midday. To get there from town, ride the Banff Transit bus ($2), which passes the hostel twice an hour during summer.

A one-time hospital, **YWCA Banff Hotel** (102 Spray Ave., 403/762-3560, www.ywcabanff.ca, dorm $45, $200-240 s or d) is a centrally located choice for budget travelers. Facilities include a laundry facility, wireless Internet, and the Great Room—a huge living area where the centerpiece is a massive stone fireplace, with writing desks and shelves stocked with books scattered throughout. Some private rooms have en suite bathrooms.

Along the main strip of accommodations and a five-minute walk to downtown is **Samesun Banff** (433 Banff Ave., 403/762-4499, www.samesun.com, dorm $70-74, $192 s or d), which offers clean and comfortable accommodations. As converted motel rooms, each dormitory has its own bathroom, and some are for females only. Guest amenities include a pub with daily food and drink specials, wireless Internet, free continental breakfast, and underground (but not heated) parking.

$100-200

Accommodations in this price range are limited. In addition to private rooms at the HI-Banff Alpine Centre and the YWCA Banff Hotel, there are the seven guest rooms at the **Elkhorn Lodge** (124 Spray Ave., 403/762-2299, www.elkhornbanff.ca, $176-330). Travelers on a budget who aren't fans of bed-and-breakfasts will find this older lodge suitable. The four small sleeping rooms, each with a bathroom, TV, and coffeemaker, are $176 s or d, while larger rooms with fridges are $315-330. Rates include a light breakfast. It's halfway up the hill to the Fairmont Banff Springs.

Blue Mountain Lodge (137 Muskrat St., 403/762-5134, www.bluemtnlodge.com, $180-300 s or d) is a rambling, older-style lodge with 10 guest rooms, each with a private bath, TV, and telephone. The Trapper's Cabin room is the most expensive, but the gabled ceiling, walls decorated with snowshoes and bearskin, and an electric fireplace create a funky mountain feel. All guests have use of shared kitchen facilities, a lounge, and Internet access while enjoying an expansive cold buffet breakfast to fuel a day of hiking.

$200-300
Mountain View B&B (347 Grizzly St., 403/760-9353, www.mountainviewbanff.ca, May-Sept., $265-300 s or d) is on a quiet residential street three blocks from the heart of downtown. The two guest rooms in the main house are simply furnished, each with a double bed, TV, sink, and bar fridge. They share a bathroom and a common area that includes basic cooking facilities (microwave, toaster, kettle) and opens to a private deck. Two additional rooms in the adjacent Carriage House are large and have en suite bathrooms. Off-street parking and a light breakfast round out this excellent choice.

$300-400
More than 100 years since Jim and Bill Brewster guided their first guests through the park, their descendants are still actively involved in the tourist industry, operating the central and very stylish ★ **Brewster's Mountain Lodge** (208 Caribou St., 403/762-2900 or 888/762-2900, www.brewstermountainlodge.com, $390-510 s or d). The building features an eye-catching log exterior with an equally impressive lobby. The western theme is continued in the 77 upstairs rooms. Standard rooms feature two queen-size beds, deluxe rooms offer a jetted tub and sitting area, and loft suites are designed for families.

Packages provide good value here, while off-season rates are slashed up to 30 percent.

The 99 guest rooms at the **Banff Inn** (501 Banff Ave., 403/762-8844, www.banffinn. com, $340-380 s or d) are no-frills modern in appearance. Pluses include underground heated parking, a large indoor whirlpool, a guest lounge with a fireplace, and free continental breakfast.

Opened as a bungalow camp in 1946, **Douglas Fir Resort** (525 Tunnel Mountain Rd., 403/762-5591 or 800/661-9267, www. douglasfir.com, from $340 s or d) is now a sprawling complex of 133 large condo-style units a 15-minute downhill walk (or short bus ride) to town. Although falling in the same price range as many of those on Banff Avenue, all units are self-contained, making them good for families, small groups, or those who want to cook their own meals. Each has a fully equipped kitchen and a living area with fireplace. Other facilities include a hot tub, an exercise room, squash and tennis courts, a grocery store, and a laundry. Infinitely more important if you have children are the indoor waterslides.

$400-500
The 134-room **Banff Ptarmigan Inn** (337 Banff Ave., 403/762-2207 or 800/661-8310, www.bestofbanff.com, from $464 s or d) is a slick, full-service hotel with tastefully decorated rooms, down comforters on all beds, the Meatball Italian restaurant, complimentary cooked breakfasts, heated underground parking, wireless Internet, and a variety of facilities to soothe sore muscles, including a spa, whirlpool, and sauna.

Since opening in 1908, the centrally located **Mount Royal Hotel** (138 Banff Ave., 403/762-3331 or 877/442-2623, www.banffjaspercollection.com, from $450 s or d) has seen various expansions. Today, guests are offered more than 130 tastefully decorated rooms and the use of a large health club with hot tub. Also on the premises is a family-style restaurant and small lounge. For a splurge, you won't find better than the one-bedroom suites (from $600).

Canalta Lodge (545 Banff Ave., 403/762-2112, www.canaltalodge.com, $460-520 s or d) is a modern mountain-style lodge where the 120 guest rooms are spacious and a relatively good value for Banff (upgrade to a king bed for $480 s or d or a Loft Suite that sleeps four for $520). A hot breakfast buffet and rooftop hot tubs are bonuses.

Toward downtown from the Banff Inn is the **High Country Inn** (419 Banff Ave., 403/762-2236 or 800/293-5142, www.banff-highcountryinn.com, $400-505 s or d), which has a heated indoor pool, spacious hot tubs, a cedar-lined sauna, and the ever-popular Ticino Swiss/Italian restaurant. All rooms are adequately furnished with comfortable beds and an earthy color scheme. The High Country's honeymoon suite ($505) is an excellent value; it features a king-size bed, fireplace, jetted tub, and a large balcony with views to Cascade Mountain.

The **Rundlestone Lodge** (537 Banff Ave., 403/762-2201 or 800/661-8630, www.rundlestone.com, $440-590 s or d) features mountain-style architecture with an abundance of raw stonework and exposed timber inside and out. At street level is a comfortable sitting area centered on a fireplace, as well as an indoor pool, a lounge-style bar, and a restaurant. Furniture and fittings in the 96 rooms are elegant, and many rooms have small balconies and gas fireplaces; some are wheelchair accessible.

The best rooms along the motel strip are at **Royal Canadian Lodge** (459 Banff Ave., 403/762-3307 or 888/778-5050, www.royalcanadianlodge.com, from $460 s or d), which features 99 luxuriously appointed rooms, heated underground parking, a lounge, a dining room where upscale Canadian specialties are the highlight, a spa/pool complex, and a landscaped courtyard.

Although the ★ **Banff Aspen Lodge** (401 Banff Ave., 403/762-4401 or 877/886-8857, www.banffaspenlodge.com, $429-479 s or d) is priced a little higher than some other properties along this section of the motel strip, value is excellent. Standard rates include a full cooked breakfast buffet, use of two outdoor hot pools, and a steam room/sauna. Rooms themselves are modern and well maintained. It's worth the extra $20-40 for a room with a balcony and mountain views.

OVER $500

At **Buffalo Mountain Lodge,** a 15-minute walk from town on Tunnel Mountain Road (700 Tunnel Mountain Rd., 403/762-2400 or 800/661-1367, www.crmr.com, $525 s or d), you'll notice the impressive timber-frame construction, as well as the hand-hewn construction of the lobby, with its vaulted ceiling and eye-catching fieldstone fireplace. The 108 rooms, chalets, and bungalows all have fireplaces, balconies, large bathrooms, and comfortable beds topped by feather-filled duvets; many have kitchens. Although rack rates start at over $500, book online to pick up summer rates around $400 including breakfast. (The lodge takes its name from Tunnel Mountain, which early park visitors called Buffalo Mountain for its shape.)

Hidden Ridge Resort (901 Hidden Ridge Way, 403/762-3544 or 800/661-1372, www.banffhiddenridge.com, from $550 s or d) sits on a forested hillside away from the main buzz of traffic. Choose from modern condo-style units or much larger premier king whirlpool tub suites. All units have wood-burning fireplaces, wireless Internet, and balconies or patios, and the condos have washer/dryer combos. In the center of the complex is a barbecue area and 30-person outdoor hot tub overlooking the valley.

Bed-and-breakfast connoisseurs will fall in love with **Buffaloberry B&B** (417 Marten St., 403/762-3750, www.buffaloberry.com, $515 s or d), a purpose-built lodging within walking distance of downtown. The home itself is a beautiful timber-and-stone structure, while inside, guests soak up mountain-style luxury in the vaulted living area, which comes complete with a stone fireplace, super-comfortable couches, and a library of local-interest books.

The spacious rooms come with niceties such as pillow-top mattresses, TV/DVD combos, heated bathroom floors, and bathrobes. Breakfast is equally impressive. Buffaloberry is also the only Banff bed-and-breakfast with heated underground parking.

Two blocks from downtown is **Moose Hotel & Suites** (345 Banff Ave., 403/762-2638 or 800/563-8764, www.moosehotelandsuites.com, from $600-1,200 s or d), which opened in 2016. Even the standard rooms are air-conditioned and come with luxuries such as rain showers. The one- and two-bedroom suites all have balconies, gas fireplaces, and basic cooking facilities. Other features include outdoor and indoor hot pools; a day spa with a private outdoor hot pool; a central courtyard with lots of outdoor seating, a firepit, and a restored 1908 home used for special events; and a classy yet well-priced family-style Italian restaurant.

Banff Log Cabin (226 Glen Cres., 403/762-3516, www.bannflogcabin.ca, $525 s or d) is exactly as the name suggests—a beautifully handcrafted log cabin that sleeps two comfortably. Dating to the 1970s and completely renovated since, it features a wrought-iron queen-size bed, deer-antler chandelier, full bathroom, and wall-mounted TV. Rates include a light breakfast (including freshly baked muffins) delivered to your door.

On Mountain Avenue, a short walk from the Upper Hot Springs, is **Rimrock Resort Hotel** (403/762-3356 or 888/746-7625, www.rimrockresort.com, from $830 s or d). The original hotel was constructed in 1903 but was fully rebuilt and opened as a full-service luxury resort in the mid-1990s. Guest amenities include two restaurants, two lounges, a health club, an outdoor patio, and a multistory heated parking garage. Each of the 345 well-appointed rooms is decorated with earthy tones offset by brightly colored fabrics. They also feature picture windows, a king-size bed, comfortable armchair, writing desk, two phones, a minibar, and a hair dryer. Since the hotel is set high above the Bow Valley, views for the most part are excellent, most notably from Suite Infinity, which costs $3,000 per night.

The 770-room **Fairmont Banff Springs** (405 Spray Ave., 403/762-2211 or 800/257-7544, www.fairmont.com, from $1,200 s or d) is Banff's best-known accommodation. Earlier this century, the hotel came under the ownership of Fairmont Hotels and Resorts, losing its century-old tag as a Canadian Pacific hotel and in the process its ties to the historic railway company that constructed the original hotel back in 1888. Even though the rooms have been modernized, many date to the 1920s, and as is common in older establishments, these accommodations are small (Fairmont rooms are 14.4 square meters/155 square feet). But room size is only a minor consideration when staying in this historic gem. With 12 eateries, four lounges, a luxurious spa facility, a huge indoor pool, elegant public spaces, a 27-hole golf course, tennis courts, horseback riding, and enough twisting, turning hallways, towers, and shops to warrant a detailed map, you'll not want to spend much time in your room. (Unless, of course, you are in the eight-room presidential suite.) During summer, rack rates for a regular Fairmont room are $1,200, discounted to around $600 or less the rest of the year. Many summer visitors stay as part of a package—the place to find these is on the website www.fairmont.com. Packages may simply include breakfast, while others will have you golfing, horseback riding, or relaxing in the spa.

Along the Bow Valley Parkway and Vicinity

The Bow Valley Parkway is the original route between Banff and Lake Louise. It is a beautiful drive in all seasons, and along its length are several accommodations, each a viable alternative to staying in Banff.

Johnston Canyon Resort (403/762-2971 or 888/378-1720, www.johnstoncanyon.com,

---

1: Moose Hotel & Suites **2:** Shadow Lake Lodge **3:** Rimrock Resort Hotel **4:** Park Interpretive Program in the summer

mid-May-early Oct., $370-780 s or d) is 26 kilometers (16 miles) west of Banff at the beginning of a short trail that leads to the famous canyon. The 42 cabins are older but have been thoroughly renovated on the inside, giving them a distinctive alpine charm. The larger cabins have multiple bedrooms and kitchens. On the grounds are tennis courts, a barbecue area, and a gift store. Resort dining options vary from munching on a burger and fries at the counter of an old-time cafeteria to enjoying pan-fried rainbow trout in a dining room that oozes alpine charm. Basic two-person duplex cabins are $370, two-person cabins with a gas fireplace and sitting area are $460, and offerings go up in price to $780 for a classic bungalow complete with two bedrooms, cooking facilities, and heritage-style furnishings—still reasonable when compared to downtown Banff prices.

Constructed by the Canadian Pacific Railway in 1922, ★ **Storm Mountain Lodge** (Hwy. 93, 403/762-4155, www.stormmountainlodge.com, daily in summer, Thurs.-Mon. only the rest of the year, $365-495 s or d) features 14 historic cabins restored to their former rustic glory. Each has its original log walls, along with a log bed, covered deck, a wood-burning fireplace, and bathroom with claw-foot tub. They don't have phones, Internet, or TVs, so there's little to distract you from the past. Look for fall and spring deals that include a breakfast and dinner for around the room-only price in summer. Outside, the wilderness beckons, with Storm Mountain as a backdrop. The lodge is at Vermilion Pass, a 25-minute drive from Banff or Lake Louise (head west from the Castle Mountain interchange). The lodge restaurant (8am-10:30am, 11:30am-3pm, and 5pm-8:30pm daily) is one of my favorite places to eat in the park.

At Castle Junction, 32 kilometers (20 miles) northwest of Banff, is **Castle Mountain Chalets** (403/762-3868 or 877/762-2281, www.castlemountain.com, $505-770 s or d). Set on 1.5 hectares (four acres), this resort is home to a collection of magnificent log chalets. Each has high ceilings, beautifully handcrafted log interiors, at least two beds, a stone fireplace, a full kitchen with dishwasher, a bathroom with hot tub, and satellite TV. Part of the complex has a grocery store, barbecue area, and the only gas between Banff and Lake Louise.

BACKCOUNTRY ACCOMMODATIONS

Shadow Lake Lodge (403/762-0116 or 866/762-0114, www.shadowlakelodge.com, mid-June-Sept.) is 13 kilometers (eight miles) from the nearest road. Access is on foot or, in winter, on skis. The lodge is near picturesque Shadow Lake, and many hiking trails are nearby. Dating to 1928, the oldest structure has been restored as a rustic yet welcoming lounge area, complete with wood-burning fireplace and library. Guests overnight in 12 newer, comfortable cabins, each with a queen or king bed. Guests share bathroom facilities, but these are modern and kept spotless. The daily rate, including three meals served buffet-style and afternoon tea, is $730-850 s or d per night. The trailhead is along the Trans-Canada Highway, 19 kilometers (12 miles) west of Banff, at the Redearth Creek parking area.

Campgrounds

Within Banff National Park, 13 campgrounds hold more than 2,400 sites. Although the town of Banff has five of these facilities with more than 1,500 sites in its immediate vicinity, most fill by early afternoon. The three largest campgrounds are strung out over 1.5 kilometers (0.9 mile) along Tunnel Mountain Road, with the nearest sites 2.5 kilometers (1.6 miles) from town. Sites at most campgrounds can be reserved through the **Parks Canada Reservation Service** (877/737-3783, www.reservation.pc.gc.ca) starting in mid-January, and it's strongly recommended that you do reserve if you require electrical hookups or want to stay at one of the more popular campgrounds, such as Two Jack Lakeside. Although some sites are available for those without reservations, they fill fast each day (especially in July and August).

Open fires are permitted in designated areas throughout all campgrounds, but you must purchase a firewood permit ($8.80 per site per night) to burn wood, which is provided at no cost. For general camping information, stop at the **Banff Visitor Centre** (224 Banff Ave., 403/762-1550) or go to the Parks Canada website, www.pc.gc.ca, and follow the links to Banff National Park.

AROUND THE TOWN OF BANFF

Closest to town is **Tunnel Mountain Campground,** which is three campgrounds rolled into one. The location is a lightly treed ridge east of downtown, with views north to Cascade Mountain and south to Mount Rundle. From town, follow Tunnel Mountain Road east to beyond the Douglas Fir Resort (which is within walking distance for groceries, liquor, and laundry). If you're coming in off the Trans-Canada Highway from the east, bypass town completely by turning left onto Tunnel Mountain Road at the Banff Rocky Mountain Resort. Approaching from this direction, the first campground you pass is the park's largest, with 622 well-spaced, relatively private sites ($29 per site), each with a fire ring and picnic table. Other amenities include drinking water, hot showers, and kitchen shelters. This campground has no hookups. It is open mid-May-early September. Less than one kilometer (0.6 mile) farther along Tunnel Mountain Road toward town is a signed turnoff ("Hookups") that leads to a registration booth for two more campgrounds. Unless you have a reservation from Parks Canada Reservation Service (877/737-3783, www.reservation.pc.gc.ca), you'll be asked whether you require an electrical hookup ($33 per site) or a site with power, water, and sewer ($39 per site), and then sent off into the corresponding campground. The power-only section (closest to town) stays open year-round, the other mid-May-September. Both have hot showers but little privacy between sites.

Along Lake Minnewanka Road northeast of town are two campgrounds offering fewer services than the others, but with sites that offer more privacy. The pick of the two is **Two Jack Lakeside Campground** (June-mid-Sept., $33 per site), for which you will need advance reservations. It features 80 sites tucked into trees at the south end of Two Jack Lake, an extension of Lake Minnewanka. Facilities include hot showers, kitchen shelters, drinking water, and flush toilets. It's just over 6 kilometers (3.7 miles) from the Trans-Canada Highway underpass. The much larger **Two Jack Main Campground** (mid-June-mid-Sept., $23 per site; no reservations) is a short distance farther along the road, with 381 sites spread throughout a shallow valley. It offers the same facilities as Two Jack Lakeside, sans showers. If you arrive in Banff without campground reservations, Two Jack Main is probably your best chance of getting a campsite, but no guarantees.

BOW VALLEY PARKWAY

Along Bow Valley Parkway between the town of Banff and Castle Junction are two campgrounds. Closest to Banff is **Johnston Canyon Campground** (early June-mid-Sept., $29 per site), between the road and the rail line, 26 kilometers (16 miles) west of Banff. It is the largest of the three campgrounds, with 140 sites, and has hot showers but no hookups. Almost directly opposite is Johnston Canyon Resort, with groceries and a restaurant, and the beginning of a trail to the park's best-known waterfalls.

Continuing 8 kilometers (5 miles) toward Lake Louise, **Castle Mountain Campground** (late June-Aug., $23 per site) is also within walking distance of a grocery store (no restaurant), but it has just 44 sites and no showers. Services are limited to flush toilets, drinking water, and kitchen shelters.

INFORMATION

Many sources of information are available on the park and its commercial facilities. Once you've arrived, the best place to make your first stop is the **Banff Visitor Centre** (224 Banff Ave., 8am-8pm daily mid-May-Sept., 9am-5pm daily Oct.-mid-May). This central complex houses information desks for **Parks Canada** (403/762-1550) and the **Banff/Lake Louise Tourism Bureau** (403/762-0270), as well as a retail outlet that stocks guidebooks, maps, and bear spray.

National Park Information

On the right-hand side of the **Banff Visitor Centre** is a row of desks staffed by Parks Canada employees. They will answer all your queries regarding Banff's natural wonders and advise you of trail closures. If you haven't already done so, you can purchase a day or annual pass here, or check for available backcountry campsites. Also here, you can pick up park brochures or wander down the back to peruse park maps, view a free slideshow, and watch videos about the park. All questions pertaining to the national park itself can be answered here, or check out the Parks Canada website (www.pc.gc.ca).

To report wildlife sightings, call **Banff Dispatch** (403/762-1470), in the industrial park at the north entrance to town. The **weather office** (403/762-2088) offers updated forecasts. If you want to *see* the weather in Banff, check out the gondola webcam at www.banffjaspercollection.com.

Tourism Information

In the **Banff Visitor Centre,** across the floor from Parks Canada, is a desk for **Banff Lake Louise Tourism** (403/762-8421, www.banfflakelouise.com). This organization represents businesses and commercial establishments in the park. Here you can find out about accommodations and restaurants, and have any other questions answered. To answer the most frequently asked question here: the **restrooms** are downstairs.

Newspapers

Look for the free *Crag and Canyon* each Wednesday. It's been keeping residents and visitors informed about park issues and town gossip for more than a century. The *Rocky Mountain Outlook* is another free weekly newspaper (Thursday) that offers coverage of mountain life and upcoming events. Both are available on stands at businesses throughout town.

BOOKS AND MAPS

The Canadian Rockies are one of the most written about, and definitely the most photographed, regions in Canada. As a walk along Banff Avenue will confirm, there is definitely no lack of postcards, calendars, and coffee-table books about the area.

Summerthought Publishing (www.summerthought.com) is a local company that has been publishing the authoritative *Canadian Rockies Trail Guide* since 1971 as well as history books authored by Ted (E. J.) Hart, a former director of the Whyte Museum.

Purchase waterproof and tear-resistant **Gem Trek** (www.gemtrek.com) hiking maps through the company website in advance of your trip, or at visitor centers, bookstores, and outdoor retailers throughout Banff National Park.

Bookstores

On Banff's busiest thoroughfare, **Banff Visitor Centre** (224 Banff Ave., 8am-8pm daily mid-May-Sept., 9am-5pm daily Oct.-mid-May) has a selection of the best hiking guides as well as maps and scenic books.

The **Whyte Museum Shop** (111 Bear St., 403/762-2291, 10am-5pm daily) specializes in regional natural and human history books, and also has a good selection of historic prints.

Library

The **Banff Public Library** (opposite Central Park at 101 Bear St., 403/762-2661, 10am-8pm Mon.-Thurs., 10am-6pm Fri., 11am-5pm Sat., 1pm-5pm Sun.) boasts an extensive collection of nonfiction books, many about the park and its environs, which makes it an excellent rainy-day hangout. It also has a large collection of magazines and newspapers. Internet access is free.

SERVICES

The **post office** (9am-5:30pm Mon.-Fri.) is on the corner of Buffalo and Bear Streets opposite Central Park. The general-delivery service here is probably among the busiest in the country, due to the thousands of seasonal workers in the area.

Major banks can be found along Banff Avenue and are generally open 9:30am-4pm Monday-Thursday, 9am-5pm Friday. The **Bank of Montreal** (107 Banff Ave., 403/762-2275) allows cash advances with MasterCard, while the **CIBC** (98 Banff Ave., 403/762-3317) accepts Visa. **Freya's Currency Exchange** is in the Clock Tower Mall (108 Banff Ave., 403/762-4652, 11am-7pm daily).

The only downtown laundry is **Cascade Coin Laundry** (317 Banff Ave., 403/762-3444, 7:30am-10pm daily), on the lower level of the Cascade Shops.

Mineral Springs Hospital (301 Lynx St., 403/762-2222) has 24-hour emergency service. **Rexall Drug Store,** on the lower level of the Cascade Shops (317 Banff Ave., 403/762-2245), is open from 9am until 8pm daily.

Get online access at all Banff lodgings, at most downtown cafés, or head to the **Banff Public Library** (101 Bear St., 403/762-2661, 10am-8pm Mon.-Thurs., 10am-6pm Fri., 11am-5pm Sat., 1pm-5pm Sun.).

GETTING THERE

The town of Banff is along the Trans-Canada Highway 128 kilometers (80 miles) west of Calgary and 836 kilometers (519 miles) east of Vancouver. Allow 90 minutes and 10 hours, respectively. From Jasper in the north, the Icefields Parkway leads 230 kilometers (143 miles) south to Lake Louise, from where it's a farther 56 kilometers (35 miles) southeast to Banff. As there are speed restrictions and often heavy traffic on this route, allow at least four hours to travel from Jasper to Banff. If you're driving to Banff from the United States, the best approach route depends on your starting point. Although it may not appear so from looking quickly at a map, the best way to reach Banff from Seattle is to take I-5 north to Vancouver and then the Trans-Canada Highway west (total distance is 965 kilometers/600 miles). From Colorado or other Rocky Mountain states, head north on Highway 93, crossing into Canada north of Kalispell, Montana, from where it's 430 kilometers (267 miles) to Banff along Highway 93/95 via Cranbrook and Kootenay National Park.

From Calgary International Airport

Calgary International Airport, 128 kilometers (80 miles) east, is the closest airport to Banff National Park. **Banff Airporter** (403/762-3330 or 888/449-2901, www.banffairporter.com) offers door-to-door service between the airport and Banff for adult $72, child $36. The earliest service back to the airport departs Banff at 5:30am. **Brewster Express** (403/762-6700 or 866/606-6700, www.banff-jaspercollection.com) shuttles between the airport and Banff National Park twice daily, stopping at Banff, then continuing to Lake Louise. Calgary to Banff is adult $72, child $36. This shuttle delivers guests to all major Banff hotels. Adjacent desks at Calgary airport's Arrivals level take bookings for both companies, but it's best to reserve a seat by booking over the phone or online in advance.

GETTING AROUND

Most of the sights and some hiking trailheads are within walking distance of town. **Roam Transit** (403/762-0606, www.roam-transit.com) operates bus service along two routes through the town of Banff: one from the Banff Gondola north along Banff Avenue, the other from the Fairmont Banff Springs to the Tunnel Mountain campgrounds. Mid-May-September, buses run twice an hour between 7am and midnight. Roam buses also run out to Lake Minnewanka, to Canmore, and to Lake Louise.

Cabs around Banff are reasonably priced: flag drop is $6, then it's $3 per kilometer. A ride from the Banff bus depot to accommodations on Tunnel Mountain will run around $12, same to the Fairmont Banff Springs, more after midnight. Call **Banff Taxi** (403/762-4444).

The days when a row of horse-drawn

Parking Tips

The downtown core of Banff is busy year-round, but especially so between late June and early September after 10am. If you're staying in a motel along Banff Avenue or on Tunnel Mountain, don't drive into town—**walk** or catch a **Banff Transit bus** (ask at your accommodation for a schedule).

If you do drive into downtown, don't let not finding a parking spot on Banff Avenue ruin your holiday. Head to the **Fenlands Banff Recreation Centre** on Mount Norquay Road, the large parking lot on the east side of the Banff Railway Station, or the **parking garage** at the corner of Bear and Lynx Streets.

For travelers with **RVs** or **trailers,** finding a downtown parking spot can be a challenge. If you're planning on staying at one of the campgrounds on Tunnel Mountain, check in first, then walk or catch the Banff Transit bus (departs the campground every 30 minutes, $2) to downtown. If you must bring your rig into town, try the RV-only parking spots on Railway Avenue opposite the railway station and at the corner of Lynx and Wolf Streets.

The website **www.banffparking.ca** is an excellent resource that includes real-time updates of various parking areas, including the number of empty stalls at parking lots through town.

buggies eagerly awaited the arrival of wealthy visitors at the CPR station have long since passed, but the **Trail Rider Store** (132 Banff Ave., 403/762-4551, 9am-5pm daily) offers visitors rides around town in a beautifully restored carriage. Expect to pay from $140 per carriage for a short loop along the Bow River.

Car Rental

Plan on renting a vehicle before you reach the park. In addition to high pricing for walk-in customers, the main catch is that local companies don't always offer unlimited mileage, especially for larger and premium vehicles. **Avis** and **Budget** share a desk at street level in Cascade Shops (317 Banff Ave., 403/762-3222). The other agency represented in Banff is **Hertz** (Fairmont Banff Springs, 405 Spray Ave., 403/762-2027). Reservations for vehicles in Banff should be made well in advance, especially in July and August.

Lake Louise and Vicinity

Lake Louise is 56 kilometers (35 miles) northwest of Banff along the Trans-Canada Highway, or a little bit longer if you take the quieter Bow Valley Parkway. The hamlet of Lake Louise, composed of a small mall, hotels, and restaurants, is in the Bow Valley, just west of the Trans-Canada Highway. The lake itself is 200 vertical meters (660 vertical feet) above the valley floor, along a winding, paved 4-kilometer (2.5-mile) road. Across the valley is Canada's second-largest ski resort, also called Lake Louise. It's a world-class facility renowned for diverse terrain, abundant snow, and breathtaking views.

When you see the first flush of morning sun hit Victoria Glacier, and the impossibly steep northern face of Mount Victoria reflected in the sparkling, emerald-green waters of Lake Louise, you'll understand why this lake is regarded as one of the world's seven natural wonders. Overlooking the magnificent scene, Fairmont Chateau Lake Louise is without a doubt one of the world's most photographed hotels. Apart from staring, photographing, and videotaping, the area has plenty to keep you busy. Nearby you'll find some of the park's best hiking, canoeing, and horseback riding. Only a short distance away is

Lake Louise and Vicinity

To Jasper National Park

To Skoki Lodge

To Field and Golden

Kicking Horse Pass

ICEFIELDS PARKWAY

Herbert Lake

Bow

93

Pipestone

River

Whitehorn Mountain

LAKE LOUISE

Corral

Creek

Ross Lake

(CLOSED TO VEHICLES)

ALBERTA
BRITISH COLUMBIA

Mt Niblock

LAKE AGNES TRAIL

Little Beehive

SEE "LAKE LOUISE" MAP

LAKE LOUISE

Lipalian Mtn

Banff

National

Park

Lake Agnes

Mt Whyte

Big Beehive

Louise

Creek

BOW VALLEY PARKWAY

PLAIN OF SIX GLACIERS TEAHOUSE

Lake Louise

LAKE LOUISE

93

MORAINE LAKE

River

BOW VALLEY

BAKER CREEK MOUNTAIN RESORT

Fairview Mtn

Saddleback

TRANS-CANADA HIGHWAY

Mt Victoria 3,459m

Victoria Glacier

Mt Aberdeen

Creek

PARKWAY

Abbot Pass

The Mitre

Paradise

Valley

Lake Annette

Creek

To Lake O'Hara

Mt Lefroy

Giant Steps

Paradise

Mt Temple

RD

To Banff

Lake Oesa

Bow Range

Sentinel Pass

Larch Valley

Moraine

Valley of the Ten Peaks

Opabin Lake

Pinnacle Mtn

LARCH VALLEY TRAIL

Panorama Ridge

Hungabee Mountain

Eiffel Peak

MORAINE LAKE LODGE

Mt Biddle

Wenkchemna Peak

Eiffel Lake

MORAINE LAKE

Mt Babel

Consolation Lakes

Yoho National Park

Neptuak Mtn

Wenkchemna Glacier

0   1 mi

0   1 km

Deltaform Mtn

Mt Tuzo

Mt Fay

Kootenay National Park

Mt Allen

Mt Bowlen

Mt Little

Taylor Lake

Quadra Mountain

© MOON.COM

Lake Louise

© MOON.COM

Moraine Lake, not as famous as Lake Louise but rivaling it in beauty.

From Lake Louise the Trans-Canada Highway continues west, exiting the park over Kicking Horse Pass (1,647 meters/5,400 feet) and passing through Yoho National Park to Golden. Highway 93, the famous Icefields Parkway, begins one kilometer (0.6 mile) north of the village and heads northwest through the park's northern reaches to Jasper National Park.

Transit and Parking

Lake Louise and Moraine Lake are very busy during summer. My advice is simple: Prebook transportation or plan on arriving very early

to be assured a parking spot. Transportation options have increased in the last few years and continue to evolve. You should check the Parks Canada webpage at pc.gc.ca/banff-now before arriving for up-to-date traffic and parking status throughout the park and shuttle information. At the time of publication, there were two ways to reach Lake Louise and Moraine Lake by shuttle bus. From various pickup points in Banff, **Roam Transit** (403/762-0606, www.roamtransit.com) has service to both lakes throughout summer for $10 each way. Make reservations online to be assured a seat, although these are not required. From Lake Louise Ski Resort, across the valley from the village, Parks Canada operates an inexpensive shuttle bus to both lakes. Reservations are required on this service.

If you do feel the need to drive up to either lake, plan on arriving at **Lake Louise** before 7am—and preferably before 6am. Parking is $11.70 per vehicle June to mid-October between 7am and 7pm. There is no charge outside these times. For **Moraine Lake,** you will need to arrive even earlier—on many summer mornings the parking lot is full by 5am, at which point Moraine Lake Road is closed. When the parking lots at both lakes are full, visitors will be turned back.

SIGHTS

TOP EXPERIENCE

★ Lake Louise

In summer, about 10,000 visitors per day make the journey from the Bow Valley floor up to Lake Louise, famous for its stunning turquoise coloring. By 7am the tiered parking lot is often full (see Transit and Parking, above). An alternative to the road is one of two hiking trails that begin in the village and end at the public parking lot. From here several paved trails lead to the lake's eastern shore. From these vantage points the dramatic setting can be fully appreciated. The lake is 2.4 kilometers (1.5 miles) long, 500 meters (1,640 feet) wide, and up to 90 meters (295 feet) deep. Its cold waters reach a maximum temperature of 4°C (39°F) in August.

Fairmont Chateau Lake Louise is a tourist attraction in itself. Built by the CPR to take the pressure off the popular Banff Springs Resort, the château has seen many changes over the years, yet it remains one of the world's great mountain resorts. No one minds the hordes of camera- and phone-toting tourists who traipse through each day—and there's really no way to avoid them. The immaculately manicured gardens between the château and the lake make an interesting foreground for the millions of Lake Louise photographs taken each year. At the

lakeshore boathouse, canoes are rented for $135 per hour.

The snow-covered peak at the back of the lake is **Mount Victoria** (3,459 meters/11,350 feet), which sits on the Continental Divide. Amazingly, its base is more than 10 kilometers (6.2 miles) from the eastern end of the lake. Mount Victoria, first climbed in 1897, remains one of the park's most popular peaks for mountaineers. Although the difficult northeast face (facing the château) was first successfully ascended in 1922, the most popular and easiest route to the summit is along the southeast ridge, approached from Abbot Pass.

★ Moraine Lake

Although less than half the size of Lake Louise, Moraine Lake is just as spectacular and worthy of just as much time. It is up a winding road 13 kilometers (8 miles) off Lake Louise Drive. Its rugged setting, nestled in the Valley of the Ten Peaks among the towering mountains of the main ranges, has provided inspiration for millions of people from around the world since Walter Wilcox became the first white man to reach its shore in 1899. Wilcox's subsequent writings, such as "no scene has given me an equal impression of inspiring solitude and rugged grandeur," guaranteed the lake's future popularity. Although Wilcox was a knowledgeable man, he named the lake on the assumption that it was dammed by a glacial moraine deposited by the retreating Wenkchemna Glacier. In fact, the large rock pile that blocks its waters was deposited by major rockfalls from the Tower of Babel to the south. The lake often remains frozen until June, and the access road is closed all winter. A trail leads along the lake's northern shore, and canoes are rented for $120 per hour from the concession below Moraine Lake Lodge.

Parking at Moraine Lake is even more limited than at Lake Louise. If you arrive at the beginning of the Moraine Lake Road after 6am most days, expect the road to be closed until vehicles begin leaving. I can't stress this enough—if you want to see Moraine Lake during July and August, arrive before 6am or park at the overflow lot and take the shuttle.

Sightseeing Gondola

During summer, the main ski lift at the **Lake Louise resort** (403/522-3555 or 877/253-6888, www.skilouise.com) whisks visitors up the face of Mount Whitehorn to Whitehorn Lodge in either open chairs or enclosed gondola cars. At an altitude of more than 2 kilometers (1.2 miles) above sea level, the view from the top—across the Bow Valley, Lake Louise, and the Continental Divide—is among the most spectacular in the Canadian Rockies. Short trails lead through the forests, across open meadows, and, for the energetic, to the summit of Mount Whitehorn, more than 600 vertical meters (1,970 vertical feet) above. Visitors are free to walk these trails, but it pays to join a guided walk if you'd like to learn about the surrounding environment. After working up an appetite (and working off breakfast), head to the teahouse in the Whitehorn Lodge, try the outdoor barbecue, or, back at the base area, enjoy lunch at the **Lodge of the Ten Peaks,** the resort's impressive post-and-beam day lodge. The lift operates 9am-4pm daily May-September, with extended summer hours of 9am-5pm July-August (adult $44, child $22). Ride-and-dine packages are an excellent deal. Free shuttles run from Lake Louise accommodations to the day lodge.

SIDE TRIP: YOHO NATIONAL PARK

West of Banff and near Lake Louise, is Yoho National Park in British Columbia. Lake O'Hara is 26 kilometers (16 miles) from Lake Louise. Emerald Lake is a little farther west, 39 kilometers (24 miles), but with a more direct route along the Trans-Canada Highway, it only takes about 30 minutes to get there from Lake Louise.

★ Lake O'Hara

Nestled in a high bowl of lush alpine meadows, Lake O'Hara, 11 kilometers (6.8 miles) from the nearest public road, is surrounded by dozens of smaller alpine lakes and framed by spectacular peaks permanently mantled in snow. As if that weren't enough, the entire area is webbed by a network of hiking trails established during the 20th century by luminaries such as Lawrence Grassi. Trails radiate from the lake in all directions; the longest is just 7.5 kilometers (4.7 miles), making Lake O'Hara an especially fine hub for day hiking. What makes this destination all the more special is that a quota system limits the number of visitors.

TRANSPORTATION AND SERVICES

Most visitors take the shuttle bus along a road closed to the public to reach Lake O'Hara. The departure point is a signed parking lot 15 kilometers (9.3 miles) east of Field and three kilometers (1.9 miles) west of the Continental Divide. Buses for day visitors depart between mid-June and early October at 8:30am and 10:30am, returning at 2:30pm, 4:30pm, and 6:30pm. To book a seat, visit www.reservation.pc.gc.ca or call the dedicated reservations line (250/343-6433). Reservations are made through a lottery system that is open through March for the summer season; check the website for details. Reservations are only required for the inbound shuttle; outgoing buses fill on demand. If you are camping at Lake O'Hara, you do not require a separate booking for the bus.

All times—bus departures and reservation center hours—are Mountain Standard Time (the same time zone as Banff).

After the 20-minute bus trip to the lake, day hikers are dropped off at **Le Relais,** a homely log shelter where books and maps are sold, including the recommended *Lake O'Hara Gem Trek* map. Hot drinks and light snacks are served—something to look forward to at the end of the day, as this is also the afternoon meeting place for the return trip.

Several overnight options are available at

1: Fairmont Chateau Lake Louise 2: Lake O'Hara
3: Moraine Lake

"Lake of Little Fishes"

During the summer of 1882, Tom Wilson, an outfitter, was camped near the confluence of the Bow and Pipestone Rivers when he heard the distant rumblings of an avalanche. He questioned Stoney Indian guides and was told the noises originated from the "Lake of Little Fishes." The following day, Wilson, led by a Stoney guide, hiked to the lake to investigate. He became the first white man to lay eyes on what he named Emerald Lake. Two years later, the name was changed to Lake Louise, honoring Princess Louise Caroline Alberta, daughter of Queen Victoria.

A railway station known as Laggan was built where the rail line passed closest to the lake, 6 kilometers (3.7 miles) away. Until a road was completed in 1926, everyone arrived by train. The station's name was changed to Lake Louise in 1913 to prevent confusion among visitors. In 1890, a modest two-bedroom wooden hotel replaced a crude cabin that had been built on the shore of the lake as word of its beauty spread. After many additions, a disastrous fire, and the addition of a concrete wing in 1925, the château of today took shape, minus a convention center that opened in 2004.

the lake, including the **Elizabeth Parker Hut** (403/678-3200, www.alpineclubofcanada.ca), **Lake O'Hara Lodge** (250/343-6418, www.lakeohara.com), and a campground (see below for information on making campground reservations), but each should be booked well in advance.

Emerald Lake

Outfitter Tom Wilson stumbled upon stunning Emerald Lake while guiding Major A. B. Rogers through the Kicking Horse River Valley in 1881. He was led to the lake by his horse, which had been purchased from local Indigenous people. He later surmised that the horse had been accustomed to traveling up to the lake, meaning that the horse's former owners must have known about the lake before the white man arrived.

One of the jewels of the Canadian Rockies, the beautiful lake is surrounded by a forest of Engelmann spruce, as well as many peaks more than 3,000 meters (9,840 feet) high. It is covered in ice most of the year but comes alive with activity for a few short months in summer when hikers, canoeists, and horseback riders take advantage of the magnificent surroundings. **Emerald Lake Lodge** (250/343-6321 or 800/663-6336, www.crmr.com) is grand, offering a restaurant, café, lounge,

and recreation facilities for both guests and nonguests.

HIKING

The variety of hiking opportunities in the vicinity of Lake Louise and Moraine Lake is surely equal to those of any area on the face of the earth. The region's potential for outdoor recreation was first realized in the late 1800s, and it soon became the center of hiking activity in the Canadian Rockies. This popularity continues today; trails here are among the most heavily used in the park. Hiking is best early or late in the short summer season. Head out early in the morning to miss the strollers, high heels, dogs, and bear bells that you'll surely encounter during the busiest periods.

The two main trailheads are at Fairmont Chateau Lake Louise and Moraine Lake. Two trails lead from the village to the château (a pleasant alternative to driving the steep and busy Lake Louise Drive). Shortest is the 2.7-kilometer (1.7-mile) **Louise Creek Trail.** It begins on the downstream side of the point where Lake Louise Drive crosses the Bow River, crosses Louise Creek three times, and ends at the Lake Louise parking lot. The other trail, **Tramline,** is longer (4.5 km/2.8 mi) but not as steep. It begins behind the railway station and follows the route of a narrow-gauge railway that once transported guests from the CPR line to Chateau Lake Louise.

Bow River Loop

Length: 7 kilometers/4.3 miles (1.5-2 hours) round-trip
Elevation gain: minimal
Rating: easy
Trailheads: various points throughout Lake Louise village, including behind Samson Mall

This loop follows both banks of the Bow River southeast from the railway station. Used by joggers and cyclists to access various points in the village, the trail also links the railway station to the Lake Louise Alpine Centre, Post Hotel, Samson Mall, both campgrounds, and the Louise Creek and Tramline Trails to Lake Louise. Interpretive signs along its length provide information on the Bow River ecosystem.

Louise Lakeshore

Length: 2 kilometers/1.2 miles (30 minutes) one-way
Elevation gain: none
Rating: easy
Trailhead: Lake Louise, 4 kilometers (2.5 miles) from Trans-Canada Highway

Probably the busiest trail in all the Canadian Rockies, this one follows the north shore of Lake Louise from in front of the château to the west end of the lake. Here numerous braided glacial streams empty their silt-filled waters into Lake Louise. Along the trail's length are benches for sitting and pondering what English mountaineer James Outram once described as "a gem of composition and of coloring…perhaps unrivalled anywhere."

Plain of Six Glaciers

Length: 5.3 kilometers/3.3 miles (90 minutes) one-way
Elevation gain: 370 meters/1,215 feet
Rating: moderate
Trailhead: Lake Louise

Hikers along this trail are rewarded not only with panoramic views of the glaciated peaks of the main range but also with a rustic trail's-end teahouse serving homemade goodies baked on a wooden stove. For the first 2 kilometers (1.2 miles), the trail follows the Louise Lakeshore Trail to the western end of the lake. From there it begins a steady climb through a forest of spruce and subalpine fir. It enters an open area where an avalanche has come tumbling down (now a colorful carpet of wildflowers), then passes through a forested area into a vast wasteland of moraines produced by the advance and retreat of Victoria Glacier. Views of surrounding peaks continue to improve until the trail enters a stunted forest. Eventually the trail arrives at the **Plain of Six Glaciers Teahouse** (9am-5pm daily mid-June-early Oct., cash only). It operates the same way now as it did back when it was built by the CPR at the turn of the 20th century: Supplies are packed in by horse, and all cooking is done in a rustic kitchen.

After resting, continue one kilometer (0.6 mile) to the end of the trail on the narrow top of a lateral moraine. From here the trail's namesakes are visible. From left to right, the glaciers are Aberdeen, Upper Lefroy, Lower Lefroy, Upper Victoria, Lower Victoria, and Pope's. Between Mount Lefroy (3,441 meters/11,290 feet) and Mount Victoria (3,459 meters/11,350 feet) is Abbot Pass, named for Phillip Abbot, who died attempting to climb Mount Lefroy in 1896.

★ Lake Agnes

Length: 3.6 kilometers/2.2 miles (90 minutes) one-way
Elevation gain: 400 meters/1,312 feet
Rating: moderate
Trailhead: Lake Louise

This moderately strenuous hike is one of the park's most popular. It begins in front of the château, branching right near the beginning of the Louise Lakeshore Trail. For the first 2.5 kilometers (1.6 miles), the trail climbs steeply, switchbacking through a forest of subalpine fir and Engelmann spruce, crossing a horse trail, passing a lookout, and leveling out at tiny Mirror Lake. Here the old, traditional trail veers right (use it if the ground is wet or snowy), while a more direct route veers left to the Plain of the Six Glaciers. The final elevation gain along both trails is made easier by a flight of steps beside Bridal Veil Falls. The trail ends at its namesake subalpine lake, which is nestled in a hanging valley. It's also where you'll find the rustic **Lake Agnes Teahouse** (8am-5pm daily early June-mid-Oct., cash only), which offers homemade soups, healthy sandwiches, and a wide assortment of teas.

From the teahouse, a 1-kilometer (0.6-mile) trail leads to Little Beehive and impressive views of the Bow Valley. Another trail leads around the northern shore of Lake Agnes, climbing to Big Beehive or joining the Plain of the Six Glaciers Trail, just 3.2 kilometers (two miles) from the château and 2.1 kilometers (1.3 miles) from the teahouse at the end of that trail.

Big Beehive

Length: 5 kilometers/3.1 miles (2 hours) one-way
Elevation gain: 520 meters/1,710 feet
Rating: moderate
Trailhead: Lake Louise

The lookout atop the larger of the two "beehives" is one of the best places to admire the Bow Valley, which lies over 500 meters (1,640 feet) directly below. The various trails to the summit have one thing in common: All are steep. But the rewards are worth every drop of sweat along the way. The most popular route follows the Lake Agnes Trail for the first 3.6 kilometers (2.2 miles) to Lake Agnes. From the teahouse, a trail leads to the western end of the lake, then switchbacks steeply up an exposed north-facing ridge. At the crest of the ridge, the trail forks. To the right it descends to the Plain of Six Glaciers Trail; to the left it continues 300 meters (0.2 mile) to a log gazebo. Across Lake Louise is Fairview Mountain (2,745 meters/9,000 feet), and behind this peak is the distinctive shape of Mount Temple (3,549 meters/11,645 feet). Views also extend up the lake to Mount Lefroy and northeast to the Lake Louise Ski Resort. Views from the edge of the cliff are spectacular, but be very careful—it's a long, long way down. By returning down the Lake Louise side

of the Big Beehive, the loop is 11.5 kilometers (7.1 miles).

Saddleback

Length: 3.7 kilometers/2.3 miles (90 minutes) one-way
Elevation gain: 600 meters/1,970 feet
Rating: moderate/difficult
Trailhead: boathouse, Lake Louise

This trail climbs the lower slopes of Fairview Mountain from beside the boathouse on Lake Louise, ending in an alpine meadow with a view of Mount Temple from across Paradise Valley. Four hundred meters (0.2 mile) from the trailhead, the trail forks. Keep left and follow the steep switchbacks through a forest of Engelmann spruce and subalpine fir until reaching the flower-filled meadow. The meadow is actually a pass between Fairview Mountain (to the northwest) and Saddle Mountain (to the southeast). Although most hikers are content with the awesome views from the pass and return along the same trail, it is possible to continue to the summit of Fairview (2,745 meters/9,000 feet), a further climb of 400 vertical meters (1,310 vertical feet). The barely discernible, switchbacking trail to the summit begins near a stand of larch trees above the crest of Saddleback. As you would expect, the view from the top is stupendous; Lake Louise is more than one kilometer (0.6 mile) directly below. This option is for strong, experienced hikers only. From the Saddleback, the trail descends into Sheol Valley, then into Paradise Valley. The entire loop would be 15 kilometers (9.3 miles).

Paradise Valley

Length: 18 kilometers/11.2 miles (6 hours) round-trip
Elevation gain: 380 meters/1,250 feet
Rating: moderate/difficult
Trailhead: Moraine Lake Road, 3.5 kilometers (2.2 miles) from Lake Louise Drive

This aptly named trail makes for a long day hike, but it can be broken up by overnighting

---

1: Louise Lakeshore Trail **2:** Lake Agnes **3:** Larch Valley **4:** looking over Skoki Lakes

at the backcountry campground at the far end of the trail. The trail climbs slowly for the first five kilometers (3.1 miles), crossing Paradise Creek numerous times and passing the junction of a trail that climbs the Sheol Valley to Saddleback. After five kilometers (3.1 miles), the trail begins a steep ascent to **Lake Annette.** It's a typical subalpine lake in a unique setting, nestled against the near-vertical 1,200-meter (3,940-foot) north face of snow- and ice-capped **Mount Temple** (3,549 meters/11,645 feet), one of the 10 highest peaks in the Canadian Rockies. This difficult face was successfully climbed in 1966, relatively late for mountaineering firsts. The lake is a worthy destination in itself (allow yourself four hours round-trip from the trailhead). For those looking for a full day's outing, continue beyond the lake into an open avalanche area that affords views across Paradise Valley. Look and listen for pikas and marmots among the boulders. The trail eventually begins a steep descent to reach a series of cascades known as the **Giant Steps.**

★ Larch Valley

Length: 2.9 kilometers/1.8 miles (60 minutes) one-way
Elevation gain: 400 meters/1,310 feet
Rating: moderate
Trailhead: Moraine Lake, 13 kilometers (8 miles) from Lake Louise Drive

In mid- to late September, when the larch trees have turned a magnificent gold and the sun is shining, few spots in the Canadian Rockies can match the beauty of this valley, but don't expect to find much solitude. Although the most popular time for visiting the valley is fall, it is a worthy destination all summer, when the open meadows are filled with colorful wildflowers. The trail begins just past Moraine Lake Lodge and climbs fairly steeply, with occasional glimpses of Moraine Lake below. After reaching the junction of the Eiffel Lake Trail, keep right, passing through an open forest of larch and into the meadow beyond. The range of larch is restricted within the park, and this is one of the few areas

where they are prolific. Mount Fay (3,235 meters/10,615 feet) is the dominant peak on the skyline, rising above the other mountains that make up the Valley of the Ten Peaks. Continue up a further one kilometer (0.6 mile) to the two Minnestimma Lakes, where views back to the Ten Peaks are unforgettable.

Sentinel Pass

Length: 5.8 kilometers/3.6 miles (2-3 hours) one-way
Elevation gain: 725 meters/2,380 feet
Rating: moderate/difficult
Trailhead: Moraine Lake

Keen hikers should consider continuing through the open meadows of Larch Valley to Sentinel Pass (2,608 meters/8,560 feet), one of the park's highest trail-accessible passes. The length and elevation gain listed are from Moraine Lake. Once in Larch Valley, you're halfway there and have made over half of the elevation gain. Upon reaching Larch Valley, take the formed trail that winds through the open meadow. Beyond the Minnestimma Lakes, the trail switchbacks for 1.2 kilometers (0.7 mile) up a steep scree slope to the pass, sandwiched between Pinnacle Mountain (3,067 meters/10,060 feet) and Mount Temple (3,549 meters/11,645 feet). From the pass most hikers opt to return along the same trail, although with advance planning it is possible to continue into Paradise Valley and back to the Moraine Lake access road, a total of 17 kilometers (10.6 miles) one-way.

Eiffel Lake

Length: 5.6 kilometers/3.5 miles (2 hours) one-way
Elevation gain: 400 meters/1,310 feet
Rating: moderate/difficult
Trailhead: Moraine Lake

Eiffel Lake is small, and it looks even smaller in its rugged and desolate setting, surrounded by the famed Valley of the Ten Peaks. For the first 2.4 kilometers (1.5 miles), follow the Larch Valley Trail, then fork left. Most of the elevation gain has already been made, and the trail remains relatively level before emerging onto an open slope from where each of the 10 peaks can be seen. From left to right the peaks are Fay, Little, Bowlen, Perren, Septa, Allen, Tuzo, Deltaform, Neptuak, and Wenkchemna. The final two peaks are divided by Wenkchemna Pass (2,605 meters/8,550 feet), a further 4 kilometers (2.5 miles) and 360 vertical meters (1,180 vertical feet) above Eiffel Lake. The lake itself soon comes into view. It lies in a depression formed by a rockslide from Neptuak Mountain. The lake is named for Eiffel Peak (3,085 meters/10,120 feet), a rock pinnacle behind it, which with a little imagination could be compared to the Eiffel Tower in Paris.

Consolation Lakes

Length: 3 kilometers/1.9 miles (1 hour) one-way
Elevation gain: 65 meters/213 feet
Rating: easy/moderate
Trailhead: beside the restrooms at Moraine Lake parking lot

This short trail begins with a crossing of Moraine Creek at the outlet of Moraine Lake and ends at a pleasant subalpine lake. The first section of the trail traverses a boulder-strewn rock pile—the result of rockslides on the imposing Tower of Babel (3,100 meters/10,170 feet)—before entering a dense forest of Engelmann spruce and subalpine fir and following Babel Creek to the lower lake. The wide valley affords 360-degree views of the surrounding jagged peaks, including Mount Temple back down the valley and Mounts Bident and Quadra at the far end of the lakes.

Skoki Valley

Length: 14.4 kilometers/8.9 miles (5 hours) one-way
Elevation gain: 775 meters/2,540 feet
Rating: moderate/difficult
Trailhead: end of Fish Creek Road, off Whitehorn Road 1.8 kilometers (1.1 miles) north of Lake Louise interchange

The trail into historic Skoki Lodge is only one of the endless hiking opportunities tucked behind the Lake Louise Ski Resort, across the valley from all hikes detailed previously. The first 3.4 kilometers (2.1 miles) of the trail are along a gravel access road. Guests of Skoki Lodge ride a shuttle for this first stretch,

lessening the hiking distance to 11 kilometers (6.8 miles). From the end of the road, the trail climbs to Boulder Pass, passing the Hidden Lake Junction and Halfway Hut (a rustic shelter; no camping), above Corral Creek. The pass harbors a large population of pikas and hoary marmots. The trail then follows the north shore of Ptarmigan Lake before climbing again to Deception Pass, named for its false summit. It then descends into Skoki Valley, passing a side trail to the Skoki Lakes and eventually reaching Skoki Lodge. Just over one kilometer (0.6 mile) beyond the lodge is a campground, an excellent base for exploring the region for those equipped for backcountry camping.

OTHER SUMMER RECREATION

In Lake Louise, "summer fun" means hiking—and lots of it. You may see small fish swimming along the shore of Lake Louise, but the fishing in this lake and all others in the area is poor due to the super-cold glacial water. Talking of cold water, everyone is invited to take a swim in Lake Louise to celebrate the country's national holiday, **Canada Day** (July 1). You don't need to be Canadian to join in—just brave.

Through summer, **Brewster Adventures** (403/762-5454, www.brewsteradventures. com) offers two-hour horseback rides to the end of Lake Louise for $120, half-day rides to **Lake Agnes Teahouse** for $200, and all-day rides up **Paradise Valley,** including lunch, for $350.

WINTER RECREATION

Lake Louise is an immense winter playground, offering one of the world's premier alpine resorts, unlimited cross-country skiing, ice-skating, sleigh rides, and nearby heli-skiing. Between November and May, accommodation prices are reduced by up to 60 percent (except Christmas holidays). Lift-and-lodging packages begin at $180 per person, and you'll always be able to get a table at your favorite restaurant.

Lake Louise Ski Resort

Canada's answer to U.S. megaresorts is **Lake Louise Ski Resort** (403/522-3555 or 877/253-6888, www.skilouise.com), which opens in mid-November and operates until early or mid-May. The nation's second-largest ski resort (behind only Whistler/Blackcomb) comprises 1,700 hectares (4,200 acres) of gentle trails, mogul fields, long cruising runs, steep chutes, and vast bowls filled with famous Rocky Mountain powder.

The resort, which has more than 100 named runs, is made up of four distinct faces. The front side has a vertical drop of 1,000 meters (3,280 feet) and is served by eight lifts, including four high-speed quads and western Canada's only six-passenger chairlift. The four back bowls are each as big as many midsize resorts and are all well above the tree line. Larch and Ptarmigan faces have a variety of terrain, allowing you to follow the sun as it moves across the sky or escape into trees for protection on windy days. Each of the three day lodges has a restaurant and bar. Ski and snowboard rentals, clothing, and souvenirs are available in the Lodge of the Ten Peaks, a magnificent post-and-beam day lodge that overlooks the front face.

Lift tickets per day are adult $140, senior $120, youth $100, and child younger than 12 $60. Free guided tours of the mountain are available three times daily; inquire at customer service. Free shuttle buses run regularly from Lake Louise accommodations to the hill. From Banff, free shuttles run from many hotels to the resort. For information on packages and multiday tickets that cover all three national park resorts, go to www.skibig3.com.

Cross-Country Skiing

The most popular cross-country skiing areas are on Lake Louise, along Moraine Lake Road, and in Skoki Valley at the back of the Lake Louise ski area. For details and helpful trail classifications, pick up a copy of *Cross-Country Skiing—Nordic Trails in Banff National Park* from the Lake Louise Visitor Centre. Before heading out, check the weather forecast at the visitors center or call 403/762-2088. For avalanche reports, call 403/762-1460.

Ice-Skating and Sleigh Rides

Of all the ice-skating rinks in Canada, the one on frozen Lake Louise, in front of the château, is surely the most spectacular. Spotlights allow skating after dark, and on special occasions hot chocolate is served. Skates are available in the château at **Chateau Mountain Sports** (403/522-3628); $16 for the day, plus $8 for a helmet.

Brewster Adventures (403/762-5454, www.brewsteradventures.com) offers rides in traditional horse-drawn sleighs along the shores of Lake Louise beginning from in front of the château. Although blankets are supplied, you should still bundle up. The one-hour ride is $45 per person, $35 for children. Reservations are necessary. The rides are scheduled hourly December through March from 10am on weekends and from 1pm on weekdays, with the last ride between 6pm and 8pm.

NIGHTLIFE

The **Sir Norman Lounge** in the Post Hotel (200 Pipestone Dr., 403/522-3989, 2pm-11pm daily) oozes mountain style and upscale charm. It's cozy, quiet, and the perfect place to relax in front of a fire with a cocktail before moving on to the adjacent fine-dining restaurant. Not your scene? Hang out with seasonal workers at the **Lake Louise Village Grill & Bar** (upstairs in Samson Mall, 403/522-9011, 8am-2am daily in summer, 11am-2am daily the rest of the year) or travelers from around the world at the **Explorer's Lounge** (Lake Louise Inn, 210 Village Rd., 403/522-3791, 11am-2am daily) for dancing to recorded music after 10pm. Up at the Fairmont Chateau Lake Louise is **Alpine Social** (111 Lake Louise Dr., 403/522-1601, 5pm-midnight daily), with fine wines, fancy cocktails, and a full menu.

FOOD

Other guidebooks encourage readers to "eat at your hotel." Not only is this not helpful, it's misleading. The village of Lake Louise may exist only to serve travelers, but there are good dining options serving all budgets.

Casual

If you don't feel like a cooked breakfast, start your day off at ★ **Laggan's Mountain Bakery** (Samson Mall, 403/552-2017, 7am-7pm daily, until 4pm outside of summer, lunches $8-12), *the* place to hang out with a coffee and a freshly baked breakfast croissant, pastry, cake, or muffin. The chocolate brownie is delicious (order two slices to save having to line up twice). If the tables are full, order takeout and enjoy your meal on the riverbank behind the mall.

For a casual meal, head to **Bill Peyto's Cafe** in the Lake Louise Alpine Centre (203 Village Rd., 403/522-2200, 7am-10pm daily, $13-25), where the food is consistent and well priced. A huge portion of poutine is $11, pasta is $15-20, and stir-fries range $16-20.

Across the Trans-Canada Highway, the **Lodge of the Ten Peaks,** at the base of the Lake Louise Ski Resort (403/522-3555, $12-20, 8am-4pm daily mid-May-early Oct., lunches $12-16), is open 8am-11am daily for a large and varied breakfast buffet, followed by cafeteria-style lunch service, with food best enjoyed out on the covered balcony. The lodge also has a café where you can grab coffee and muffins.

European

In 1987, the ★ **Post Hotel** (200 Pipestone Dr., 403/522-3989 or 800/661-1586, www.posthotel.com) was expanded to include a luxurious new wing. The original log building was renovated as a rustic, timbered dining room (6:30pm-10pm daily, $34-52) linked to the rest of the hotel by an intimate lounge. Although the dining room isn't cheap, it's a favorite of locals and visitors alike. The chef specializes in European cuisine, preparing several Swiss dishes (such as veal zurichoise) to make co-owner George Schwarz feel less homesick. He's also renowned for his presentation of Alberta beef, Pacific salmon, and Peking duck. The 32,000-bottle cellar is one of the finest in Canada. Reservations are essential for dinner.

Canadian

Over one hundred years ago, visitors departing trains at Laggan Station were eager to get to the Chateau Lake Louise as quickly as possible to begin their adventure. Today guests from the château, other hotels, and even people from as far away as Banff are returning to dine in ★ **The Station Restaurant** (200 Sentinel Rd., 403/522-2600, 11:30am-4pm and 5pm-9pm daily, $25-48). Although the menu is not extensive, it puts an emphasis on creating imaginative dishes with a combination of Canadian produce and Asian ingredients. Lighter lunches include a Caesar salad topped with roasted garlic dressing—perfect for those planning an afternoon hike. In the evening, expect entrées like a memorable pan-seared salmon smothered in basil pesto.

Fairmont Chateau Lake Louise

Within this famous lakeside hotel is a choice of eateries and an ice-cream shop. For all château dining reservations, call 403/522-1601.

The **Poppy Brasserie** has obscured lake views and is the most casual place for a meal. Breakfasts (6:30am-10am daily), offered buffet-style ($38 per person), are expensive for light eaters. Dinners (5:30am-9pm daily, $34-52) are à la carte. The **Walliser Stube** (5:30pm-9:30pm daily, $38-55) is an elegant two-story wine bar decorated with rich wood paneling and solid oak furniture. It offers a simple menu of German dishes as well as a number of classic fondues. The **Lakeview Lounge** (11am-10pm daily, lunches $24-36) has floor-to-ceiling windows with magnificent lake views. Choose this dining area for lunch or afternoon tea (noon-3pm daily, reservations required, $56 per person, or $66 with a glass of champagne).

The **Fairview Bar and Restaurant**

(5:30pm-9:30pm daily, $42-62) has a lot more than just a fair view. As the château's signature dining room, it enjoys the best views and offers the most elegant setting.

ACCOMMODATIONS AND CAMPING

In summer, accommodations at Lake Louise are even harder to come by than in Banff, so it's essential to make reservations well in advance. Any rooms not taken by early afternoon will be the expensive ones.

Under $100

With beds for $100 less than anyplace else in the village, the 164-bed **HI-Lake Louise Alpine Centre** (203 Village Rd., 403/522-2200 or 866/762-4122, www.hihostels.ca) is understandably popular. Of log construction, with large windows and high vaulted ceilings, the lodge is a joint venture between the Alpine Club of Canada and Hostelling International Canada. Beyond the reception area is Bill Peyto's Cafe, the least-expensive place to eat in Lake Louise. Upstairs is a large timber-frame lounge area and guide's room—a quiet place to plan your next hike or browse through the large collection of mountain literature. Other amenities include Wi-Fi, a laundry, a game room, and a wintertime ski shuttle. The rooms are modern, with comfortable beds. Most rooms have four or five beds, with private room configurations including two singles, doubles with en suites, and family rooms. Members of Hostelling International pay $62 per person per night (nonmembers $66) for a dorm bed or from $190 s or d ($200 for nonmembers) in a private room. Rates are discounted to $50 for a dorm and $140 s or d for a private room October-May, including throughout the extremely busy winter season. The hostel is open year-round, with check-in after 3pm. In summer and on weekends during the winter season, advance bookings (up to six months) are essential. The hostel is on

Village Road, less than one kilometer (0.6 mile) from Samson Mall.

$300-400

Historic **Deer Lodge** (109 Lake Louise Dr., 403/410-7417 or 800/661-1595, www.crmr.com, $390-600 s or d) began life in 1921 as a teahouse, with rooms added in 1925. Facilities include a rooftop hot tub with glacier views, game room, restaurant (breakfast and dinner), and bar. The least-expensive rooms are older and don't have phones. Rooms in the $300 range are considerably larger, or pay $440 for a heritage-themed Tower Room. Deer Lodge is along Lake Louise Drive, up the hill from the village, and just a five-minute walk from the lake itself.

Over $400

★ **Baker Creek Mountain Resort** (403/522-3761, www.bakercreek.com, $600-900 s or d) lies along the Bow Valley Parkway 10 kilometers (6.2 miles) from Lake Louise back toward Banff. Each of the log chalets has a kitchenette, separate bedroom, fireplace, and outside deck (complete with cute wood carvings of bears climbing over the railings). The Trapper's Cabin is a huge space with a log bed, antler chandelier, wood-burning fireplace, double-jetted tub, and cooking facilities. A lodge wing has eight luxurious suites, each with richly accented log work, a deck, microwave and fridge, and a deluxe bathroom. (Check the website for great off-season deals.)

An excellent option for families and those looking for old-fashioned mountain charm is ★ **Paradise Lodge and Bungalows** (105 Lake Louise Dr., 403/522-3595, www.paradiselodge.com, mid-May-early Oct., from $440 s or d). This family-operated lodge provides outstanding value in a wonderfully tranquil setting. Spread out around well-manicured gardens are 21 attractive cabins in four configurations. Each has a rustic yet warm and inviting interior, with comfortable beds, a separate sitting area, and an en suite bathroom. Each cabin has a small fridge, microwave, and coffeemaker, while the larger ones have

---

1: descending from Boulder Pass 2: Post Hotel
3: Skoki Lodge 4: Lake Agnes Teahouse

full kitchens and separate bedrooms. Instead of television, children are kept happy with a playground that includes a sandbox and jungle gym. The least-expensive cabins, complete with a classic cast-iron stove/fireplace combo, are $440 s or d, or pay $500 for a cabin with a big deck and sweeping valley views. Twenty-four luxury suites, each with a fireplace, TV, one or two bedrooms, and fabulous mountain views, start at $440, or $480 with a kitchen. The Temple Suite, with all of the above as well as a large hot tub, is $500. To get there from the valley floor, follow Lake Louise Drive toward the Fairmont Chateau Lake Louise for 3 kilometers (1.9 miles); the lake itself is just one kilometer (0.6 mile) farther up the hill.

Aside from the château, the **Lake Louise Inn** (210 Village Rd., 403/522-3791 or 800/661-9237, www.lakelouiseinn.com, from $445 s or d) is the village's largest lodging, with more than 200 units spread throughout five buildings. Across from the lobby, in the main lodge, is a gift shop and an activities desk, and beyond is a pizzeria, restaurant, bar, and indoor pool. Most rates booked online include breakfast.

On the valley floor, **Mountaineer Lodge** (101 Village Rd., 403/522-3844, www.mountaineerlodge.com, $400-530 s or d) offers large, functional guest rooms, many with mountain views and all with wireless Internet access. On the downside, the rooms have no phones or air-conditioning, and there is no elevator.

Originally called Lake Louise Ski Lodge, the ★ **Post Hotel** (200 Pipestone Dr., 403/522-3989 or 800/661-1586, www.posthotel.com, $500-1,000 s or d) is one of only a handful of Canadian accommodations that have been accepted into the prestigious Relais & Châteaux organization. Bordered to the east and south by the Pipestone River, it may lack views of Lake Louise, but it is as elegant—in a modern, woodsy way—as the château. Each bungalow-style room is furnished with Canadian pine and has a balcony. Many rooms have whirlpools and fireplaces, while some have kitchens. Other facilities include the upscale Temple Mountain Spa, an indoor pool, a steam room, and a library. The hotel has 17 different room types, with 26 different rates depending on the view. Between the main lodge and the Pipestone River are four sought-after cabins, each with a wood-burning fireplace.

The famously fabulous **Fairmont Chateau Lake Louise** (111 Lake Louise Dr., 403/522-3511 or 866/540-4413, www.fairmont.com, from $1,200), a historic 500-room hotel on the shore of Lake Louise, has views equal to any mountain resort in the world. But all this historic charm and mountain scenery come at a price. Rooms on the Fairmont Gold Floor come with a private concierge and upgraded everything for a little over $1,400. Official rates drop as low as $500 s or d outside of summer, with accommodation and ski pass packages sometimes advertised for around $500 d. Children younger than 18 sharing with parents are free, but if you bring a pet, it'll be an extra $85 per night.

At the lake for which it's named, 4 kilometers (2.5 miles) from the valley floor, is super-luxurious **Moraine Lake Lodge** (Moraine Lake Rd., 403/522-3733 or 877/522-2777, www.morainelake.com, June-Sept., from $1,000-1,100 s or d). Designed by renowned architect Arthur Erickson, the lodge is a bastion of understated charm, partially obscured from the masses of day-trippers who visit the area and yet taking full advantage of its location beside one of the world's most photographed lakes. The decor reflects the wilderness location, with an abundance of polished log work and solid, practical furnishings in heritage-themed rooms. The rooms have no TVs or phones; instead, guests take guided nature walks, have unlimited use of canoes, and are pampered with gourmet breakfast and afternoon tea.

TOP EXPERIENCE

Backcountry Accommodations

If you're prepared to lace up your hiking boots for a true mountain experience, consider spending time at ★ **Skoki Lodge**

(403/256-8473 or 800/258-7669, www.skoki.com, late June-early Oct. and late Dec.-mid-Apr., $260-500 pp), north of the Lake Louise ski resort and far from the nearest road. Getting there requires an 11-kilometer (6.8-mile) hike or ski, depending on the season. The lodge is an excellent base for exploring nearby valleys and mountains. It dates to 1931, when it operated as a lodge for local Banff skiers, and is now a National Historic Site. Accommodations are rustic (propane heat but no electricity) but comfortable, with mostly twin beds in the main lodge and cabins that sleep up to five. Washroom facilities are outside and communal. Rates include three meals daily, including a picnic lunch that guests build from a buffet-style layout before heading out hiking or skiing. The dining room and lounge center on a wood-burning fire, where guests come together each evening to swap tales from the trail and mingle with the convivial hosts.

Campgrounds

Exit the Trans-Canada Highway at the Lake Louise interchange, 56 kilometers (35 miles) northwest of Banff, and take the first left beyond Samson Mall and under the railway bridge to reach **Lake Louise Campground,** within easy walking distance of the village. The campground is divided into two sections by the Bow River but is linked by the Bow River Loop hiking trail that leads into the village along either side of the river. Individual sites throughout are close together, but some privacy and shade are provided by towering lodgepole pines. Just under 200 serviced (powered) sites ($39) are grouped together at the end of the road; this section also has showers and flush toilets. Across the river are 216 unserviced sites ($35), each with a fire ring and picnic table. Amenities include kitchen shelters and a modern bathroom complex with hot showers. A dump station is near the entrance to the campground ($8 per use). An interpretive program runs throughout the summer (9pm Wed.-Mon.) in the outdoor theater. Sites should be booked well in advance by contacting the **Parks Canada Reservation Service** (877/737-3783, www.reservation.pc.gc.ca). The serviced section of this campground is open year-round, the unserviced section mid-May-September.

INFORMATION AND SERVICES
Information
Lake Louise Visitor Centre (403/522-3833, 8am-8pm daily mid-June-Aug., 8am-6pm daily mid-May-mid-June and Sept., 9am-4pm daily the rest of the year) is beside Samson Mall on Village Road. This excellent Parks Canada facility has interpretive exhibits, slide and video displays, and staff on hand to answer questions, recommend hikes suited to your ability, and issue camping passes to those heading out into the backcountry. Look for the stuffed (literally) female grizzly and read her fascinating but sad story.

Services
Although Lake Louise has no banks, there's a currency exchange in the Fairmont Chateau Lake Louise and a cash machine in the Samson Mall grocery store. Camping supplies and bike rentals are available from **Wilson Mountain Sports** (Samson Mall, 403/522-3636, 8am-8pm daily).

The closest **hospital** is in Banff (403/762-2222). For the local **RCMP,** call 403/522-3811.

GETTING THERE

The village of Lake Louise is beside the Trans-Canada Highway 56 kilometers (35 miles) northwest of Banff and 184 kilometers (115 miles) west of Calgary. To access Lake Louise along the Icefields Parkway, allow around 3.5 hours from Jasper (230 kilometers/143 miles) to the north. From Vancouver, it's a drive of approximately 784 kilometers (484 miles) east along the Trans-Canada Highway to Lake Louise.

Calgary International Airport is the closest airport to Lake Louise. **Brewster Express** (403/762-6700 or 866/606-6700, www.banffjaspercollection.com) and **Banff**

Airporter (403/762-3330 or 888/449-2901, www.banffairporter.com) offer at least a couple of shuttles per day that continue beyond Banff to Lake Louise from the airport. All charge around the same: $90 each way, with a slight round-trip discount.

GETTING AROUND

Samson Mall is the commercial heart of Lake Louise village. If the parking lot out front is full, consider leaving your vehicle across the road behind the Esso gas station, where one area is set aside for large RVs. The campground, hostel, and some hotels are all within easy walking distance of Samson Mall. Fairmont Chateau Lake Louise is a 2.7-kilometer (1.7-mile) walk from the valley floor. **Lake Louise Taxi & Tours** (Samson Mall, 403/522-2020) charges $7 for flag drop, then $3.25 per kilometer. From the mall to Fairmont Chateau Lake Louise runs around $38, and to Banff $220. **Wilson Mountain Sports** (Samson Mall, 403/522-3636, 8am-7pm daily) has mountain bikes for rent from $50 per day (includes a helmet, bike lock, and water bottle) and electric bikes for $80. They also rent bear spray and climbing gear.

Icefields Parkway

The 230-kilometer (143-mile) Icefields Parkway, between Lake Louise and Jasper, is one of the most scenic, exciting, and inspiring mountain roads ever built. From Lake Louise this paved route parallels the Continental Divide, following in the shadow of the highest, most rugged mountains in the Canadian Rockies. The first 122 kilometers (76 miles) to Sunwapta Pass (the boundary between Banff and Jasper National Parks) can be driven in two hours, and the entire parkway in four hours. But it's likely you'll want to spend at least a day, probably more, stopping at each of the 13 viewpoints, hiking the trails, watching the abundant wildlife, and just generally enjoying one of the world's most magnificent landscapes. Along the section within Banff National Park are two lodges, three hostels, three campgrounds, and one gas station.

Although the road is steep and winding in places, it has a wide shoulder, making it ideal for an extended bike trip. Allow seven days to pedal north from Banff to Jasper, staying at hostels or camping along the route. This is the preferable direction to travel by bike because the elevation at the town of Jasper is more than 500 meters (1,640 feet) lower than either Banff or Lake Louise.

The parkway remains open year-round, although winter brings with it some special considerations. The road is often closed for short periods for avalanche control. Check road conditions in Banff or Lake Louise before setting out. And be sure to fill up with gas; no services are available between November and April.

SIGHTS AND DRIVES
Lake Louise to Crowfoot Glacier

The Icefields Parkway forks right from the Trans-Canada Highway just north of Lake Louise. The impressive scenery begins immediately. Just 3 kilometers (1.9 miles) from the junction is **Herbert Lake,** formed during the last ice age when retreating glaciers deposited a pile of rubble, known as a *moraine*, across a shallow valley and water filled in behind it. The lake is a perfect place for early-morning or early-evening photography, when the Waputik Range and distinctively shaped **Mount Temple** are reflected in its waters.

Traveling north, you'll notice numerous depressions in the steep, shaded slopes of the Waputik Range across the Bow Valley. The cooler climate on these north-facing slopes makes them prone to glaciation. Cirques were cut by small local glaciers. On the opposite side of the road, **Mount Hector** (3,394 meters/11,130 feet), easily recognized by its layered peak, soon comes into view.

Hector Lake Viewpoint is 16 kilometers (10 miles) from the junction. Although the lake itself is a long way from the highway, the emerald-green waters nestled below a massive wall of limestone form a breathtaking scene. **Bow Peak,** seen looking northward along the highway, is only 2,868 meters (9,410 feet) high but is completely detached from the Waputik Range, making it a popular destination for climbers. As you leave this viewpoint, look across the northeast end of Hector Lake for glimpses of **Mount Balfour** (3,246 meters/10,650 feet) on the distant skyline.

Crowfoot Glacier

The aptly named Crowfoot Glacier can best be appreciated from a viewpoint 17 kilometers (10.6 miles) north of Hector Lake. The glacier sits on a wide ledge near the top of Crowfoot Mountain, from where its glacial claws cling to the mountain's steep slopes. The retreat of this glacier has been dramatic. In the 1960s, two of the claws extended to the base of the lower cliff. Today they are a shadow of their former selves, barely reaching over the cliff edge.

Bow Lake

The sparkling, translucent waters of Bow Lake are among the most beautiful that can be seen from the Icefields Parkway. The lake was created when moraines deposited by retreating glaciers dammed subsequent meltwater. On still days, the water reflects the snowy peaks, their sheer cliffs, and the scree slopes that run into the lake. You don't need photography experience to take good pictures here! At the southeast end of the lake, a day-use area offers waterfront picnic tables and a trail to a swampy area at the lake's outlet. At the upper end of the lake, you'll find the historic Num-ti-jah Lodge and the trailhead for a walk to Bow Glacier Falls.

The road leaves Bow Lake and climbs to **Bow Summit.** As you look back toward the lake, its true turquoise color becomes apparent, and the Crowfoot Glacier reveals its unique shape. At an elevation of 2,069 meters (6,790 feet), this pass is one of the highest points crossed by a public road in Canada. It is also the beginning of the Bow River, the one you camped beside at Lake Louise, photographed flowing through the town of Banff, and fished along downstream of Canmore.

★ Peyto Lake

From the parking lot at Bow Summit, a 10-minute paved trail leads to one of the most breathtaking views you could ever imagine. Far below the viewpoint is Peyto Lake, an impossibly intense-green lake whose hues change according to season. Before heavy melting of nearby glaciers begins (in June or early July), the lake is dark blue. As summer progresses, meltwater flows across a delta and into the lake. This water is laden with finely ground particles of rock debris known as rock flour, which remains suspended in the water. It is not the mineral content of the rock flour that is responsible for the lake's unique color, but rather the particles reflecting the blue-green sector of the light spectrum. As the amount of suspended rock flour changes, so does the color of the lake.

The lake is one of many park landmarks named for early outfitter Bill Peyto. In 1898, Peyto was part of an expedition camped at Bow Lake. Seeking solitude (as he was wont to do), he slipped off during the night to sleep near this lake. Other members of the party coined the name Peyto's Lake, and it stuck.

A farther 3 kilometers (1.9 miles) along the parkway is a viewpoint from which **Peyto Glacier** is visible at the far end of Peyto Lake Valley. This glacier is part of the extensive **Wapta Icefield,** which straddles the Continental Divide and extends into the northern reaches of Yoho National Park in British Columbia.

Beside the Continental Divide

From Bow Summit, the parkway descends to a viewpoint directly across the Mistaya River

from **Mount Patterson** (3,197 meters/10,490 feet). Snowbird Glacier clings precariously to the mountain's steep northeast face, and the mountain's lower, wooded slopes are heavily scarred where rock and ice slides have swept down the mountainside.

As the parkway continues to descend and crosses Silverhorn Creek, the jagged limestone peaks of the Continental Divide can be seen to the west. **Mistaya Lake** is a 3-kilometer-long (1.9-mile-long) body of water that sits at the bottom of the valley between the road and the divide, but it can't be seen from the parkway. The best place to view it is from the Howse Peak Viewpoint at Upper Waterfowl Lake. From here the high ridge that forms the Continental Divide is easily distinguishable. Seven peaks can be seen from here, including **Howse Peak** (3,290 meters/10,790 feet). At no point along this ridge does the elevation drop below 2,750 meters (9,000 feet). From Howse Peak, the Continental Divide makes a 90-degree turn to the west. One dominant peak that can be seen from Bow Pass to north of Saskatchewan River Crossing is **Mount Chephren** (3,268 meters/10,720 feet). Its distinctive shape and position away from the main ridge of the Continental Divide make it easy to distinguish. (Look for it directly north of Howse Peak.)

To Saskatchewan River Crossing

A trail leads down to the swampy shore of **Upper Waterfowl Lake,** providing one of the park's best opportunities to view moose, which feed on the abundant aquatic vegetation. Rock and other debris that have been carried down nearby valley systems have built up, forming a wide alluvial fan, nearly blocking the Mistaya River and creating Upper Waterfowl Lake. **Lower Waterfowl Lake** gets all the attention for its beautiful turquoise hue. Continuing north is **Mount Murchison** (3,337 meters/10,950 feet), on the east side of

the parkway. Although not one of the park's highest mountains, this gray and yellow massif of Cambrian rock comprises 10 individual peaks, covering an area of 3,000 hectares (7,400 acres).

From a parking lot 14 kilometers (8.9 miles) northeast of Waterfowl Lakes Campground, a short trail descends into the montane forest to **Mistaya Canyon.** Here the effects of erosion can be appreciated as the Mistaya River leaves the floor of the Mistaya Valley, plunging through a narrow-walled canyon into the North Saskatchewan Valley. The area is scarred with potholes where boulders have been whirled around by the action of fast-flowing water, carving deep depressions into the softer limestone bedrock below.

The **North Saskatchewan River** posed a major problem for early travelers and later for the builders of the Icefields Parkway. This swift-running river eventually drains into Hudson Bay. In 1989 it was named a Canadian Heritage River. One kilometer (0.6 mile) past the bridge you'll come to a panoramic viewpoint of the entire valley. From here the Howse and Mistaya Rivers can be seen converging with the North Saskatchewan at a silt-laden delta. This is also a junction with Highway 11 (also known as David Thompson Highway), which follows the North Saskatchewan River to Rocky Mountain House and Red Deer. From this viewpoint, numerous peaks can be seen to the west. Two sharp peaks are distinctive: **Mount Outram** (3,254 meters/10,680 feet) is the closer; the farther is **Mount Forbes** (3,630 meters/11,975 feet), the highest peak in Banff National Park (and the sixth highest in the Canadian Rockies).

To Sunwapta Pass

On the north side of the North Saskatchewan River is the towering hulk of **Mount Wilson** (3,261 meters/10,700 feet), named for Banff outfitter Tom Wilson. The Icefields Parkway passes this massif on its western flanks. A pullout just past Rampart Creek Campground offers good views of Mount Amery to the west and Mounts Sarbach, Chephren, and

---

1: Bow Lake 2: Herbert Lake along the Icefields Parkway 3: Lower Waterfowl Lake 4: Peyto Lake

Murchison to the south. Beyond here is the **Weeping Wall,** a long cliff of gray limestone where a series of waterfalls tumbles more than 100 meters (330 feet) down the steep slopes of Cirrus Mountain. In winter this wall of water freezes, becoming a mecca for ice climbers.

After ascending quickly, the road drops again before beginning a long climb to Sunwapta Pass. Halfway up the 360-vertical-meter (1,180-vertical-foot) climb is a viewpoint well worth a stop (cyclists will definitely appreciate a rest). From here views extend down the valley to the slopes of Mount Saskatchewan and, on the other side of the parkway, Cirrus Mountain. Another viewpoint, farther up the road, has the added attraction of a view of Bridal Veil Falls across the valley.

A cairn at **Sunwapta Pass** (2,023 meters/6,640 feet) marks the boundary between Banff and Jasper National Parks. It also marks the divide between the North Saskatchewan and Sunwapta Rivers, whose waters drain into the Atlantic and Arctic Oceans, respectively.

★ COLUMBIA ICEFIELD (JASPER)

The largest and most accessible of 17 glacial areas along the Icefields Parkway is the 325-square-kilometer (125-square-mile) Columbia Icefield, beside the Icefields Parkway in Jasper National Park, just north of Banff. It is 132 kilometers (82 miles) north of Lake Louise and 105 kilometers (65 miles) south of the town of Jasper. It's a remnant of the last major glaciation that covered most of Canada 20,000 years ago, and it has survived because of its elevation at 1,900-2,800 meters (6,230-9,190 feet) above sea level, cold temperatures, and heavy snowfalls. From the main body of the ice cap, which sits astride the Continental Divide, six glaciers creep down three main valleys. Of these, **Athabasca Glacier** is the most accessible and can be seen from the Icefields Parkway; it is one of the world's few glaciers that you can drive right up to. It is an impressive 600 hectares (1,480 acres) in area and up to 100 meters (330 feet)

deep. The speed at which glaciers advance and retreat varies with the long-term climate. Athabasca Glacier has retreated to its current position from across the highway, a distance of more than 1.6 kilometers (one mile) in a little more than 100 years. Currently it retreats up to two meters (six feet) per year. The rubble between the toe of Athabasca Glacier and the highway is a mixture of rock, sand, and gravel known as **till,** deposited by the glacier as it retreats.

The ice field is made more spectacular by the impressive peaks that surround it. **Mount Athabasca** (3,491 meters/11,450 feet) dominates the skyline, and three glaciers cling to its flanks. **Dome Glacier** is also visible from the highway; although part of the Columbia Icefield, it is not actually connected. Instead, it is made of ice that breaks off the ice field 300 meters (980 feet) above, supplemented by large quantities of snow each winter.

No gas is available along this stretch of the Icefields Parkway. The nearest gas stations are at Saskatchewan River Crossing (Banff National Park) and in the town of Jasper, 150 kilometers (93 miles) apart, so keep your tank topped up to be safe.

Exploring the Icefield

From the Icefields Parkway, an unpaved road leads down through piles of till left by the retreating Athabasca Glacier to a parking area beside Sunwapta Lake. An interesting alternative is to leave your vehicle beside the highway and take the 1.6-kilometer (one-mile) hiking trail through the lunarlike landscape to the parking area. From this point, a short path leads up to the toe of the glacier. (Along the access road, look for the small markers showing how far the toe of the glacier reached in years past; the farthest marker is across the highway beside the stairs leading up to the Icefield Centre.)

The ice field can be dangerous for unprepared visitors. Like that of all glaciers, the broken surface of the Athabasca is especially hazardous because snow bridges can hide its deep crevasses. The crevasses are uncovered

Columbia Icefield

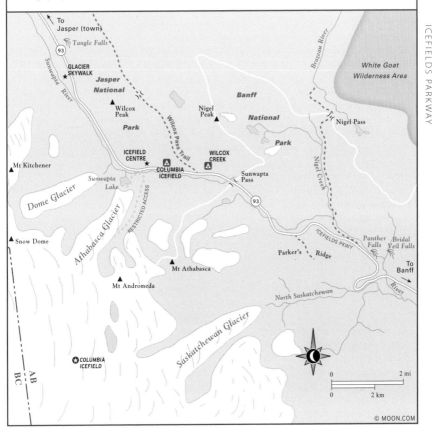

To Jasper (town)

Tangle Falls

93

GLACIER SKYWALK ★

Jasper

Sunwapta River

National

▲ Wilcox Peak

Nigel Peak ▲

Banff

Brazeau River

White Goat Wilderness Area

Park

National

Nigel Pass

ICEFIELD CENTRE ★

Wilcox Pass Trail

WILCOX CREEK

Park

▲ Mt Kitchener

COLUMBIA ICEFIELD

RESTRICTED ACCESS

Sunwapta Pass

Nigel Creek

Sunwapta Lake

93

Dome Glacier

Athabasca Glacier

ICEFIELDS PKWY

Panther Falls   Bridal Veil Falls

▲ Snow Dome

Parker's   Ridge

To Banff

▲ Mt Athabasca

▲ Mt Andromeda

North Saskatchewan

Saskatchewan Glacier

River

AB
BC

✪ COLUMBIA ICEFIELD

0   2 mi
0   2 km

© MOON.COM

as the winter snows melt. The safest way to experience the glacier firsthand is on specially developed vehicles with balloon tires that can travel over the crevassed surface. These Ice Explorers are operated by **Pursuit** (403/762-6700 or 866/606-6700, www.banff-jaspercollection.com). The 90-minute tour of Athabasca Glacier includes time spent walking on the surface of the glacier. The tour, which begins with a bus ride from the Icefield Centre, costs adult $125, child $65, and operates 9am-6pm daily May-mid-October (try to plan your tour for before 10am or after 3pm, after the tour buses have departed for the day). The ticketing office is on the main floor of the

Icefield Centre, with the surrounding area resembling an airport departure lounge—check the television screens for departure times and ensure you make your way to the correct gate. Early in the season, the glacier is still covered in a layer of snow and is therefore not as spectacular as during the summer. If you're in Banff or Jasper without transportation, consider Pursuit's day trip to the Columbia Icefield, which lasts nine hours and costs adult $260, child $140, including the Ice Explorer excursion.

Icefield Centre

The magnificent **Icefield Centre** is nestled

at the base of Mount Wilcox, overlooking the Athabasca Glacier. The building is as environmentally friendly as possible: Lights work on motion sensors to reduce electricity, some water is reused, suppliers must take their packaging with them after deliveries, and the entire building freezes in winter.

The center is the staging point for Ice Explorer tours, but before heading out onto the ice field, don't miss the **Glacier Gallery** on the lower floor. This large display area details all aspects of the frozen world, including the story of glacier formation and movement. The centerpiece is a scaled-down fiberglass model of the Athabasca Glacier, which is surrounded by hands-on displays and audiovisual presentations.

Also in the gallery is a **Parks Canada desk** (780/852-6288, 10am-5pm daily early May-late Sept.), a good source of information for northbound travelers.

On the main level is a Starbucks outlet, while upstairs is **Chalet** (9am-5pm daily May-mid-Oct.), a casual self-serve café with hot drinks, sandwiches, and other light meals. Seating is inside or out, with the outside tables offering unparalleled glacier views. Across the hallway is the modern and stylish **Altitude Restaurant** (7:30am-9:30am, 10:45am-2:45pm, and 6pm-9pm daily May-mid-Oct., $30-40), with a Canadiana-oriented menu for lunch and dinner. Relative to the remote location, the setting, service, and prices are all reasonable.

The entire Icefield Centre closes down for the winter in mid-October, reopening the following year in May. During summer, the complex (including display area) is open 9am-10pm daily, with reduced hours outside of July and August.

Columbia Icefield Skywalk

The architecturally impressive **Columbia Icefield Skywalk** projects out into the Sunwapta Canyon 280 meters (918 feet) above the valley floor around six kilometers (3.7 miles) north of the Icefield Centre. Access is by shuttle bus from the Icefield Centre (no passenger vehicles are allowed to stop at the skywalk itself). A short interpretive trail leads along the canyon edge and then out onto the glass-floored skywalk. Looking upstream from the skywalk, you can see the massive, ice-draped slopes of Mount Athabasca (3,491 m/11,450 ft) framed by the walls of the valley—a truly inspiring view of this great mountain. Directly across the valley is the ice-capped east face of Mount Kitchener. The Columbia Icefield Skywalk is operated by **Pursuit** (403/762-6700 or 866/606-6700, www.banffjaspercollection.com, 9am-6pm daily May-mid-Oct., included with the Ice Explorer bus, or adult $34, child $17).

HIKING
★ Helen Lake

Length: 6 kilometers/3.7 miles (2.5 hours) one-way
Elevation gain: 455 meters/1,500 feet
Rating: moderate
Trailhead: across the Icefields Parkway from Crowfoot Glacier Lookout, 33 kilometers (20 miles) northwest from the junction with the Trans-Canada Highway

The trail to Helen Lake is one of the easiest ways to access a true alpine environment from any highway within Banff National Park. The trail climbs steadily through a forest of Engelmann spruce and subalpine fir for the first 2.5 kilometers (1.6 miles) to an avalanche slope, reaching the tree line and the first good viewpoint after three kilometers (1.9 miles). The view across the valley is spectacular, with Crowfoot Glacier visible to the southwest. As the trail reaches a ridge, it turns sharply and passes through extensive meadows of wildflowers that are at their peak in late July and early August. The trail then crosses a photogenic stream and climbs to the glacial cirque where Helen Lake lies. Listen and look for hoary marmots along the last section of trail and around the lakeshore.

For those with the time and energy, it's

1: Columbia Icefield Skywalk 2: the Athabasca Glacier from the Icefield Centre

possible to continue an additional three kilometers (1.9 miles) to Dolomite Pass; the trail switchbacks steeply up 100 vertical meters (330 vertical feet) in less than one kilometer (0.6 mile), then descends an additional one kilometer (0.6 mile) to Katherine Lake and beyond to the pass.

Bow Glacier Falls

Length: 3.4 kilometers /2.1 miles (1 hour) one-way
Elevation gain: 130 meters/430 feet
Rating: easy
Trailhead: Num-ti-jah Lodge, Bow Lake, 36 kilometers (22.3 miles) northwest from the Trans-Canada Highway

This hike skirts one of the most beautiful lakes in the Canadian Rockies before ending at a narrow but spectacular waterfall. From the public parking lot in front of Num-ti-jah Lodge, follow the shore through to a gravel outwash area at the northwest end of the lake. Across the lake are reflected views of Crowfoot Mountain. The trail then begins a short but steep climb up the rim of a canyon before leveling out at the edge of a vast moraine of gravel, scree, and boulders. Pick your way through the 800 meters (0.5 mile) of rough ground that remains to reach the base of Bow Glacier Falls. (The namesake glacier can be seen above the falls from the trailhead, but not from the falls themselves.)

Peyto Lake

Length: 1.4 kilometer/0.9 mile (30 minutes) one-way
Elevation loss: 100 meters/330 feet
Rating: easy
Trailhead: unmarked pullout, Icefields Parkway, 2.4 kilometers (1.5 miles) north of Bow Summit

Without a doubt, the best place to view Peyto Lake is from a popular viewpoint accessible via a short trail from Bow Summit, 41 kilometers (25.5 miles) along the Icefields Parkway from the Trans-Canada Highway. The easiest way to access the actual shoreline, though, is along this short trail farther along the highway. A pebbled beach, strewn with driftwood, is the perfect setting for picnicking, painting, or just admiring the lake's quieter side. Back

at the lake lookout, a rough trail drops nearly 300 meters (980 feet) in 2.4 kilometers (1.5 miles) to the lake.

Chephren Lake

Length: 4 kilometers/2.5 miles (60-90 minutes) one-way
Elevation gain: 100 meters/330 feet
Rating: easy
Trailhead: Waterfowl Lakes Campground, Icefields Parkway, 57 kilometers (35 miles) northwest from the Trans-Canada Highway

This pale-green body of water (pronounced kef-ren) is hidden from the Icefields Parkway but easily reached. The official trailhead is a bridge across the Mistaya River at the back of Waterfowl Lakes Campground (behind site 86). If you're not registered at the campground, park at the end of the unpaved road running along the front of the campground and walk 300 meters (0.2 mile) down the well-worn path to the river crossing. From across the river, the trail dives headlong into a subalpine forest, reaching a crudely signposted junction after 1.6 kilometer (one mile). Take the right fork. This leads 2.4 kilometers (1.5 miles) to Chephren Lake, descending steeply at the end (this stretch of trail is often muddy). The lake is nestled under the buttresses of Mount Chephren. To the left, farther up the lake, is Howse Peak.

The trail to smaller **Cirque Lake** (4.5 kilometers/2.8 miles from the trailhead) branches left 1.6 kilometer (one mile) along this trail. It is less heavily used, but this lake is popular with anglers for its healthy population of rainbow trout.

Glacier Lake

Length: 9 kilometers/5.6 miles (2.5-3 hours) one-way
Elevation gain: 220 meters/770 feet
Rating: moderate
Trailhead: an old gravel pit on the west side of the highway, one kilometer (0.6 mile) west of Saskatchewan River Crossing

This 3-kilometer-long (1.9-mile-long) lake is one of the park's largest lakes not accessible by road. Although not as scenic as the more accessible lakes along the parkway, it's a pleasant destination for a full-day or overnight trip. For the first one kilometer (0.6 mile), the trail passes through an open forest of lodgepole pine to a fancy footbridge across the rushing North Saskatchewan River. From there it climbs gradually to a viewpoint overlooking the Howse River and the valley beyond, then turns away from the river for a long slog through dense forest to Glacier Lake. A primitive campground lies just over 300 meters (0.2 mile) from where the trail emerges at the lake.

Nigel Pass

Length: 7.4 kilometers/4.6 miles (2.5 hours) one-way
Elevation gain: 365 meters/1,200 feet
Rating: moderate
Trailhead: Icefields Parkway, 2.5 kilometers (1.6 miles) north of the switchback on the "Big Bend"

Park on the east side of the highway and follow the gravel road for two kilometers (1.2 miles) to the patrol cabin. Descend to two creek crossings and you quickly reach the site of Camp Parker, an old campsite used first by Indigenous hunting parties and then by mountaineers exploring the area around the Columbia Icefield. Look for carvings on trees recording these early visitors. From here the trail continues to climb steadily, only increasing in gradient for the last one kilometer (0.6 mile) to the pass. The pass (2,195 meters/7,200 feet) marks the boundary between Banff and Jasper National Parks. For the best view, scramble over the rocks to the left. To the north, the view extends down the Brazeau River Valley, surrounded by a mass of peaks. To the west (left) is Nigel Peak (3,211 meters/10,535 feet), and to the southwest are views of Parker's Ridge and the glaciated peaks of Mount Athabasca.

Parker's Ridge

Length: 2.4 kilometers/1.5 miles (1 hour) one-way
Elevation gain: 210 meters/690 feet
Rating: easy/moderate
Trailhead: Icefields Parkway, 4 kilometers (2.5 miles) south of Sunwapta Pass

From the trailhead on the west side of the highway, this wide path gains elevation quickly through open meadows and scattered stands of subalpine fir. This fragile environment is easily destroyed, so it's important that you stay on the trail. During the short alpine summer, these meadows are carpeted with red heather, white mountain avens, and blue alpine forget-me-nots. From the summit of the ridge, you look down on the 2-kilometer-wide (1.2-mile-wide) Saskatchewan Glacier spreading out below. Beyond is Castleguard Mountain, renowned for its extensive cave system.

ACCOMMODATIONS AND CAMPING
Under $100

North of Lake Louise, four hostels are spread along the Icefields Parkway: two in Banff National Park and two in Jasper National Park. Facilities at all four are limited, and beds should be reserved as far in advance as possible. For reservations, call 778/328-2220 or 866/762-4122, or book online (www.hihostels.ca). The first, 24 kilometers (15 miles) from Lake Louise, is **HI-Mosquito Creek,** which is near good hiking and offers accommodations for 32 in four- and six-bed cabins. Facilities include a kitchen, wood-heated sauna, and a large common room with fireplace. Although the hostel has no showers, guests are permitted to use those at the nearby Lake Louise Alpine Centre. Rates are $36 per night for members of Hostelling International (nonmembers $40). Check-in is 5pm-10pm, and it's open June-March.

HI-Rampart Creek, a further 64 kilometers (40 miles) along the parkway, is nestled below the snowcapped peak of Mount Wilson, with views across the North Saskatchewan River to even higher peaks along the Continental Divide. Like Mosquito Creek, it's near good hiking and has a kitchen and sauna. Its four cabins have a total of 24 bunk beds. Members pay $36 per night (nonmembers $40). It's open nightly May-March. Check-in is 5pm-10pm.

$200-300

The Crossing Resort (403/761-7000, www. thecrossingresort.com, mid-Apr.-mid-Oct., $270-340 s or d) is a large complex 87 kilometers (54 miles) north of Lake Louise and 45 kilometers (28 miles) south of the Columbia Icefield. It's also at the junction of Highway 11, which spurs east along Abraham Lake to Rocky Mountain House and Red Deer. The rooms offer a good combination of size and value but lack the historic charm of those at Num-ti-jah Lodge to the south and the views enjoyed by those at the Columbia Icefield Centre to the north. Each of the 66 units has a phone and TV. In addition to overnight rooms, The Crossing has the only gas between Lake Louise and Jasper, a self-serve cafeteria, restaurant, pub, and supersized gift shop.

Over $300

Pioneer guide and outfitter Jimmy Simpson built ★ **Num-ti-jah Lodge** (403/522-2167, www.num-ti-jah.com, late May-mid-Oct., from $355 s or d) on the north shore of Bow Lake, 40 kilometers (25 miles) north of Lake Louise, as a base for his outfitting operation in 1920. In those days, the route north from Lake Louise was nothing more than a horse trail. The desire to build a large structure when only short timbers were available led to the unusual octagonal shape of the main lodge. Simpson remained at Bow Lake, a living legend, until his death in 1972 at the age of 95. With a rustic mountain ambience that has changed little since Simpson's passing, Num-ti-jah provides a memorable overnight stay. Just don't expect the conveniences of a regular motel. Under the distinctively red, steep-pitched roof of the main lodge are 25 rooms, some that share bathrooms, and there's not a TV or phone in sight. Downstairs, guests soak up the warmth of a roaring log fire while mingling in a comfortable library filled with historical mountain literature. A dining room lined with memorabilia is open for breakfast and dinner daily ($28-48).

Campgrounds

Beyond Lake Louise, the first available camping along the Icefields Parkway is at **Mosquito Creek Campground** (late June-late Sept., $23 per site), 24 kilometers (15 miles) from the Trans-Canada Highway. Don't be scared by the name; the bugs here are no worse than anywhere else. The 32 sites are nestled in the forest, with a tumbling creek separating the campground from a hostel of the same name. Each site has a picnic table and fire ring, while other amenities include drinking water, pit toilets, and a kitchen shelter with an old-fashioned woodstove. If you're camping at Mosquito Creek and want a break from the usual camp fare, consider traveling 17 kilometers (10.6 miles) up the highway to the convivial, historic dining room at Num-ti-jah Lodge (403/522-2167, www.sntj.ca) to feast on Canadian-inspired cuisine.

Waterfowl Lakes Campground (late June-mid-Sept., $28 per site) is 33 kilometers (20 miles) north along the Icefields Parkway from Mosquito Creek. It features 116 sites between Upper and Lower Waterfowl Lakes, with a few sites in view of the lower lake. Facilities include drinking water, flush toilets, and kitchen shelters with wood-burning stoves. Rise early to watch the first rays of sun hit Mount Chephren from the shoreline of the lower lake, then plan on hiking the 4-kilometer (2.5-mile) trail to Chephren Lake—you'll be the first on the trail and back in time for a late breakfast.

Continuing toward Jasper, the Icefields Parkway passes The Crossing, a good place to gas up and buy last-minute groceries before reaching **Rampart Creek Campground** (July-Aug., $23 per site), 31 kilometers (19 miles) beyond Waterfowl Lake and 88 kilometers (55 miles) from Lake Louise. With just 50 sites, this campground fills early each afternoon. Facilities include kitchen shelters, pit toilets, and drinking water.

Nearby Parks

★ MOUNT ASSINIBOINE PROVINCIAL PARK

Named for one of the Canadian Rockies' most spectacular peaks, this 39,050-hectare (96,500-acre), roughly triangular park lies northeast of Radium Hot Springs, sandwiched between Kootenay National Park to the west and Banff National Park to the east. It's inaccessible by road; access is on foot or by helicopter. A haven for experienced hikers, the park offers alpine meadows, lakes, glaciers, and many peaks higher than 3,050 meters (10,000 feet) to explore. The park's highest peak, 3,618-meter (11,870-foot) Mount Assiniboine (seventh highest in the Canadian Rockies), is known as the "Matterhorn of the Rockies" for its resemblance to that famous Swiss landmark. The striking peak can be seen from many points well outside the boundaries of the park, including the Sunshine Village in Banff National Park.

The peak is named for the Assiniboine people, who ventured into this section of the Canadian Rockies many thousands of years before European exploration. The name Assiniboine means "stone boilers," a reference to their preferred cooking method. The mountain was sighted and named by a geological survey team in 1885, but the first ascent wasn't made until 1901.

Lake Magog is the destination of most park visitors. Here you'll find the park's only facilities and the trailheads for several interesting and varied day hikes. One of the most popular walks is along the Sunburst Valley/Nub Ridge Trail. From Lake Magog, small Sunburst Lake is reached in about 20 minutes, then the trail continues northwest a short distance to Cerulean Lake. From this lake's outlet, the trail descends slowly along the Mitchell River to a junction four kilometers (2.5 miles) from Lake Magog. Take the right fork, which climbs through a dense subalpine forest to Elizabeth Lake, nestled in the southern shadow of Nub Peak. From this point, instead of descending back to Cerulean Lake, plan on taking the Nub Ridge Trail, which climbs steadily for one kilometer (0.6 mile) to a magnificent viewpoint high above Lake Magog. From the viewpoint, it's just less than four kilometers (2.5 miles), downhill all the way, to the valley floor. The total length of this outing is 11 kilometers (6.8 miles), and as elevation gained is only just over 400 meters (1,310 feet), the trail can comfortably be completed in four hours.

Backcountry Accommodations

Getting to and staying at ★ Assiniboine Lodge (403/678-2883, www.assiniboinelodge.com, $400-580 per person) isn't cheap, but the number of repeat guests is testament to an experience that you will never forget. The mountain scenery may take most of the kudos, but the lodge's congenial atmosphere makes the stay equally memorable. Built in 1928 by the CPR, the delightfully rustic lodge is set in a lakeside meadow below its distinctive namesake peak. The main building holds six double rooms that share bathroom facilities and a dining area where hearty meals (included in the rates) are served up communal-style. Scattered in the surrounding trees are six one-room cabins that sleep 2-5 people. Each has running water and uses propane to heat and light the space. Outhouses and showers are shared.

You can reach the lodge on foot or fly in with Alpine Helicopters from a helipad in Spray Valley Provincial Park for $200 per person each way. The departure days are Wednesday, Friday, and Sunday. Lodge guests flying in may bring 18 kilograms (40 pounds) of gear, plus one pair of skis.

If you decide to hike in (or out), the charge for luggage transfers is $5 per pound (0.45 kilogram).

The operating season is late June to the first weekend of October, and then mid-February to late March, for cross-country skiing. There is a minimum stay of two nights.

Campground and Huts

Lake Magog is the park's main facility area, such as it is. A designated camping area on a low ridge above the lake's west shore provides a source of drinking water, pit toilets, and bear-proof food caches. Open fires are prohibited. Sites are $10 per person per night. Reserve a site up to four months in advance through BC Parks (https://camping.bcparks.ca).

A few hundred meters from the helicopter landing site are the **Naiset Huts,** where bunk beds cost $25 per person per night (book through Assiniboine Lodge at 403/678-2883, www.assiniboinelodge.com). The cabins contain nothing more than bunk beds with mattresses, but the modern communal kitchen has everything you will need to cook up a backcountry feast. Beds fill very quickly, so check the lodge website for reservations opening day (usually January for the upcoming summer season) and get ready to start dialing.

Information

In addition to the government agency responsible for the park (BC Parks, https://bcparks.ca), park information centers in Radium Hot Springs, Lake Louise, and Banff provide information and up-to-date trail conditions.

1: Naiset Hut at Lake Magog 2: hikers heading to Mount Assiniboine via Bryant Creek 3: Mount Assiniboine and Lake Magog

Getting There
APPROACHING THE PARK ON FOOT

Three trails provide access to **Lake Magog,** the park's largest body of water. The most popular comes in from the northeast, starting at Sunshine Village in Banff National Park and leading 29 kilometers (18 miles) via Citadel Pass to the lake. Although this trail is spectacular, it requires a strenuous, full-day hike into the park. Another approach is from the east, in Spray Valley Provincial Park (Kananaskis Country). The trailhead is at the southern end of Spray Lake; take the Mount Shark staging area turnoff 40 kilometers (25 miles) south of Canmore. By the time the trail has climbed the Bryant Creek drainage to 2,165-meter (7,100-foot) Assiniboine Pass, all elevation gain (450 meters/1,480 feet) has been made. At 27 kilometers (16.8 miles), this is the shortest approach, but its elevation gain is greater than that of the other two trails. The longest and least-used access is from Highway 93 at Simpson River in Kootenay National Park. This trail climbs the Simpson River and Surprise Creek drainages and crosses 2,270-meter (7,450-foot) Ferro Pass to the lake for a total length of 32 kilometers (20 miles).

THE EASY WAY IN: HELICOPTER

If these long approaches put visiting the park out of your reach, there's one more option: You can fly in by helicopter from the Mount Shark Heliport, at the southern end of Spray Valley Provincial Park, 40 kilometers (25 miles) southwest of Canmore. Flights depart from 11am Wednesday, Friday, and Sunday and cost $200 per person each way, including an 18-kilogram (40-pound) per-person baggage limit. Although **Alpine Helicopters** (403/678-4802, www.alpinehelicopter.com) operates the flights, all bookings must be made through **Assiniboine Lodge** (call 403/678-2883 8:30am-2:30pm Mon.-Fri., www.assiniboinelodge.com).

If you're planning on hiking into the park, Alpine Helicopters will fly your gear in for $4 per pound (0.45 kilogram). This same company, which also operates from a base in Canmore, charges $380 per person for a 30-minute flightseeing trip over the park. For more information, contact Alpine Helicopters.

SIFFLEUR WILDERNESS AREA

This remote region on the Alberta side of the Canadian Rockies lies south of Highway 11, which crosses West-Central Alberta between Rocky Mountain House and Saskatchewan River Crossing, in Banff National Park. It is completely protected from any activities that could have an impact on the area's fragile ecosystems. That includes road and trail development: No bridges have been built over the area's many fast-flowing streams, and the few old trails that do exist are not maintained. **Elk, deer, moose, cougars, wolverines, wolves, coyotes, black bears, and grizzly bears** roam the area's four main valleys, while the higher alpine elevations harbor **mountain goats and bighorn sheep.**

The main trail into the 41,200-hectare (101,800-acre) wilderness begins from a parking area two kilometers (1.2 miles) south of the Two O'Clock Creek Campground at Kootenay Plains. The area's northeastern boundary is a 7-kilometer (4.3-mile) hike from here. Even if you're not heading right into the wilderness area, the first section of this trail, which passes through Siffleur Falls Provincial Recreation Area to **Siffleur Falls,** is worth walking. The trail crosses the North Saskatchewan River via a swinging bridge and then at the 2-kilometer (1.2-mile) mark crosses the Siffleur River, reaching the falls after four kilometers (2.5 miles); allow 70 minutes one-way. These are the official Siffleur Falls, but others lie farther upstream at the 6.2-kilometer (3.9-mile) and 6.9-kilometer (4.3-mile) marks.

Once inside the wilderness area, the trail climbs steadily alongside the Siffleur River and into the heart of the wilderness.

Ambitious hikers can continue through to the Dolomite Creek area of Banff National Park, finishing at the Icefields Parkway, seven kilometers (4.3 miles) south of Bow Summit. Total length of this trail is 68 kilometers (42 miles), a strenuous five-day backcountry expedition. Another access point for the area is opposite Waterfowl Lakes Campground in Banff National Park. From here it is six kilometers (3.7 miles) up Noyes Creek to the wilderness area boundary; the trail peters out after 4.5 kilometers (2.8 miles) and requires some serious scrambling before descending into Siffleur. This trail—as with all others in the wilderness area—is for experienced hikers only.

Campground

Two O'Clock Creek Campground (May-mid-Oct., $24 per night) lies two kilometers (1.2 miles) from the park's main trailhead in Kootenay Plains Provincial Recreation Area. It is a primitive facility with a picnic shelter, firewood, and drinking water; the 24 sites each have a picnic table and firepit (firewood $4).

WHITE GOAT WILDERNESS AREA

White Goat comprises 44,500 hectares (110,000 acres) of high mountain ranges, wide valleys, hanging glaciers, waterfalls, and high alpine lakes. It lies north and west of Highway 11, abutting the north end of Banff National Park and the south end of Jasper National Park. The area's vegetation zones are easily recognizable: subalpine forests of Engelmann spruce, subalpine fir, and lodgepole pine; alpine tundra higher up. Large mammals here include a sizable population of bighorn sheep, as well as mountain goats, deer, elk, woodland caribou, moose, cougars, wolves, coyotes, black bears, and grizzly bears.

The most popular hike is the **McDonald Creek Trail,** which first follows the Cline River, then McDonald Creek to the creek's source in the heart of the wilderness area.

McDonald Creek is approximately 12 kilometers (7.5 miles) from the parking area on Highway 11, but a full day should be allowed for this section because the trail crosses many streams. From where McDonald Creek flows into the Cline River, it is 19 kilometers (11.8 miles) to the McDonald Lakes, but allow another two full days; the total elevation gain for the hike is a challenging 1,222 meters (4,000 feet). Other hiking possibilities include following the Cline River to its source and crossing Sunset Pass into Banff National Park, 17 kilometers (10.6 miles) north of Saskatchewan River Crossing, or heading up Cataract Creek and linking up with the trails in the Brazeau River area of Jasper National Park.

Siffleur River

Canmore

Long perceived as a gateway to the mountain national parks, the town of Canmore is very much a destination in itself these days.

Canmore lies in the Bow Valley, 103 kilometers (64 miles) west of Calgary, 28 kilometers (17 miles) southeast of Banff, and on the northern edge of Kananaskis Country. Its ideal mountain location and the freedom it enjoys from the strict development restrictions that apply in the nearby parks have made Canmore the fastest-growing town in Canada, with the population having more than tripled in the four decades since 1979. The permanent population is 14,000, and there are an additional 6,000 nonpermanent residents (folks who own a home in town but whose permanent address is elsewhere).

Highlights

Look for ★ to find recommended sights, activities, dining, and lodging.

★ **Coal-Mining History:** Explore Canmore's coal-mining history by walking through the residential area west of downtown. Continue up Canmore Creek past sealed mine entrances for the full effect (page 112).

★ **Grassi Lakes Trail:** A short walk is required to reach these two lakes, which are natural highlights of the Canmore region (page 114).

★ **Ha Ling Peak:** Feeling fit? Follow the trail to this summit for valley views that are unsurpassed (page 114).

★ **Golfing:** The town's three golf courses all offer something a little bit different, but they do have one thing in common—spectacular mountain scenery (page 116).

★ **Elevation Place:** The biggest and best aquatic center in the Canadian Rockies is a good place to spend a rainy afternoon—or to try your hand at indoor rock climbing (page 118).

Canmore

To Harvie Heights and Banff

TRAVEL ALBERTA INFORMATION CENTRE

WAPITI CAMPGROUND

CROSS ZEE RANCH

GOLFING

SILVERTIP

CANMORE GOLF COURSE

GOLFING

SILVER CREEK LODGE

LARCH AVE

SILVER TIP RD

SILVER TIP DR

MOUNTAIN AVE

BOW VALLEY

PALLISER TRAIL

SAGE BISTRO

17TH ST

ROCKY MOUNTAIN SKI LODGE

CRAZYWEED KITCHEN

WAPITI SPORTS/ JK BAKERY

FAIRHOLME DR

TRANS-CANADA HWY

TRAIL

RAILWAY

CPR TRESTLE BRIDGE

SEE DOWNTOWN CANMORE MAP

HOSPITAL

LADY MACDONALD COUNTRY INN

To
GRASSI LAKES TRAIL, HA LING PEAK, and Spray Valley Provincial Park (Kananaskis Country)

CANMORE NORDIC CENTRE

Bow River

6TH AVE

BASECAMP LODGE/RESORT

GEORGETOWN INN

ECLIPSE COFFEE ROASTERS

BENCHLANDS TRAIL

CREEKSIDE VILLA

BEAR AND BISON INN

MAIN ST

6TH AVE

ELEVATION PLACE

THE SHOPS OF CANMORE

COAST CANMORE HOTEL

COUGAR CREEK DR

SUMMIT CAFÉ

MINE SHAREHOLDER'S CABIN

RUNDLEVIEW DR

THREE SISTERS DR

RUNDLE DR

8TH AVE

7TH AVE

Centennial Park

5TH ST

6TH ST

5TH ST

4TH AVE

2ND ST

1ST ST

Millennium Park

Spring Creek

Policeman's Creek

Cougar Creek

BOW VALLEY TRAIL

TRANS-CANADA HWY

SPRAY LAKES RD

COAL-MINING HISTORY

Canmore Creek

Quarry Lake

Canmore Creek

HELIPORT

To
Alpine Club of Canada Clubhouse (HI-Canmore) and Grotto Canyon

1A

LAWRENCE GRASSI RIDGE

THREE SISTERS DR

WILSON WAY

Bow River

THREE SISTERS PKWY

To
Bow River Campground, Stewart Creek Golf Course, and Calgary

0   0.25 mi

0   0.25 km

© MOON.COM

Canmore in One Day

Many Canmore visitors plan their stays around a specific activity—golfers come to golf, skiers come to ski, and climbers come to climb. But if you're interests are varied, consider:

- Starting with an early-morning stroll through downtown for breakfast at one of the many cafés, such as Communitea Cafe.

- Heading out for some recreation. Depending on your interests, choose between a tee time at Stewart Creek Golf Course or a hike to crystal-clear Grassi Lakes.

- Heading to Valbella Gourmet Foods for lunch; eat in or plan a picnic beside the Bow River.

- After lunch, strolling along the riverside loop trail, and detouring up Canmore Creek to Quarry Lake if the weather is warm enough for swimming. Recover from the sun by spending the late afternoon at Elevation Place or the Canmore Museum and Geoscience Centre.

- For dinner, making reservations at Crazyweed for creative cooking or Tavern 1883 for upscale pub fare.

The surrounding mountains provide Canmore's best recreation opportunities. Hiking is excellent on trails that lace the valley and mountainside slopes, with many high viewpoints easily reached. Flowing through town, the Bow River offers great fishing, kayaking, and rafting; golfers flock to three scenic courses; and nearby Mount Yamnuska has become the most developed rock-climbing site in the Canadian Rockies. Canmore also hosted the Nordic events of the 1988 Winter Olympic Games and is the home of the Alpine Club of Canada.

PLANNING YOUR TIME

You can include Canmore in your itinerary in a variety of ways. The most obvious one is to make the town a base for your Canadian Rockies vacation. The advantages are less-crowded streets, better-priced accommodations, a choice of family-friendly lodgings, and a central location (Banff is a 15-minute drive to the west, and Kananaskis Country is a 40-minute drive southeast). Campers should keep in mind that there are much nicer campgrounds elsewhere in the region. If you decide to stay in Banff instead, there's no reason to relocate to Canmore for a night or two—simply visit the town as part of a day trip (or two).

Regardless of whether or not you stay in Canmore, there's plenty to do in the town itself for one day. Plan on two or more if you enjoy being outdoors. A two-day stay might include a morning tee time at Silvertip Golf Resort or a horseback ride at Cross Zee Ranch. After lunch at Crazyweed Kitchen, spend the afternoon exploring the main street, the museum, and the historic buildings scattered through town. The next morning, lace up your hiking boots for the walk to Grassi Lakes. Golfers will probably want to squeeze in another round of golf, this time at Stewart Creek Golf Course, but there are plenty of other choices—fishing on the Bow River, a rock-climbing lesson, or a helicopter flightseeing trip. Your two evenings could be spent swimming and climbing at Elevation Place and dining at Tavern 1883.

Previous: Ha Ling Peak; Silvertip Golf Resort; remains of Canmore's mining history.

THE LANDSCAPE

Canmore lies in the Bow Valley, flanked by mountains rising up to 1,000 meters (3,280 feet) above the valley floor. To the south and west are the distinctive peaks of the Three Sisters, Mount Lawrence Grassi, impressive Ha Ling Peak (known locally as Chinaman's Peak), and the southeastern extent of Mount Rundle. Across the valley are the Fairholme Range, Mount Lady Macdonald, and Grotto Mountain. Like the rest of the Canadian Rockies, these mountains began as layers of sedimentary rock laid down on the bed of an ancient sea. The seabed was forced upward over millions of years to create today's lofty peaks, whose sedimentary layers give them a distinct appearance. Through the valley flows the braided Bow River, heading eastward and into the Saskatchewan River system. At the north end of town, the river divides in two, leaving downtown Canmore on a low-lying island that is protected from annual spring flooding by dikes of large boulders.

HISTORY

The Hudson's Bay Company explored the Bow Valley corridor and attempted, without success, to establish a fur trade with Stoney people for most of the 1840s. In 1858 an expedition from the east, led by Captain John Palliser, sent back discouraging reports about the climate and prospects for agriculture in the valley. A few decades later, the Canadian Pacific Railway (CPR) chose the Bow Valley corridor as the route through the mountains, and the first divisional point west of Calgary was established in 1883. It was named Canmore for the 11th-century Scottish king Malcolm of Canmore.

Coal Mining

The CPR was delighted to discover that the valley was rich with coal, which it could use in its steam engines. Mining on the lower slopes of the Three Sisters and Mount Rundle commenced in 1886, attracting hundreds of miners and their families. Within a few years numerous mines operated around Canmore.

In 1899, the CPR moved its divisional point to Laggan (now Lake Louise), but the mines continued to operate, with the most productive mine located on Canmore Creek. Hotels and businesses were established, and a hospital, North West Mounted Police (NWMP) barracks, and opera house were built. The Canmore Opera House, reputed to be the only log movie house in the world, still stands and has been relocated to Calgary's Heritage Park.

Many British and European miners were attracted to the area, and the population continued to increase. A small contingent of Chinese miners also lived in Canmore. They didn't stay long, but their memory lives on in the name Chinaman's Peak. A Chinese cook, Ha Ling, was bet $50 that he couldn't climb the peak and return to Canmore in less than six hours. He did, and it became known as Chinaman's Peak; the name was changed to Ha Ling Peak in 1997.

In 1912, the Canadian Anthracite Coal Company relocated its operation from near present-day Banff to the west side of the Bow River, 5 kilometers (3.1 miles) from the rail line. **Georgetown,** a bustling little village, sprang up beside the mine. Workers enjoyed electricity and running water in cozy cabins along with their own company store, post office, and a school for the kids. Three short years later, markets dried up and the anthracite mine closed. Georgetown was abandoned, and the buildings were barged downstream to Canmore.

Recent Times

A little more than 100 years after mining commenced and less than 30 years after the last mine closed in 1979, Canmore experienced its second boom—tourism—which today shows no sign of slowing. In 1979, the population stood at 3,500; by 2020, that number had more than tripled. Half the current residents have lived in town for less than 15 years. Aside from exponential growth, the biggest news story in the last decade was a devastating flood that occurred in June 2013, when over 220 millimeters (nine inches) of rain fell in less than 36 hours, wiping out homes on the north side of town along Cougar Creek and forever changing the landscape of sections of town.

Canmore is a popular spot for moviemakers, and watching a locally filmed movie is a good way to get a taste for local scenery, even if the plotline is somewhat forgettable (such as the 2014 film *The Right Kind of Wrong*, which showcases the local mountains wonderfully). Other locally filmed big-budget movies have included *Shanghai Noon; Grizzly Falls; Mystery, Alaska; The Edge; Wild America; The Last of the Dogmen; Legends of the Fall; Snow Dogs; Open Range; The Assassination of Jesse James by the Coward Robert Ford;* and the 2016 Leonardo DiCaprio film *The Revenant.*

Sights and Recreation

Canmore spreads across both sides of the Trans-Canada Highway, with downtown Canmore occupying an island in the middle of the Bow River. Although development sprawls in all directions, large tracts of forest remain intact, including along the river, where paths lead beyond built-up neighborhoods and into natural areas. The most expansive of these is 37,340-hectare (92,220-acre) **Bow Valley Wildland Provincial Park,** which comprises pockets along the valley floor as well as most of the surrounding mountain slopes along both sides of the valley.

SIGHTS

Through booming times, the original core of Canmore, on the southwestern side of the Trans-Canada Highway, has managed to retain much of its original charm. Many historic buildings line the downtown streets, while other buildings from the coal-mining days are being preserved at their original locations around town. The best way to get downtown from the Trans-Canada Highway is to take Railway Avenue from Highway 1A and drive down 8th Street, also known as Main Street. Parking is easiest one street back along 7th Street, where one parking lot—at 6th Avenue—is designated for RVs.

Downtown

The first building of interest at the east end of the main street is Canmore's original **NWMP Barracks** (609 8th St., 403/678-1955, 10am-4pm Thurs.-Mon., donation), built in 1892.

It is one of the few such posts still in its original location, even though at the time of its construction the building was designed as a temporary structure to serve the nascent coal-mining town. The interior is decorated with period furnishings, while out back is a thriving garden filled with the same food crops planted by the post's original inhabitants. The post sits across from Policeman's Creek, a shallow body of water alive with ducks. **Ralph Connor United Church,** a little farther down 8th Street, was built in 1890 and is now a Provincial Historic Site. The church is named for its first reverend, Charles Gordon, who used the pen name Ralph Connor for the 35 books he authored. **Canmore Hotel,** on the corner of 8th Street and 7th Avenue, was built in 1891 (at a time when three hotels already operated), has been recently renovated, and is open for thirsty townsfolk and travelers alike.

Around the corner from the hotel, inside the impressive Civic Centre complex, is the **Canmore Museum and Geoscience Centre** (902 7th Ave., 403/678-2462, 10am-4pm daily in summer, 10am-4pm Thurs.-Mon. the rest of the year, adult $5, senior and child $3). This facility highlights the region's rich geological history and its importance to the growth of the town and related industries. Geological formations along three local hikes are described, which, along with a small fossil display, microscopes, and computer resources, make this facility an interesting rainy-day diversion.

Downtown Canmore

MALLARD ALLEY

SAFEWAY/
SAVE ON FOODS

ROCKY MOUNTAIN
FLATBREAD CO

RAILWAY AVE

NUTTERS

10TH ST

7TH AVE

BASECAMP
SUITES

COMMUNITEA
CAFÉ

PAINTBOX
LODGE

Policeman's

DRAKE
INN

TAVERN
1883

9TH ST

ARTSPLACE

TOWN HALL/
MUSEUM

BELLA
CRUSTA

ROSE
AND CROWN

ROCKY MOUNTAIN
BAGEL CO.

MAIN ST

Creek

THE
WOOD

CAFÉ
BOOKS

CANMORE
HOTEL

GRIZZLY
PAW PUB

LAMPHOUSE
HOTEL

MAIN ST

POST
OFFICE

BEAMER'S
COFFEE BAR

CHEF'S STUDIO
JAPAN

RALPH CONNOR
UNITED CHURCH

NWMP
BARRACKS

SPRING

Spring

CREEK

DR

8TH AVE

7TH AVE

7TH ST

6TH AVE

Creek

MALCOLM
HOTEL

ST. MICHAEL'S
HALL

0   100 yds

0   100 m

6TH ST

Centennial Park

© MOON.COM

★ Coal-Mining History

Several scenic and historic sights lie across the Bow River from downtown, including the remains of various mining operations. To get there, walk south along 8th Avenue for 500 meters (0.3 mile) to the Bow River. With a pedestrian-only bridge and paved paths on both sides of the river leading in either direction, this is a good point to stop and get oriented. A pleasant loop can be made by walking north and crossing the river at the old **CPR trestle bridge,** which once served local mines. Follow the trail back downstream past the **Mine Shareholders' Cabin,** a log structure built in 1914.

In the same vicinity, a trail leads off from Three Sisters Drive up Canmore Creek, passing the remains of a mine site that was first worked in 1891. Beyond the visible coal seam and crumbling concrete foundations is a picturesque waterfall tucked below a residential development. Backtrack 300 meters (0.2 mile) from the end of the trail and climb the wooden steps, crossing Spray Lakes Road to **Quarry Lake.** This small lake lies in an open meadow and is a popular sunbathing and swimming spot.

HIKING

The hiking trails around Canmore are usually passed by in favor of those of its famous neighbors, but some interesting trails do exist. Paved paths around town are suitable for walking, bicycling, and, in winter, skiing. They link Policeman's Creek with the Canmore Golf & Curling Club, the Canmore

1: Canmore Hotel **2:** Canmore Museum and Geoscience Centre **3:** Bow River

Nordic Centre, and Riverview Park on the Bow River.

★ Grassi Lakes

Length: 2 kilometers/1.2 miles (40 minutes) one-way
Elevation gain: 300 meters/980 feet
Rating: easy/moderate
Trailhead: Spray Village, beyond the Nordic center, 6 kilometers (3.7 miles) west of downtown off Spray Lakes Road

This trail climbs to two small lakes below Ha Ling Peak. From the parking lot just off Spray Lakes Road, take the left fork 150 meters (0.1 mile) along the trail. It climbs steadily to stairs cut into a cliff face before leading up to a bridge over Canmore Creek and to the lakes. Interpretive signs along the trail point out interesting aspects of the Bow Valley and detail the life of Lawrence Grassi, who built the trail in the early 1920s. With Ha Ling Peak as a backdrop, these gin-clear, spring-fed lakes are a particularly rewarding destination. Behind the upper lake, an easy scramble up a scree slope leads to four pictographs (ancient rock paintings) of human figures. They are on the first large boulder in the gorge. An alternate return route is down a rough access road between the hiking trail and Spray Lakes Road, passing a broken-down log cabin along the way.

★ Ha Ling Peak

Length: 3.5 kilometers/2.2 miles (90 minutes) one-way
Elevation gain: 810 meters/2,700 feet
Rating: moderate/difficult
Trailhead: Goat Creek parking lot, Spray Lakes Road, 9 kilometers (5.6 miles) west of Canmore

Ha Ling Peak is the impressive pinnacle of rock that rises high above Canmore to the southwest. While the sheer eastern face is visible from town, this trail winds up the back side of the mountain and ends in a saddle with stunning views across the Bow Valley. Leaving your vehicle at the Goat Creek Trailhead, cross the road, then walk up to and over the canal to search out the trail, which was rerouted and more clearly marked in 2019. The trail climbs steadily through subalpine forest of Engelmann spruce before breaking out above the tree line, where views north extend down the glacially carved Goat Creek Valley. The trail then forks; the left fork climbs unforgivingly to Ha Ling Peak, but hikers are rewarded with views no less spectacular by continuing to the right along a lightly marked trail that ends at a saddle. On a clear day, the panorama afforded from this viewpoint is worth every painful step. Take care on the return journey; stay high and to the right, and watch for rock cairns and colored flagging to ensure you enter the trees at the right spot.

Cougar Creek

Length: 9.5 kilometers/6 miles (4 hours) one-way
Elevation gain: 550 meters/1,800 feet
Rating: moderate
Trailhead: corner of Benchlands Trail and Elk Run Boulevard, east side of Trans-Canada Highway

This unofficial trail follows a valley carved deeply into the Fairholme Range by Cougar Creek, both of which were changed dramatically by flooding in 2013. The length and elevation gain listed are to a high ridge on the boundary of Banff National Park. Few hikers reach this point, with most content to turn around within an hour's travel. The first section of trail runs alongside an artificial channel that acts as a conduit for runoff in years of high snowfall. It's dry most of summer, but extra care should be taken in spring. Cross just before the mouth of the canyon. From this point, the rough trail crosses the creek bed 10 times in the first 3 kilometers (1.9 miles) to a major fork. Stay within the left valley, continuing up and around the base of Mount Charles Stewart. From this point the valley walls close in, and it's a steep climb up to the boundary of Banff National Park. On the return journey, continue beyond the parking lot to the Summit Café, where you can relax on the patio with a cool drink.

Mount Lady Macdonald

Length: 3.5 kilometers/2.1 miles (90 minutes) one-way

Alpine Club of Canada

The Alpine Club of Canada (ACC), like similar clubs in the United States and Great Britain, is a nonprofit mountaineering organization whose objectives include encouraging mountaineering through educational programs, exploring and studying alpine and glacial regions, and preserving mountain flora and fauna.

The club was formed in 1906, mainly through the tireless campaign of its first president, Arthur Wheeler. A list of early members reads like a Who's Who of the Canadian Rockies—Bill Peyto, Tom Wilson, Byron Harmon, Mary Schäffer—names familiar to all Canadian mountaineers. Today the club's membership includes 3,000 alpinists from throughout Canada.

The original clubhouse was near the Banff Springs Hotel, but in 1980 a new clubhouse was built on benchland at the edge of Canmore to serve as the association's headquarters. The club's ongoing projects include operating the Canadian Alpine Centre in partnership with Hostelling International (which calls the property the Lake Louise Alpine Centre), maintaining a system of 20 huts throughout the backcountry of the Canadian Rockies, and publishing the annual *Canadian Alpine Journal*—the country's only record of mountaineering accomplishments.

For further information and membership details, contact the **Alpine Club of Canada** (403/678-3200, www.alpineclubofcanada.ca).

Elevation gain: 850 meters/2,790 feet
Rating: moderate/difficult
Trailhead: corner of Benchlands Trail and Elk Run Boulevard, east side of Trans-Canada Highway

Named for the wife of Canada's first prime minister, this peak lies immediately north of Canmore. Follow Cougar Creek to where the canyon begins and look for a faint trail winding up a grassy bank to the left. Once on the trail, take the steepest option at every fork, then a sharp right 300 meters (0.2 mile) after the trail bursts out into a cleared area. This section is steep, climbing through a rock band to the mountain's southern ridge, which you'll follow the rest of the way. The distance and elevation listed are to an unused helipad below the main summit. It's a steep, unrelenting slog, but views across the Bow Valley are stunning. From this point, the true summit is another 275 vertical meters (900 vertical feet) away, along an extremely narrow ridge that drops away precipitously to the east.

Grotto Canyon

Length: 2 kilometers/1.2 miles (40 minutes) one-way
Elevation gain: 60 meters/200 feet
Rating: easy
Trailhead: Grotto Pond, Highway 1A, 12 kilometers (7.5 miles) east of Canmore

This is one of the most interesting trails around Canmore. From Grotto Pond, this trail first follows a power-line road behind the Baymag plant. Then at a signed intersection, it takes off through the woods to the mouth of the canyon. No official trail traverses the canyon; hikers simply follow the creek bed through the towering canyon walls. Around 300 meters (0.2 mile) into the canyon, look for pictographs to the left. At the 2-kilometer (1.2-mile) mark, the canyon makes a sharp left turn at Illusion Rock, where water cascades through a narrow chasm and into the main canyon. Many hikers return from this point (the hike becomes strenuous), but through the next section of canyon, the valley opens up, passing hoodoos and a cave. It's 6.5 kilometers (4 miles) from the trailhead to the end of the valley, with most of the 680 meters (2,230 feet) of elevation gained in the last 2 kilometers (1.2 miles).

Heart Creek

Length: 2 kilometers/1.2 miles (40 minutes) one-way
Elevation gain: 80 meters/260 feet
Rating: easy
Trailhead: Lac des Arcs interchange, Trans-Canada Highway, 15 kilometers (9.3 miles) east of Canmore

This well-formed trail is signposted from the

Lac des Arcs interchange. The trail parallels the highway eastward until reaching a fork. The trail to the right follows Heart Creek for just over one kilometer (0.6 mile), crossing the creek seven times on narrow log bridges. It ends at a cleared area below a spot where Heart Creek is forced through a narrow cleft. Those tempted to continue farther can cross the creek, scramble up a steep, forested ridge, and then descend the other side to link up with the creek upstream of the gorge. Cross the creek again for views of another narrow chasm.

Helicopter Tours and Hiking

The least expensive way to take to the skies around Canmore is on a 12-minute flight with **Alpine Helicopters** (91 Bow Valley Trail, 403/678-4802, www.alpinehelicopter. com), which costs $150 per person. Pay $330 per person and you'll spend 30 minutes in the air, which is enough time to circumnavigate the spectacular peak of Mount Assiniboine. The heliport is along Highway 1A south of downtown. Try to book ahead for these trips; they're very popular with travelers staying in Banff, where there is no flightseeing.

Heli-hiking is the summer alternative to heli-skiing—a helicopter does the hard work, and you get to hike in a remote alpine region that would usually entail a long, steep hike to access. Although Alpine Helicopters does the flying, reservations are made through **White Mountain Adventures** (403/760-4403, www.whitemountainadventures.com). Options include 10 minutes of flight time and 3-4 hours of guided above-the-tree-line hiking for $600 per person.

OTHER RECREATION
Canmore Nordic Centre

This sprawling complex on the outskirts of Canmore was built for the 1988 Winter Olympic Games. The cross-country skiing and biathlon (combined cross-country skiing and rifle shooting) events were held here, and today the center remains a world-class training ground for Canadian athletes in a variety of disciplines. Even in summer, long after the snow has melted, the place is worth a visit. An interpretive trail leads down to and along the west bank of the Bow River to the barely visible remains of Georgetown, a once-bustling coal-mining town. Many other trails lead around the grounds, and it's possible to hike or bike along the Bow River all the way to Banff. Mountain biking is extremely popular on 70 kilometers (43.5 miles) of trails. Bike rentals are available at **Trail Sports** (below the day lodge, 403/678-6764, www.trailsports. com, 9am-6pm daily, $60 for two hours, $80 per same-day return for a full-suspension bike). In summer, you can also play disc golf (Frisbees are available at Trail Sports). Snowmaking guarantees a ski season running November-March, with rentals and instruction available through Trail Sports.

Fishing

The **Bow River** near Canmore has fair fishing for brown (catch-and-release only) and brook trout, including right downtown between the old railway bridge and Rundle Drive. Follow Highway 1A east from town to access the best river fishing, as well as **Gap Lake** and **Grotto Pond;** the latter is stocked with rainbow trout. The Bow River is renowned for its rainbow trout fishing. This occurs downstream of Canmore toward Calgary and beyond **Ghost Lake,** which holds healthy populations of lake, rainbow, and brown trout.

For all your fishing needs, head to **Wapiti Sports** (1506 Railway Ave., 403/678-5550, 9am-5pm Mon.-Sat., 9am-3pm Sun.), which stocks bait and tackle and sells licenses.

★ Golfing

As with golfing elsewhere in the Canadian Rockies, book all tee times well in advance but also try to be flexible, because two of Canmore's three courses offer weekday and twilight discounts. The golfing season in Canmore runs early May-late September.

1: Grassi Lakes **2:** Canmore Nordic Centre **3:** hiking Ha Ling Peak **4:** Elevation Place

Silvertip (2000 Silvertip Trail, 403/678-1600 or 877/877-5444, www.silvertipresort.com) spreads across a series of wide benches between the valley floor and the lower slopes of Mount Lady Macdonald. It is generally recognized as one of Canada's finest resort courses, but more tellingly, it boasts a slope rating of 153, one of the highest of any course in North America. Needless to say, the layout is challenging, with the most distinct feature being an elevation change of 200 meters (660 feet) between the lowest and highest points on the course. Adding to this challenge are narrow, sloping, tree-lined fairways; numerous water hazards; 74 bunkers; and a course length of a frightening 7,300 yards from the back markers. High-season greens fees are $185, which includes a mandatory cart and use of the driving range.

Stewart Creek Golf Club (4100 Stewart Creek Dr., 403/609-6099 or 877/993-4653, www.stewartcreekgolf.com), another newer layout, lies across the valley in the Three Sisters Mountain Village development. It is shorter than Silvertip but still measures more than 7,000 yards from the back tees. The fairways are relatively wide, but positioning of tee shots is important, and the course is made more interesting by hanging greens, greenside exposed rock, and historic mine shafts. Greens fees are $215, with twilight rates of $160. These rates include use of a power cart and practice facility.

Canmore Golf & Curling Club (2000 8th Ave., 403/678-4785, www.canmoregolf.net) is an 18-hole course with a modern clubhouse and practice facility. It is an interesting layout, with scenic panoramas and water on some holes. Greens fees are $99.

Horseback Riding

Nestled on a wide bench on the northeastern side of town, **Cross Zee Ranch** (2500 Palliser Trail, 403/678-4171, www.crosszeeranch.ca) has been guiding visitors through the valley since the 1950s. From expansive stables, rides pass through thickly wooded areas, along colorful meadows, and to high lookouts. Options include Ranger Ridge and Bone Gully (one hour, $60 per person), Sunny Bench (90 minutes, $80), and the Great Aspens ride (two hours, $100).

Climbing

Hundreds of climbing routes have been laid out around Canmore. **Mount Yamnuska,** which rises 900 meters (2,950 feet) above the valley floor east of town along Highway 1A, is the most developed site. Climbers also flock to **Ha Ling Peak, Cougar Creek,** the area behind **Grassi Lakes,** and **Grotto Canyon.** Canmore is home to many qualified mountain guides.

Yamnuska (403/678-416, www.yamnuska.com) offers basic rock-climbing courses and instruction for all ability levels on ice climbing, mountaineering, and trekking. A good introduction to rock climbing is the weekend-long Outdoor Rock Intro course, which costs $425. Unique to the company are three-month-long courses that take in all aspects of mountain-oriented skills.

★ Elevation Place

Between the Trans-Canada Highway and downtown Canmore, **Elevation Place** (700 Railway Ave., 403/678-8920, 6am-9pm Mon.-Fri., 8:30am-9pm Sat.-Sun.) is a large recreation center whose architecturally pleasing design mimics the surrounding mountains. It's a fantastic place for all ages to enjoy—whether swimming, climbing, or working out. The facility is anchored by a large aquatic center, with a lap pool, a leisure pool complete with a beach-like entry, a lazy river, and waterslides. The climbing gym features over 1,000 square meters (10,700 square feet) of climbing surface up to 15 meters (45 feet) high, as well as routes for children as young as four. Entry is adult $8, senior $6, child $5, with climbing wall access and equipment rental extra. Also within Elevation Place are a large fitness facility, the town library, an art gallery featuring local artists, and a café.

Entertainment and Events

NIGHTLIFE

Canmore doesn't have anywhere near the number of bars that nearby Banff is so famous for, but no one ever seems to go thirsty. **The Wood** (838 8th St., 403/678-3404, 11am-10pm daily) has a beer garden that catches the afternoon sun and is especially busy on weekends. One block north of the main street is **Tavern 1883** (709 9th St., 403/609-2000, 11:30am-10pm Mon.-Tues., 11:30am-1am Wed.-Sun.), where the owners have done an admirable job of creating a stylish western ambience within the confines of an early 1900s residence. Also notable is the patio, which feels a world away from the nearby bustle of the main street. Arrive between 3pm and 5pm Sunday to Wednesday to enjoy happy-hour prices (beer, wine, appetizers just $6), and stop by Thursday night for open mic, Friday for live music, and Saturday for a DJ.

The **Grizzly Paw Pub** (622 8th St., 403/678-9983, 11am-10pm daily) brews its own beer, with six year-round offerings and various seasonals produced in-house (look for special winter brews around Christmas). The lighter Grumpy Bear Honey Wheat Ale suits most tastes. The brewpub has a pleasant patio facing the main street, although it gets especially busy on summer evenings.

At the north end of the main street is the **Drake Inn** (909 Railway Ave., 403/678-5131, 10am-2am daily), with a small outdoor patio and bands most nights. Across the road, at the **Rose and Crown** (749 Railway Ave., 403/678-5168, 11am-2am daily), you'll find a beer garden. Both these bars have midweek drink specials and a couple of pool tables each.

FESTIVALS AND EVENTS

Canmore's small-town pride lives on through a busy schedule of festivals and events, which are nearly always accompanied by parades of flag-waving kids, free downtown pancake breakfasts, and an evening shindig somewhere in town.

Winter

Throughout the winter months, locals play **hockey** on ponds and rinks scattered throughout the valley. Things get a little more serious at home games of the **Canmore Eagles** (www.canmoreeagles.com), a Junior A club that plays at the recreation center along 8th Avenue between October and March. The New Year is ushered in with **Party on the Pond,** with skating, wagon rides, fireworks, and bonfires on and around the frozen pond beside 10th Street; the fun starts at 5:30pm.

Summer

Canada Day (July 1) is celebrated with a pancake breakfast, parade, various activities in Centennial Park, and 10:30pm fireworks.

On the Heritage Day long weekend, the first weekend of August, Canmore hosts a **Folk Music Festival** (www.canmorefolkfestival.com), which starts on Saturday and runs through Monday evening. This event, which attracts more than 15,000 fans, features national and international acts performing in Centennial Park, musical workshops, and a free pancake breakfast beside the post office on Heritage Day. Day passes are $65-75, or purchase a three-day pass for $185.

The first Sunday of September is the **Canmore Highland Games** (403/678-9454, www.canmorehighlandgames.ca), a day of dancing, eating, and caber tossing culminating in a spectacular and noisy parade of pipe bands throughout the grounds of Centennial Park; the event attracts more than 10,000 spectators. The grand finale is the *ceilidh,* a traditional Scottish celebration involving loud beer-drinking, foot-stomping music, which takes place under a massive tent set up in the park for the occasion.

Fall

Beginning at the end of every summer, artsPlace (950 8th Ave., 403/609-2623, www.artsplacecanmore.com) curates a full schedule of arts-oriented festivities, including workshops, displays, and walking tours throughout the town.

Food

The restaurant scene has come a long way in Canmore since the late 1990s. While you can still get inexpensive bar meals at the many pubs, other choices run the gamut, from the lively atmosphere of dining in the front yard of a converted residence to organic gourmet pizza.

GROCERIES

Save on Foods and **Safeway** (both 8am-10pm daily) are large grocery stores on Railway Avenue. Both have in-house bakeries, butchers, and delis, along with a surprisingly wide selection of fresh seafood at Save on Foods.

GOURMET GOODIES

Near Save on Foods, **Nutter's** (900 Railway Ave., 403/678-3335, 9am-7pm Mon.-Fri., 10am-6pm Sat., 10am-5pm Sun.) is chock-full of bulk bins—a great place to stock up for hiking trips.

Away from the downtown core, **JK Bakery** (1514 Railway Ave., 403/678-4232, 7:30am-5pm Mon.-Sat., lunches $8-12) supplies regular and European-style breads to shops and restaurants throughout the Canadian Rockies. A café out front serves up soups, sandwiches, and pastries, and also sells gourmet breads over the counter.

Tucked away in an industrial park beyond the south end of Bow Valley Trail is ★ **Valbella Gourmet Foods** (104 Elk Run Blvd., 403/678-4109, 8am-6pm Mon.-Fri., 9am-5pm Sat., lunches $9-14). Valbella mainly supplies gourmet meats to Bow Valley restaurants and grocery stores; head there for Canadian specialties such as buffalo, venison, and salmon; fresh cuts of marinated Alberta beef, lamb, chicken, and pork; and cured sausages. In the café off to one side, the same top-notch ingredients are used to make well-priced sandwiches.

CAFÉS AND COFFEE SHOPS

The **Rocky Mountain Bagel Company** (830 8th St., 403/678-9978, 7am-5pm daily) is a popular early-morning gathering spot. With a central location, it's always busy but manages to maintain an inviting atmosphere. It's the perfect place to start the day with a good strong coffee and fruit-filled muffin.

In 1994, Michael Beamer was the first to introduce gourmet coffee to the Canmore population with the opening of **Beamer's Coffee Bar.** Although the original location is now closed, it has been replaced by two new Beamer's Coffee Bars: one downtown (737 7th Ave., 403/609-0111, 6am-7pm daily) and another in the Shops of Canmore complex (300 Old Canmore Rd., 403/675-0116, 6am-8pm daily), which has lots of outdoor seating.

★ **Communitea Cafe** (1001 6th Ave., 403/678-6818, 9am-7pm daily, lunches $9-15) is a bright, welcoming space with lots of comfortable seating. As the name suggests, tea is the specialty, with over 80 blends to choose from, but the coffee is also good and the food outstanding. The menu features lots of creative, healthy choices, including pad Thai, an organic Indian-spiced chicken burger, and a goat cheese and beet quesadilla.

Across the railway from downtown, **Eclipse Coffee Roasters** (702 Bow Valley Trail, 403/678-7777, 7:30am-5:30pm daily) is generally regarded as having the best coffee in town. Beans are sourced from single-origin suppliers and roasted in-house. Also away from downtown, near where Cougar Creek enters Canmore from the Fairholme Range, is the **Summit Café** (1001 Cougar Creek Dr., 403/609-2120, 6:30am-1:30pm daily, breakfasts $9-16). Best known for generous breakfasts, it also features a health-conscious lunch menu including lots of salads, but many people come just to soak up the sun on the outside deck or relax with a cup of coffee.

CANADIAN

Canmore has many top-notch restaurants, and one of the best is ★ **Tavern 1883** (709 9th St., 403/609-2000, 11:30am-10pm daily, $17-33), a family-friendly venue that is part pub and part restaurant. The food is great, and so is the restaurant itself. Earthy tones, hardwood floors, rustic furniture, and a large deck out front create a modern western ambience unequaled in Canmore. The menu takes its inspiration from across Canada, with an emphasis on freshly prepared Canadian produce. Choose from dishes such as elk burger, grilled bison and prawns, or poutine (thick french fries covered with cheese curds and gravy).

★ **Crazyweed Kitchen** (1600 Railway Ave., 403/609-2530, 11:30am-10pm Wed.-Sun., $24-47) dishes up creative culinary fare that gets rave reviews from even cultured Calgarians. From the busy open kitchen, all manner of creative dishes are on offer: prawn curry in a coconut broth, masala-spiced baby back ribs, and Moroccan lamb sirloin topped with beet hummus. Healthy portions are served at tables inside or out. Also notable is the extensive wine list.

The innovative Canadian-oriented cuisine and flawless presentation make **Sage Bistro** (1712 Bow Valley Trail, 403/678-4878, 5pm-9pm Mon.-Fri., 10am-9pm Sat.-Sun., $32-46) a longtime Canmore favorite for well-priced dining in a comfortable setting. The main dining room is at street level in a two-story log building, while upstairs is a wine lounge with a tapas menu and three small patios that enjoy mountain views. Mains include familiar favorites with a local

twist: steelhead trout with a lemon-caper rub and braised lamb shank with seasonal vegetables. Finish up with a sampler platter of crème brûlées (the mango-passionfruit combo is my favorite).

GOURMET PIZZA

Downtown, ★ **Bella Crusta** (903 6th Ave., 403/609-3366, noon-4pm Tues.-Sat.), a hole-in-the-wall place just off the main street, is the purveyor of the best gourmet pizza in the Bow Valley and also creates delicious focaccia sandwiches to go. Heated slices to go are $5, or pay around $20 for a family-size version and heat it yourself; the friendly staff recommends doing so on a barbecue grill.

Rocky Mountain Flatbread Co. (838 10th St., 403/609-5508, 11:30am-8pm Sun.-Thurs., 11:30am-9pm Fri.-Sat., $20-25) is a lovely space decorated in natural tones and dominated by a wood-fired clay oven in one corner. The oven is also the main attraction when it comes to the food—gourmet flatbread-style pizzas for mostly under $20. My advice: Start with a bowl of made-from-scratch chicken noodle soup, then move on to the apple chicken pizza.

ASIAN

Duck down an alleyway off the main street to **Chef's Studio Japan** (709 8th St., 403/609-8383, noon-2:30pm Sat.-Sun. and 5pm-9pm daily, $14-20), a Japanese restaurant with a distinctive artsy feel. Seating is at a sushi counter or at regular tables surrounded by original art. The cuisine is not overly inventive, but the portions are generous and the tempura—always a good litmus test—is light and delicate.

Wild Orchid Bistro (Silver Creek Lodge, 1818 Mountain Ave., 403/679-2029, 4pm-9pm Mon.-Fri., noon-9pm Sat.-Sun., $16-30) is my favorite Japanese restaurant in the Canadian Rockies. It features all the usual choices, all expertly crafted in the open kitchen, as well as many with a western twist. Perfect presentation, mountain views, and a large deck add to the appeal.

Accommodations and Camping

Canmore's population boom has been mirrored by the construction of new hotels and motels. Most of the newer lodgings are on Bow Valley Trail (Highway 1A). As with all resort towns in the Canadian Rockies, reservations should be made as far in advance as possible in summer.

In addition to dozens of vacation rentals (www.airbnb.ca), more than 40 bed-and-breakfasts operate in Canmore. They are all small, family-run affairs with only one or two rooms (a local town bylaw limits the number of guest rooms in private homes to just two). During summer, they fill every night. For a full list of B&Bs, check the website of the **Canmore/Bow Valley Bed and Breakfast Association** (www.bbcanmore.com) for one that suits your needs.

Although hotel pricing in Canmore may be higher than you're used to, it is definitely much cheaper than nearby Banff, so much of the local business is overflow from the adjacent park. Additionally, outside the busiest summer period (mid-June-mid-Sept.), room rates are slashed considerably, especially at the more expensive accommodations; with a little bit of searching, expect to find rates that include two lift tickets (at either the Banff or Kananaskis ski resorts) for little more than the room-only rate during summer.

IN AND AROUND THE TOWN OF CANMORE
Under $100

Located in an iconic main-street building that dates to 1890, the **Canmore Hotel** (738 Main St., 403/688-7888, www.thecanmore-hotel.com, dorms $60, from $180 s or d) was thoroughly renovated in 2018. It features a western-style bar, two patios, and upstairs lodging. Choices are bunk beds in dorms that sleep between 4 and 10 guests, and a few private rooms with shared bathrooms.

HI-Canmore (403/678-3200, www.

hihostels.ca) is an excellent hostel-style accommodation at the base of Grotto Mountain. Affiliated with Hostelling International, the lodge is part of the headquarters for the Alpine Club of Canada, the country's national mountaineering organization. In addition to sleeping up to 46 people in seven rooms, it has a kitchen, an excellent library, a laundry room, bar, sauna, and lounge area with a fireplace. Rates are $40 per night for members of Hostelling International or the Alpine Club (nonmembers $45). Private rooms are $100 s or d for members (nonmembers $110). Alpine Club membership is inexpensive and includes a discount at the Lake Louise Alpine Centre. To get here from downtown, follow Bow Valley Trail southeast; the hostel is signposted to the left, 500 meters (0.3 mile) after passing under the Trans-Canada Highway.

$200-300

Also at the edge of Canmore's downtown core is the **Drake Inn** (909 Railway Ave., 403/678-5131 or 800/461-8730, www.drakeinn.com, $275-350 s or d). It offers 26 bright and cheerfully decorated motel rooms. Well worth an extra $10 are Creekside Rooms, featuring private balconies overlooking Policeman's Creek.

★ **Silver Creek Lodge** (1818 Mountain Ave., 403/678-4242 or 877/598-4242, www.silvercreekcanmore.ca, $250-470 s or d) provides hotel and suite accommodations within a larger condominium development. Aside from modern kitchen-equipped condos (from $350), many with separate bedrooms and mountain views, highlights include the highly recommended Wild Orchid Bistro, spa services, outdoor hot tubs with mountain views, and underground parking.

Named for one of the valley's original coal-mining communities, the **Georgetown Inn** (1101 Bow Valley Trail, 403/678-3439 or 866/695-5955, www.georgetowninn.ca, $255-350 s or d) is set up as a country inn of times gone by, complete with a pub-style dining room open daily for breakfast, lunch, and dinner. Each of the 20 guest rooms has its own individual charm, with a modern twist on decor that features lots of English antiques.

Across from the Georgetown, **Lady Macdonald Country Inn** (1201 Bow Valley Trail, 403/678-3665 or 800/567-3919, www.ladymacdonald.com, $280-350 s or d) exudes a welcoming atmosphere and offers personalized service not experienced in the larger properties. Its 10 rooms are all individually furnished, with the smallest, the Palliser Room, featuring elegant surroundings and a magnificent wrought-iron bed. The largest of the rooms is the Three Sisters, which has bright, welcoming pastel-colored decor, a king bed, a two-way gas fireplace, a hot tub, and uninterrupted views of its namesake. Rates include a hearty hot breakfast in a country-style breakfast room.

★ **Paintbox Lodge** (629 10th St., 403/609-0482 or 888/678-6100, www.paintboxlodge.com, $275-400 s or d) has the same upscale charm as the Bear and Bison but enjoys a more central location, just one block from the main street. The lobby itself—exposed hand-hewn timbers, slate tiles, and unique pieces of mountain-themed art—is an eye-catching gem. The upscale mountain decor continues through the five large guest rooms, each lavishly decorated with muted natural colors and a tasteful selection of heritage artifacts. Rooms also boast beds draped with the finest linens, bathrooms anchored by a deep soaking tub, and wireless Internet access. The more expensive rooms have fireplaces and balconies.

$300-400

A newcomer to the Canmore lodging scene, **Basecamp Resorts** (855/219-4707, www.basecampresorts.com) does a wonderful job of providing comfortable accommodations for all budgets. Regardless of the room type, you'll be staying in environmentally constructed buildings while enjoying locally sourced coffee and bathroom products. At

Basecamp Lodge (1002 Bow Valley Trail, $309-389) reserve motel-style rooms with simple, clean décor, and take advantage of the sauna or free bikes. Larger rooms here are an excellent value; for example, two king beds and a fireplace is $379. Adjacent to the Lodge is **Basecamp Resort** (1102 Bow Valley Trail, $329-800), where every unit has a full-size kitchen and some have balconies with mountain views. Communal facilities include barbecues and a rooftop hot tub. Units range from studios to three bedrooms. Closer to downtown, **Basecamp Suites** (798 10th St., $340-770) also has full kitchens in every unit as well as multi-room suites.

Not only can you rent one- and two-bedroom units with full kitchens at **Rocky Mountain Ski Lodge** (1711 Bow Valley Trail, 403/678-5445 or 800/665-6111, www.canmoreskilodge.com, $330-470 s or d), but there's also plenty of outdoor space for kids to run around, including a small playground. Also on the property are a barbecue and picnic area, and a laundry.

After an ambitious renovation, an older motel along the main street has been reimagined as the **Lamphouse Hotel** (610 8th St., 855/219-4707, www.lamphousehotel.com, $329-369 s or d), with 25 upscale rooms, each featuring original artwork, super-comfortable beds, gourmet coffee machines, and 55-inch TVs.

If you have up to $300 per night to spend on accommodations, I strongly recommend you consider ★ **Bear and Bison** (705 Benchlands Trail, 403/678-2058, www.bearandbisoninn.com, $340-460 s or d), offering a unique mountain ambience impossible to find in a regular motel. This elegant lodging has 10 guest rooms in three different themes. Timber and stone surroundings are complemented by rich heritage tones throughout. Each room has a king-size four-poster bed, jetted tub, fireplace, and private balcony or patio. The lounge has a high vaulted ceiling, a welcoming open fire, and panoramic picture windows. Guests also enjoy an inviting library and a private garden complete with an

oversized hot tub. Rates include baked goods on arrival, predinner drinks, and a breakfast you will remember for a long time.

In the vicinity of Bear and Bison, **Creekside Villa** (709 Benchlands Trail, 403/609-5522, www.creeksidevilla.ca, $309-349 s or d) is a modern, mountain-style lodge featuring lots of exposed timber. The 12 rooms are elegant in their simplicity; 8 have lofts. Facilities include a lounge with roaring log fire, a small exercise room, a whirlpool, and a steam room. Rates include a gourmet continental breakfast that will set you up for the day.

One of Canmore's best lodgings is the ★ **Malcolm Hotel** (321 Spring Creek Dr., 403/812-0680, malcolmhotel.ca, $440-700), which opened in 2018. A short walk from downtown, it's in a delightful location, with its public areas and some guest rooms enjoying forest and creek views. The 124 guest rooms are sleek, modern, and spacious. When booking, check for upgrade opportunities for only a few extra bucks (look for private balconies and mountain views). Other amenities include a heated outdoor pool, two outdoor hot tubs, a firepit, fitness room, restaurant, and lounge.

HARVIE HEIGHTS

Lodging in Harvie Heights, 8 kilometers (5 miles) west of Canmore and less than one kilometer (0.6 mile) from the entrance to Banff National Park, is limited but well priced.

Over $300

Banff Boundary Lodge (1000 Harvie Heights Rd., 403/678-9555, www.banffboundarylodge.ca, $300-380 s or d) is a newish property where each of the 42 units have one or two bedrooms, a comfortable lounge area with TV/DVD, and a full kitchen. Other facilities include an outdoor hot tub, barbecue area, and laundry. Outside of summer, rates drop to around $180, an excellent value.

CAMPGROUNDS
In Town

Along the Bow Valley Trail toward Banff is the town-operated **Wapiti Campground** (100 Ray McBride St., 403/678-9511 or 866/366-2267, www.wapiticamping.com, May-mid-Oct., $32-42), beside the Travel Alberta Visitor Information Centre and across the road from the Legacy Trail bike path linking Banff and Canmore. Facilities are limited to washrooms with showers ($3) and firepits. Highway noise will be a problem for light sleepers, but the location is central.

Other Campgrounds

East of Canmore are three park-like campgrounds operated by **Bow Valley Park Campgrounds** (403/673-2163, www.bowvalleycampgrounds.com). Each has pit toilets, kitchen shelters, and firewood for sale at $10 per bundle. **Bow River Campground** (mid-April-Oct., walk-in tent sites $31, power and water $39) is 3 kilometers (1.9 miles) east of Canmore at the Three Sisters Parkway overpass; **Three Sisters Campground** (May-mid-Oct., $31 per site) is accessed from Deadman's Flats, a farther 4 kilometers (2.5 miles) east, but it has a pleasant treed setting; and **Lac des Arcs Campground** (May-mid-Oct., $31 per site) slopes down to the edge of a large lake of the same name 7 kilometers (4.3 miles) farther east toward Calgary. Make reservations up to 90 days in advance through **Alberta Parks** (877/537-2757, www.reserve.albertaparks.ca).

Information and Services

INFORMATION

The best source of pre-trip information (apart from this book, of course) is **Tourism Canmore Kananaskis** (www.explorecanmore.ca). A **Travel Alberta Information Centre** (2801 Bow Valley Trail, 403/678-5277, 8am-8pm daily May-Sept., 9am-6pm daily Oct.), just off the Trans-Canada Highway on the west side of town, provides plenty of information about Canmore—and other destinations throughout the province—upon your arrival.

The *Rocky Mountain Outlook* and *Crag and Canyon* are both filled with local issues and entertainment listings; both weekly newspapers are available free on stands throughout the valley.

Canmore Library (700 Railway Ave., 403/678-2468, 10am-8pm Mon.-Fri., 10am-5pm Sat.-Sun.) is in Elevation Place on the southeast side of downtown.

At the top end of the main street, **Café Books** (826 Main St., 403/678-0908, 10am-6pm daily, later in summer) stocks an excellent selection of Canadiana, including hiking guides, coffee-table-style pictorials, Canadian Rockies cookbooks, and calendars, as well as nonfiction by local authors. Search out children's books toward the back. Part of Café Books is **Chapter Two,** an adjacent room dedicated to an interesting collection of used books.

SERVICES

The **post office** (801 8th St., 9am-5pm Mon.-Fri., 9am-noon Sat.) is on the busiest downtown intersection, beside Rusticana Grocery. **Canmore Hospital** is along Bow Valley Trail (403/678-5536). For the **RCMP,** call 403/678-5516.

In addition to all lodgings and cafés, wireless Internet is free at the **Canmore Library** (700 Railway Ave., 403/678-2468, 10am-8pm Mon.-Fri., 10am-5pm Sat.-Sun.).

Getting There and Around

GETTING THERE

Canmore is beside the Trans-Canada Highway (Hwy. 1), 103 kilometers (66 miles) west of Calgary and 28 kilometers (14 miles) east of Banff. Allow just over 1 hour to drive from downtown Calgary and around 1.5 hours from Calgary International Airport.

Banff Airporter (403/762-3330, www.banffairporter.com) offers service between Canmore's Coast Hotel and Calgary International Airport. The cost from Calgary is around $68 one-way. A desk at the airport's Arrivals level takes bookings, but it's best to reserve a seat by booking over the phone or online in advance.

GETTING AROUND

The most enjoyable way to get around Canmore is on foot or bike, on the extensive trail network winding throughout the town and on to Banff via the Legacy Trail. **Gear Up** (1302 Bow Valley Trail, 403/678-1636, 9am-6pm daily) rents front- and full-suspension mountain bikes, as well as canoes and kayaks. For a cab, call **Three Sisters Taxi** (403/493-9990).

Background

The Landscape

The Rocky Mountains rise from the dense forests of central Mexico and run north through the U.S. states of New Mexico, Colorado, Wyoming, and Montana. Continuing north across the 49th parallel (the U.S.-Canada border), the range forms a natural border between the Canadian provinces of British Columbia and Alberta. Mountainous British Columbia is Canada's westernmost province, extending to the Pacific Ocean, while Alberta, to the east, is mostly prairie. The provincial boundary is the Continental Divide, an imaginary line that runs along the Rockies' highest peaks. Although it is a subjective matter, perhaps most would agree that this particular stretch of the Rocky Mountains—the Canadian Rockies—is the most spectacular segment. North of British Columbia and Alberta, the Rockies descend to their northern terminus in the boreal forests of northern Canada.

The Canadian Rockies are relatively low compared to other well-known mountain ranges of the world; the highest peak, Mount Robson, tops out at 3,954 meters (12,970 feet). Running parallel to the mountains along their eastern edge is a series of long, rolling ridges known as the foothills. To the west is the Rocky Mountain Trench, a long, wide valley that in turn is bordered to the west by various subranges of the Columbia Mountains.

GEOLOGY

The Rocky Mountains began rising 75 million years ago, making them relatively young compared to the world's major mountain ranges. But to fully appreciate the geology of the Rockies, you must look back many hundreds of millions of years, to the Precambrian era. At this time, about 700 million years ago, the Pacific Ocean covered most of the western provinces and states. The ocean advanced, then receded, several times over the next half-billion years. Each time the ocean flooded eastward it deposited layers of silt and sand on its bed—layers that built up with each successive inundation. Starting approximately 550 million years ago, the oceans began to come alive with marine invertebrates and the first crustaceans. As these creatures died and sank to the ocean floor, they added to the layers of sediment. Over time, the ever-increasing sediment load compressed the underlying layers into sandstone, shale, and quartzite.

Birth of the Rockies

Some 200 million years ago, the stability of the ocean floor began wavering along the West Coast of North America, culminating 75 million years ago as two plates of the earth's crust collided. According to plate tectonics theory, the earth's crust is broken into several massive chunks (plates) that are always moving and occasionally bump into each other. This isn't something that happens overnight; a plate may move only a few centimeters over thousands of years. In the case of the Rockies, the Pacific Plate butted into the North American Plate and was forced beneath it. The land at this subduction zone was crumpled and thrust upward, creating the Rocky Mountains. Layers of sediment laid down on the ocean floor over the course of hundreds of millions of years were folded, twisted, and squeezed; great slabs of rock broke away, and in places older strata were pushed on top of younger. By the beginning of the Tertiary period, around 65 million years ago, the present form of mountain contours was established and the geological framework of the mountains was in place.

The Ice Ages

No one knows why, but around one million years ago the world's climate cooled a few degrees. Ice caps formed in Arctic regions and slowly moved south over North America and Eurasia. These advances, followed by retreats, occurred four times. The final major glaciation began moving south 35,000 years ago. A sheet of ice up to 2,000 meters (6,560 feet) deep covered all but the highest peaks of the Rocky Mountains. The ice scoured the terrain, destroying all vegetation as it crept slowly forward. In the mountains, these rivers of ice carved hollows, known as **cirques,** into the slopes of the higher peaks. They rounded off lower peaks and reamed out valleys from their pre-glacier V shape to the trademark, postglacial U shape. The retreat of this ice sheet, beginning around 12,000 years ago, also radically altered the landscape. Rock and debris that had been picked up by the ice on its march forward melted out during the

---

Previous: Skoki Lakes, near Lake Louise.

retreat, creating high ridges known as lateral and terminal **moraines.** Many of these moraines blocked natural drainages, resulting in the formation of lakes. Meltwater drained into rivers and streams, incising deep channels into the sedimentary rock of the plains. Today, the only remnants of this ice age are the scattered ice fields along the Continental Divide, including the 325-square-kilometer (125-square-mile) Columbia Icefield.

Waterways

Water in its various forms has had a profound effect on the appearance of the Canadian Rockies. In addition to the scouring action of the glaciers, flowing water in rivers and streams has, over the millennia, deeply etched the landscape. The process continues today.

The flow of water is directly related to **divides,** or high points of land that dictate the direction of water flow. The dominant divide in the Canadian Rockies, and indeed North America, is the Continental Divide. The natural boundary created by this divide forms the Alberta-British Columbia border, while other, less obvious divides form borders of many parks of the Canadian Rockies. The five national parks are classic examples of this scenario. The divides forming the boundaries of Banff National Park encompass the entire upper watershed of the **Bow River.** The Bow flows southward through the park, then heads east out of the mountains and into the Saskatchewan River system, whose waters continue east to Hudson Bay and the Atlantic Ocean. The Bow River is fed by many lakes famed for their beauty, including **Bow, Louise,** and **Moraine.** To the south, the rivers of Kananaskis Country and Waterton Lakes National Park also drain into the Saskatchewan River system.

The boundary between Jasper and Banff National Parks is an important north-south divide. The **Columbia Icefield,** a remnant of the last ice age, lies on either side of this divide. Runoff from the south side of the ice field flows south into the Saskatchewan River system, while runoff from the north side forms

the upper headwaters of the **Athabasca River** system. The Athabasca flows north through Jasper National Park and into the Mackenzie River system, which continues north to the Arctic Ocean. All water draining off the western slopes of the Continental Divide ends up in the Pacific Ocean via two major river systems: the **Columbia** and the **Fraser.** The mighty Columbia makes a wide northern loop before heading south into the U.S. state of Washington and draining into the Pacific Ocean. Along the way it picks up the waters of the **Kootenay River,** which begins high in Kootenay National Park and makes a lazy loop south through Montana and Idaho before joining the Columbia at Castlegar, British Columbia, and the **Kicking Horse River,** which flows down from the divides that form the borders of Yoho National Park.

CLIMATE

More than any other factor, prevailing moisture-laden westerlies blowing across British Columbia from the Pacific Ocean dictate the climate of the Canadian Rockies.

Elevation and, to a lesser degree, latitude are two other factors affecting the climate within the mountain ecosystem. Elevations vary from 1,383 meters (4,540 feet) above sea level at the town of Banff to 1,500 meters (4,920 feet) at Lake Louise to 3,618 meters (11,870 feet) at the summit of Mount Assiniboine. As a general rule, temperatures fall 5°C (9°F) for every 1,000 meters (3,280 feet) of elevation gained. Another interesting phenomenon occurring in the Canadian Rockies is the **temperature inversion,** in which a layer of warm air sits on top of a cold air mass. During these inversions, high- and low-country roles are reversed; prairie residents can be shivering and bundling up, while their mountain fellows are sunning themselves in short sleeves.

The Seasons

Summer in the mountains is short, but the days are long. With up to 17 hours of daylight around the summer solstice of June 21, this is an ideal time for travel and camping out. The months on either side of summer are ideal for touring, especially September, when rainfall is minimal. Winter is cold, but the skiing and snowboarding are fantastic.

January is usually the coldest month, when Banff's average temperature is -10°C (14°F). In winter, extended spells of -30°C (-22°F) are not uncommon anywhere in the mountains, and temperatures occasionally drop below -40°C (-40°F). The coldest temperature recorded was -52°C (-62°F), in Lake Louise on January 25, 1950. Severe cold weather is often accompanied by sunshine; the cold is a dry cold, unlike the damp cold experienced in coastal regions. Cold temperatures and snow can be expected through mid-March.

Although March, April, and May are the official months of spring, snow often falls in May, many lakes may remain frozen until June, and snow cover on higher mountain hiking trails remains until early July. During this period of the year, the mountains are often affected by low-pressure weather patterns from the southeast, creating continuous days of rain, especially in the south.

Things warm up in summer. July is the hottest month, with Banff and Canmore's average daytime temperature topping out above 23°C (73°F). On hot days, the temperature can hit 30°C (86°F) along lower-elevation valleys; in late June 2021 the region experienced its hottest temperatures on record—smashing old records by multiple degrees on consecutive days. Temperature highs that week included 37.8°C (100°F) in Banff, 38.2°C (101°F) in Canmore, and 41.2°C (106°F) in downtown Jasper. Again, because of the dryness of the air, these temperatures are more bearable here than in coastal regions experiencing the same temperatures.

By late September, the mountain air begins to have a distinct chill. October brings the highest temperature variations of the year; the thermometer can hit 30°C (86°F) but also dip as low as -20°C (-4°F). Mild weather can continue until early December, but generally the first snow falls in October, and by mid-November winter has set in.

Plants

Botanists divide the Canadian Rockies into three distinct vegetation zones (also called **biomes**): montane, subalpine, and alpine. The boundaries of these zones are determined by several factors, the most important being altitude. Latitude and exposure are also factors, but less so. Typically, within any 1,500 meters (4,920 feet) of elevation change, you'll pass through each of the three zones. Conifers (evergreens) predominate in the montane and subalpine, whereas above the tree line, in the alpine, only low-growing hardy species survive.

MONTANE

The foothills, along with most major valleys below an elevation of about 1,500 meters (4,920 feet), are primarily cloaked in montane forest. **Aspen, balsam poplar,** and **white spruce** thrive here. **Lodgepole pine** is the first species to emerge after fire. Its hard seed cones are sealed by a resin that is melted only at high temperatures. When fire races through the forest, the resin melts and the cones release their seeds. The lodgepole is named for its straight, slender trunk, which was used as a center pole for tepees. On dry, south-facing slopes, **Douglas fir** is the climax species. Where sunlight penetrates the forest, such as along riverbanks, flowers like **lady's slipper, Indian paintbrush,** and **saxifrage** are common. Large tracts of **fescue grassland** are common at lower elevations. The montane forest holds the greatest diversity of life of any vegetation zone and is prime winter habitat for larger mammals. But this is the habitat where most development occurs and therefore is often much changed from its natural state.

SUBALPINE

Subalpine forests occur where temperatures are lower and precipitation higher than in the montane. In the Canadian Rockies, this is generally 1,500-2,200 meters (4,920-7,220 feet) above sea level. The upper limit of the subalpine zone is the tree line. Approximately half the flora of the mountains falls within this zone. The climax species are **Engelmann spruce** and **subalpine fir** (recognized by its spire-like crown), although extensive forests of **lodgepole pine** occur in areas that have been scorched by fire in the last 100 years. Before lodgepole pines take root in fire-ravished areas, fireweed blankets the scorched earth. At higher elevations, stands of **larch**

are seen. Larches are deciduous conifers—unlike those of other evergreens, their needles turn a golden-orange color each fall, producing a magnificent display for photographers.

ALPINE

The alpine zone extends from the tree line to mountain summits. The upper limit of tree growth in the Canadian Rockies varies between 1,800 and 2,400 meters (5,900 and 7,900 feet) above sea level, dropping progressively to the north until it meets the treeless tundra of the Arctic. Vegetation at these high altitudes occurs only where soil has been deposited. Large areas of alpine meadows burst with color for a short period each summer as **lupines, mountain avens, alpine forget-me-nots, avalanche lilies, moss campion,** and a variety of **heathers** bloom.

Animals

One of the biggest attractions of the Canadian Rockies is the abundance of wildlife, especially large mammals such as elk, moose, bighorn sheep, and bears, which are all widespread and easily viewed throughout the mountains.

THE DEER FAMILY
Mule Deer and White-Tailed Deer

Mule deer and white-tailed deer are similar in size and appearance. Their color varies with the season but is generally light brown in summer, turning dirty gray in winter. While both species are considerably smaller than elk, the mule deer is a little stockier than the white-tailed deer. The mule deer has a white rump, a white tail with a dark tip, and large mulelike ears. It inhabits open forests along valley floors. The town of Banff has a healthy population of mule deer. The white-tailed deer's tail is dark on top, but when the animal runs, it holds its tail erect, revealing an all-white underside.

Whitetails frequent thickets along rivers and lakes.

Elk

The elk, or **wapiti,** is the most widespread and common of the larger mammals living in the Canadian Rockies. It has a tan body with a dark brown neck, dark brown legs, and a white rump. This second-largest member of the deer family weighs 250-450 kilograms (550-1,000 pounds) and stands 1.5 meters (five feet) at the shoulder. Beginning each spring, bulls grow an impressive set of antlers, covered in what is known as velvet. The velvet contains nutrients that stimulate antler growth. By fall, the antlers have reached their full size and the velvet is shed. Rutting season takes place between August and October; listen for the shrill bugles of the bulls serenading the females. During the rut, randy males will challenge anything with their antlers and can be dangerous. The bulls shed their antlers each spring, but don't relax too much because, also in spring, females protecting their young can be equally dangerous. Large herds of elk live in and around the town of Banff, often nonchalantly wandering along streets and feeding on tasty plants in residential gardens.

Moose

The giant of the deer family is the moose, an awkward-looking mammal that appears to have been designed by a cartoonist. It has the largest antlers of any animal in the world, stands up to 1.8 meters (six feet) at the shoulder, and weighs up to 500 kilograms (1,100 pounds). Its body is dark brown, and it has a prominent nose, long spindly legs, small eyes, big ears, and an odd flap of skin called a bell dangling beneath its chin. Apart from all that, it's good-looking. Each spring, the bull begins to grow palm-shaped antlers that by August will be fully grown. Moose are solitary animals preferring marshy areas and weedy lakes, but they are known to wander to higher elevations searching out open spaces in summer. They forage in and around ponds on willows, aspens, birches, grasses, and all aquatic vegetation. They are not particularly common in the park, numbering around 70-80. Although they may appear docile, moose will attack humans if they feel threatened.

BEARS

The two species of bears present in the mountains—black bears and grizzlies—can be differentiated by size and shape. Grizzlies are larger than black bears and have a flatter, dish-shaped face and a distinctive hump of muscle behind their neck. Color is not a reliable way to tell them apart. Black bears are not always black. They can be brown or cinnamon, causing them to be confused with the brown-colored grizzly.

Black Bears

If you spot a bear feeding beside the road, chances are it's a black bear. These mammals are widespread throughout all forested areas of the Canadian Rockies. Their weight varies considerably, but males average 150 kilograms (330 pounds) and females 100 kilograms (220

pounds). Their diet is omnivorous, consisting primarily of grasses and berries but supplemented by small mammals. They are not true hibernators, but in winter they can sleep for up to a month at a time before changing position. During this time, their heartbeat drops to 10 beats per minute, their body temperature drops, and they lose up to 30 percent of their body weight. Females reach reproductive maturity after five years; cubs, usually two, are born in late winter, while the mother is still asleep.

Grizzly Bears

Grizzlies, second largest of eight recognized species of bears worldwide (only polar bears are larger), have disappeared from most of North America but are widespread throughout the Canadian Rockies, numbering around 60-70 in the region. Grizzlies are only occasionally seen by casual observers; most sightings occur in alpine and subalpine zones, although sightings at lower elevations are not unusual, especially when snow falls early or late. The bears' color ranges from light brown to almost black, with dark tan being the most common. On average, males weigh 200-350 kilograms (440-770 pounds). The bears eat small and medium-size mammals, and berries in fall. Like black bears, they sleep through most of the winter. When they emerge in early spring, the bears scavenge carcasses of animals that succumbed to the winter, until the new spring vegetation becomes sufficiently plentiful. Females first give birth at four years old, and then every three years, with cubs remaining with their mother for 2-3 years.

WILD DOGS AND CATS
Coyotes

The coyote is often mistaken for a wolf when in fact it is much smaller, weighing up to only 15 kilograms (33 pounds). It has a pointed nose and a long, bushy tail. Its coloring is a mottled mix of brown and gray, with lighter-colored legs and belly. The coyote is a skillful and crafty hunter, preying mainly on rodents. Coyotes have the remarkable ability to hear

Wildlife and You

An abundance of wildlife is one of the biggest draws of Banff National Park. To help preserve this precious resource, obey fishing and hunting regulations, and use common sense.

Do not feed the animals. Many animals may seem tame, but feeding them endangers yourself, the animal, and other visitors, as animals become aggressive when looking for handouts (even the smallest critters, such as squirrels).

Store food safely. When camping, keep food in your vehicle or out of reach of animals. Just leaving it in a cooler isn't good enough.

Keep your distance. Although it's tempting to get close to wildlife for a better look or a photograph, it disturbs the animal and, in many cases, can be dangerous.

Drive carefully. The most common cause of premature death for larger mammals is being hit by vehicles.

---

the movement of small mammals under the snow, allowing them to hunt these animals without actually seeing them. They are often seen patrolling the edges of highways and crossing open meadows in low-lying valleys.

Wolves

Wolves that inhabit the Canadian Rockies are larger than coyotes and larger than the wolves of eastern Canada. They weigh up to 60 kilograms (132 pounds), stand up to one meter (3.2 feet) high at the shoulder, and resemble large huskies or German shepherds. Their color ranges from snow white to brown or black; those in the Canadian Rockies are, most often, shades of gray. They usually form packs of up to eight members, traveling, hunting, and resting together, and adhering to a hierarchical social order. As individuals, they are complex and intriguing, capable of expressing happiness, humor, and loneliness.

Once the target of a relentless campaign to exterminate the species, the wolf has made an incredible comeback in the Canadian Rockies; today about 120 wolves roam the region, including one pack occasionally seen in winter along the Bow Valley Parkway between Banff and Lake Louise.

Cougars

Rarely encountered by casual hikers, cougars (known in other parts of North America as mountain lions, pumas, or catamounts)

measure up to 1.5 meters (five feet) long. The average male weighs 75 kilograms (165 pounds) and the female 40-55 kilograms (90-120 pounds). Cougars are versatile hunters whose acute vision takes in a peripheral span in excess of 200 degrees. They typically kill a large mammal such as an elk or deer every 12-14 days, eating part of it and caching the rest. Their diet also includes chipmunks, ground squirrels, snowshoe hares, and occasionally porcupines. Their athletic prowess puts Olympians to shame. They can spring forward more than 8 meters (26 feet) from a standstill, leap 4 meters (13 feet) into the air, and safely jump from a height of 20 meters (65 feet).

The cougar is a solitary animal with distinct territorial boundaries. This limits its population density, which in turn means that its overall numbers are low. They are most common at lower elevations of the Bow Valley.

Lynx

The elusive lynx is identifiable by its pointy black ear tufts and an oversized tabby cat appearance. The animal has broad, padded paws that distribute its weight, allowing it to float on the surface of snow. It weighs up to 10 kilograms (22 pounds) but appears much larger because of its coat of long, thick fur. The lynx, uncommon but widespread throughout the region, is a solitary creature that prefers the cover of subalpine forests, feeding mostly at night on snowshoe hares and other small mammals.

OTHER LARGE MAMMALS
Mountain Goats

The remarkable rock-climbing ability of these nimble-footed creatures allows them to live on rocky ledges or near-vertical slopes, safe from predators. They also frequent the alpine meadows and open forests of the Canadian Rockies, where they congregate around natural salt licks. The goats stand one meter (3.2 feet) at the shoulder and weigh 65-130 kilograms (140-290 pounds). Both sexes possess a peculiar beard, or rather, goatee. Both sexes have horns. It is possible to determine the sex by the shape of the horns; those of the female grow straight up before curling slightly backward, whereas those of the male curl back in a single arch. The goats shed their thick coats each summer, making them look ragged, but by fall they've regrown a fine, new white woolen coat.

Bighorn Sheep

Bighorn sheep are some of the most distinctive mammals of the Canadian Rockies. Easily recognized by their impressive horns, they are often seen grazing on grassy mountain slopes or at salt licks beside the road. The color of their coat varies with the season; in summer, it's a brownish-gray with a cream-colored belly and rump, turning lighter in winter. Fully grown males can weigh up to 120 kilograms (270 pounds), while females generally weigh around 80 kilograms (180 pounds). Both sexes possess horns, rather than antlers like members of the deer family. Unlike antlers, horns are not shed each year and can grow to astounding sizes. The horns of rams are larger than those of ewes and curve up to 360 degrees. The spiraled horns of an older ram can measure longer than one meter (3.2 feet) and weigh as much as 15 kilograms (33 pounds). During the fall mating season, a hierarchy is established among the rams for the right to breed ewes. As the males face off

against each other to establish dominance, their horns act as both a weapon and a buffer against the head-butting of other rams. The skull structure of the bighorn, rams in particular, has become adapted to these head-butting clashes, keeping the animals from being knocked unconscious.

Bighorn sheep are particularly tolerant of humans and often approach parked vehicles; although they are not especially dangerous, as with all mammals, you should not approach or feed them.

Bison

Before the arrival of Europeans, millions of bison roamed the North American plains, with some entering the valleys of the Canadian Rockies to escape harsh winters. Several factors contributed to their decline, including the combined presence of explorers, settlers, and Indigenous peoples. By the late 1800s they were wiped out, and since then a few attempts at reintroduction have taken place, including in the remote Panther River Valley of Banff National Park in 2017. In the ensuing years, numbers there have increased steadily from the 31 bison initially released.

SMALL MAMMALS
Beavers

One of the animal kingdom's most industrious mammals is the beaver. Growing to a length of 50 centimeters (20 inches) and tipping the scales at around 20 kilograms (44 pounds), it has a flat, rudderlike tail and webbed back feet that enable it to swim at speeds up to 10 kph (6 mph). The exploration of western Canada can be directly attributed to the beaver, whose pelt was in high demand in fashion-conscious Europe in the early 1800s. The beaver was never entirely wiped out from the mountains, and today the animals can be found in almost any forested valley with flowing water. Beavers build their dam walls and lodges of twigs, branches, sticks of felled trees, and mud. They eat the bark and smaller twigs of deciduous plants and store branches under water, near the lodge, as a winter food supply.

Squirrels

Several species of squirrels are common in the Canadian Rockies. The **golden-mantled ground squirrel,** found in rocky outcrops of subalpine and alpine regions, has black stripes along its sides and looks like an oversized chipmunk. Most common is the **Columbian ground squirrel,** which lives in burrows, often in open grassland. It is recognizable by its reddish legs, face, and underside, and a flecked, grayish back. The bushy-tailed **red squirrel,** the bold chatterbox of the forest, leaves telltale shelled cones at the base of conifers. Another member of the species, the nocturnal **northern flying squirrel,** glides through the montane forests of mountain valleys but is rarely seen.

Hoary Marmots

High in the mountains, above the tree line, hoary marmots are often seen sunning themselves on boulders in rocky areas or meadows. They are stocky creatures, weighing 4-9 kilograms (9-19 pounds). When danger approaches, these large rodents emit a shrill whistle to warn their colony. Marmots are active only for a few months each summer, spending up to nine months a year in hibernation.

Porcupines

This small, squat animal is easily recognized by its thick coat of quills. It eats roots and leaves but is also known as being destructive around wooden buildings and vehicle tires. Porcupines are common and widespread throughout all forested areas, but they're hard to spy because they feed most often at night.

Other Rodents

Widespread throughout western Canada, **muskrats** make their mountain home in the waterways and wetlands of all low-lying valleys. They are agile swimmers, able to stay submerged for up to 12 minutes. They grow to a length of 35 centimeters (18 inches), but the best form of identification is the tail, which is black, flat, and scaly. Closely related to muskrats are **voles,** which are often mistaken for mice. They inhabit grassed areas of most valley floors.

Shrews

A member of the insectivore family, the **furry shrew** has a sharp-pointed snout and is closely related to the mole. It must eat almost constantly because it is susceptible to starvation within only a few hours of its last meal. Another variety present throughout the region, the **pygmy shrew** is the world's smallest mammal; it weighs just four grams (0.1 ounce).

Pikas

Pikas, like rabbits, are lagomorphs, which are distinguished from rodents by a double set of incisors in the upper jaw. The small, grayish pika is a neighbor to the marmot, living among the rubble and boulders of scree slopes above timberline.

Weasels

The weasel family, comprising 70 species worldwide, is large and diverse, but in general, all members have long, slim bodies and short legs, and all are carnivorous and voracious eaters, consuming up to one-third of their body weight each day. Many species can be found in the Canadian Rockies, including the **wolverine,** largest of the weasels worldwide, weighing up to 20 kilograms (44 pounds). Known to Indigenous peoples as *carcajou* (evil one), the wolverine is extremely powerful, cunning, and cautious. This solitary creature inhabits forests of the subalpine and lower alpine regions, feeding on any available meat, from small rodents to the carcasses of larger mammals. Rarely sighted by humans, the wolverine is a true symbol of the wilderness.

The **fisher** has the same habitat as the wolverine but is much smaller, reaching just five kilograms (11 pounds) in weight and growing up to 60 centimeters (24 inches) in length. This nocturnal hunter preys on small birds and rodents, but reports of fishers bringing down small deer have been made. Smaller still is the **marten,** which lives most of its life in the trees of the subalpine forest, preying on birds, squirrels, mice, and voles. Weighing just one kilogram (2.2 pounds) is the **mink,** once highly prized for its fur. At home in or out of water, it feeds on muskrats, mice, voles, and fish. Mink numbers in the Canadian Rockies are low.

As well as being home to the largest member of the weasel family, the region also holds the smallest—the **least weasel** (the world's smallest carnivore), which grows to a length of just 20 centimeters (8 inches) and weighs a maximum of 60 grams (2 ounces). Chiefly nocturnal, it feeds mostly on mice and lives throughout open wooded areas, but it is not particularly common.

REPTILES AND AMPHIBIANS

Two species of snakes, the **wandering garter snake** and the **red-sided garter snake** (North America's northernmost reptile), are found at lower elevations in the Canadian Rockies. **Frogs** are also present; biologists have noted two different species, which are also found at the lower elevations in the Canadian Rockies.

FISH

Local lakes and rivers hold a variety of fish, most of which belong to the trout and salmon family and are classed as cold-water species—that is, they inhabit waters where the temperature ranges 4-18°C (39-64°F). The predominant species, the **rainbow trout,** is not native to the mountains; it was introduced from more northern Canadian watersheds as a sport fish and is now common throughout lower-elevation lakes and rivers. It has an olive-green back and a red stripe running along the center of its body. Only three species of trout are native to the mountains. One of these, the **bull trout,** is Alberta's provincial fish. Throughout the mid-1900s, this truly native Canadian trout was perceived as a predator of more favored introduced species and was mostly removed. Today, what

was once the most widespread trout east of the Continental Divide is confined to the headwaters of the Canadian Rockies' river systems and is classed as a threatened species. While the bull trout has adapted to the harsh conditions of its reduced habitat, its continuing struggle for survival can be attributed to many factors, including a scarcity of food and a slow reproductive cycle. Bull trout grow to 70 centimeters (27 inches) in length and weigh up to 10 kilograms (22 pounds).

The **lake trout,** which grows to 20 kilograms (44 pounds), is native to large, deep lakes throughout the mountains. Identified by a silvery-gray body and irregular white splotches along its back, this species grows slowly, taking up to 8 years to reach maturity and living up to 25 years. Named for a bright red dash of color that runs from below the mouth almost to the gills, the **cutthroat trout** is native to southern Alberta's mountain streams, but it has been introduced to high-elevation lakes and streams on both sides of the Canadian Rockies. **Brown trout** are present in the Bow River and its slower tributaries, but are not native to Banff National Park. They were introduced in 1925 and have thrived ever since. Its body is a golden-brown color, and it is the only trout with both black and red spots. The **brook trout** is a colorful fish identified by a dark-green back with pale-colored splotches and purple-sheened sides. It is native to eastern Canada but was introduced to the mountains as early as 1903 and is now widespread throughout lakes and streams on the Alberta side of the Continental Divide. **Golden trout** were introduced to a few mountain lakes around 1960 as a sport fish. They are a smallish fish, similar in color to rainbow trout.

BIRDS

Bird-watching is popular in the mountains, thanks to the approximately 300 resident bird species and the millions of migratory birds that pass through each year. All it takes is a pair of binoculars, a good book detailing species, and patience. Dense forests hide many species, making them seem less common than they actually are.

Raptors

A wide variety of raptors are present in the Canadian Rockies—some call the mountains home year-round, while others pass through during annual spring and fall migrations. **Golden eagles** migrate across the Canadian Rockies, heading north in spring to Alaska and crossing back over in fall en route to Midwest wintering grounds. Golden eagles—more than 10,000 of them annually—soar high above the mountains on thermal drafts. **Bald eagles** also soar over the Canadian Rockies during annual migrations; mature birds can be distinguished from below by their white head and tail (immature birds resemble the dark-brown-colored golden eagle). **Ospreys** spend summers in the region, nesting high up in large dead trees, on telephone poles, or on rocky outcrops, but always overlooking water. They feed on fish, hovering up to 50 meters (160 feet) above water, watching for movement, then diving into the water, thrusting their legs forward and collecting prey in their talons.

Distinct from all previously listed species is a group of raptors that hunt at night. Best known as owls, these birds are rarely seen because of their nocturnal habits but are widespread throughout forested areas of the mountains. Most common is the **great horned owl,** identified by its prominent "horns," which are actually tufts of feathers. Also present are the **snowy owl** and, in the north of the region, the **great gray owl,** the largest of the owls, which grows to a height of 70 centimeters (27.6 inches).

Other Birds

Bird-watchers will be enthralled by the diversity of eastern and western bird species in the Canadian Rockies. Widespread are **magpies, sparrows, starlings, grouse, ravens,** and **crows. Blackbirds, finches, thrushes, hummingbirds, woodpeckers, flycatchers,** and 28 species of **warblers** are common in forested areas. **Ptarmigan** are common in open meadows above the tree line. A popular campground visitor, the cheeky **gray jay** is similar in appearance to the curious **Clark's nutcracker.**

History

THE EARLIEST INHABITANTS

Human habitation of the Canadian Rockies began at the end of the last ice age, approximately 11,000 years ago. The descendants of the people who migrated from northeast Asia across a land bridge spanning the Bering Strait had fanned out across North America, and as the receding ice cap began to uncover the land north of the 49th parallel, groups of people moved northward with it, in pursuit of large mammals at the edge of the melting ice mass. The mountain landscape then was far different from what it is today. Forests were nonexistent; the retreating ice had scoured the land, and

most of the lower valleys were carpeted in tundra.

The following gives an overview of the people and their cultures. To learn more, plan on visiting Banff's **Buffalo Nations Luxton Museum.**

The Kootenay

The Kootenay (other common spellings include Kootenai, Kootenae, and Kutenai) were the first human beings to enter the Canadian Rockies. Once hunters of buffalo on the great American plains, they were pushed westward by fierce enemies. As the ice cap melted, they moved north, up the western edge of the Rocky Mountains. This migration was by no means fast—perhaps only 40 kilometers (25 miles) in each generation—but about 10,000 years ago the first Kootenay arrived in the Columbia River Valley. They were hunters and gatherers, wintering along the Columbia and Kootenay River Valleys, then moving to higher elevations during the warmer months. Over time they developed new skills, learning to fish the salmon-rich rivers using spears, nets, and simple fish weirs. The Kootenay were a serious people with few enemies. They mixed freely with the Shuswap. They regularly traveled east over the Rockies to hunt—to the wildlife-rich Kootenay Plains or farther south to the Great Plains in search of bison. But as the fearsome Blackfoot extended their territory westward to the foothills of present-day Alberta, the Kootenay made fewer trips onto the plains. By the early 1700s, they had been driven permanently back to the west side of the Continental Divide.

The Stoney

The movement of humans into the mountains from the east was much more recent. Around 1650, the mighty Sioux nation began splintering, with many thousands moving north into present-day Canada. Although these immigrants called themselves Nakoda (people), other tribes called them Assiniboine (people who cook with stones) because their traditional cooking method was to heat stones in a fire, place the hot stones in a rawhide or birchbark basket with water, and cook meat and vegetables in the hot water. The white people translated *Assiniboine* as Stone People, or Stoney for short.

Slowly, generation after generation, smaller groups of the Stoney moved westward along the Saskatchewan River system, allying themselves with the Cree but keeping their own identity. They pushed through the Blackfoot territory of the plains and reached the Rockies' foothills about 200 years ago. There they split into bands, moving north and south along the foothills and penetrating the wide valleys where hunting was productive. They lived in small family-like groups and

developed a lifestyle different from that of the Plains Indians, diversifying their skills and becoming less dependent on buffalo. Moving with the seasons, they gathered berries in fall and became excellent hunters of mountain animals. They traveled over the mountains to trade with the Shuswap but rarely ventured onto the plains, home of the warlike Piegan, Blackfoot, and Blood bands of the Blackfoot Confederacy. The Stoney were a steadfast yet friendly people. Alexander Henry the Younger reported in 1811 that the Stoney, "although the most arrant horse thieves in the world, are at the same time the most hospitable to strangers who arrive in their camps."

As the great buffalo herds were decimated, the Stoney were affected less than the Plains Indians, but the effect of white settlers' intrusion on their lifestyle was still apparent. The missionaries of the day found their teachings had more effect on the mountain people than on those of the plains, so they intensified their efforts on the Stoney. Reverend John McDougall gained their trust and in 1873 built a small mission church by the Bow River at Morleyville. When the Stoney were presented with Treaty 7 in 1877, they chose to locate their reserve around the Morleyville church. Abandoning their nomadic lifestyle, they quickly became adept at farming. The Stoney were almost self-sufficient on the reserve.

EUROPEAN SETTLEMENT

In 1670, the British government granted the Hudson's Bay Company the right to govern Rupert's Land, roughly defined as all the land that drained into Hudson Bay. A vast area of western Canada, including present-day Manitoba, Saskatchewan, Alberta, Northwest Territories, and Nunavut, fell under that definition. The land was rich in fur-bearing mammals, which both the British and the French sought to exploit for profit. The Hudson's Bay Company first built forts around Hudson Bay and encouraged Indians to bring furs to the posts. But soon, French fur traders based in

David Thompson: Canadian Explorer

One of Canada's greatest explorers, David Thompson was a quiet, courageous, and energetic man who drafted the first comprehensive and accurate map of western Canada. He arrived in Canada from England as a 14-year-old apprentice clerk for the Hudson's Bay Company. With an inquisitive nature and a talent for wilderness navigation, he quickly acquired the skills of surveying and mapmaking. Indigenous peoples called him Koo-koo-sint, which translates as "the man who looks at stars."

Between 1786 and 1812, Thompson led four major expeditions into western Canada—the first for the Hudson's Bay Company and the last three for its rival, the North West Company. The longest and most important one was the last, during which he traveled up and crossed the Continental Divide at **Howse Pass.** After descending into the Columbia River Valley, he established Kootenae House on Lake Windermere, using this outpost for a five-year odyssey of exploration of the entire Columbia River system. In the process, he discovered **Athabasca Pass,** which for the next 40 years was the main route across the Canadian Rockies to the Pacific Ocean.

In 1813, Thompson began work on a master map covering the entire territory controlled by the North West Company. The map was four meters (13 feet) long and two meters (7 feet) wide, detailing more than 3.9 million square kilometers (1.5 million square miles). On completion it was hung out of public view in the council hall of a company fort in the east. Years later, after his death in 1857, the map was discovered, and Thompson became recognized as one of the world's greatest land geographers.

Montreal began traveling west to secure furs, forcing their British rivals to do the same. On one such trip, Anthony Henday became the first white man to view the Canadian Rockies when, on September 11, 1754, he climbed a ridge above the Red Deer River near present-day Innisfail. Henday returned to the east the following spring, bringing canoes loaded with furs and providing reports of snowcapped peaks.

In 1792, Peter Fidler became the first in a long succession of Europeans to actually enter the mountains. The following year, Alexander Mackenzie became the first man to cross the continent, traveling the Peace and Fraser River watersheds to reach the Pacific Ocean. Mackenzie's traverse was long and difficult, so subsequent explorers continued to seek an easier route farther south. In 1807, David Thompson set out from Rocky Mountain House, traveling up the North Saskatchewan River to Howse Pass, where he descended to the Columbia River. He established a small trading post near Windermere Lake, but warring Piegan and Kootenay forced him to search out an alternate pass to the north. In 1811, he discovered Athabasca Pass, which was used as the main route west for the next 40 years.

In 1857, with the fur trade in decline, the British government sent Captain John Palliser to investigate the agricultural potential of western Rupert's Land. During his three-year journey, Palliser explored many of the watersheds leading into the mountains, including one trip up the Bow River and over Vermilion Pass into the area now encompassed by Kootenay and Yoho National Parks.

The Dominion of Canada

By the 1860s, some of the eastern provinces were tiring of British rule, and a movement was abuzz to push for Canadian independence. The British government, wary of losing Canada as it had lost the United States, passed legislation establishing the Dominion of Canada. At that time, the North-West Territories, as Rupert's Land had become known, was a foreign land to those in eastern Canada; life out west was primitive with no laws, and no outpost held more than a couple dozen residents. But in an effort to solidify the

Dominion, the government bought the North-West Territories back from the Hudson's Bay Company in 1867. In 1871, British Columbia agreed to join the Dominion as well, but only on the condition that the federal government build a railway to link the fledgling province with the rest of the country.

The Coming of the Railway

The idea of a rail line across the continent, replacing canoe and cart routes, was met with scorn by those in the east, who saw it as unnecessary and uneconomical. But the line pushed westward, reaching Winnipeg in 1879 and what was then Fort Calgary in 1883.

Many routes across the Continental Divide were considered by the Canadian Pacific Railway (CPR), but Kicking Horse Pass, surveyed by Major A. B. Rogers in 1881, got the final nod. The line and its construction camps pushed into the mountains, reaching Siding 29 (known today as Banff) early in the fall of 1883 and Laggan (Lake Louise) a couple of months later. They then crossed the divide and reached the Field construction camp in the summer of 1884. The following year, on November 7, 1885, the final spike was laid, opening up the lanes of commerce between British Columbia and the rest of Canada. In 1914, rival company Grand Trunk Pacific Railway completed a second rail line across the Rockies, to the north through what is now Jasper National Park.

PARKS AND TOURISM
The Park of Today Take Shape

In 1883, three CPR workers stumbled upon hot springs at the base of Sulphur Mountain, near where the town of Banff now lies. This was the height of the Victorian era, when the great spa resorts of Europe were attracting hordes of wealthy clients. With the thought of developing a similar-style resort, the government designated a 2,600-hectare (6,425-acre) reserve around the hot springs, surveyed a townsite, and encouraged the CPR to build a world-class hotel there. In 1887, Rocky Mountains Park was officially created, setting

aside 67,300 hectares (166,300 acres) as a "public park and pleasure ground for the benefit, advantage, and enjoyment of the people of Canada." The park was later renamed Banff. It was Canada's first national park and only the third national park in the world.

The First Tourists Arrive

In the era the parks were created, the Canadian Rockies region was a vast wilderness accessible only by rail. The parks and the landscape they encompassed were seen as economic resources to be exploited rather than as national treasures to be preserved. Logging, hunting, and mining were permitted inside park boundaries; all but Kootenay National Park had mines operating within them for many years (the last mine, in Yoho National Park, closed in 1952). To help finance the rail line, the CPR began encouraging visitors to the mountains by building grand mountain resorts: Mount Stephen House in 1886, the Banff Springs Hotel in 1888, a lodge at Lake Louise in 1890, and Emerald Lake Lodge in 1902. Knowledgeable locals, some of whom had been used as guides and outfitters during railway construction, offered their services to the tourists the railway brought. Tom Wilson, "Wild" Bill Peyto, Jim and Bill Brewster, the Otto Brothers, and Donald "Curly" Phillips are synonymous with this era, and their names grace everything from pubs to mountain peaks.

Early Mountaineering

Recreational mountaineering has been popular in the Canadian Rockies for more than 100 years. Reports of early climbs on peaks around Lake Louise spread, and by the late 1880s the area had drawn the attention of both European and American alpinists. Many climbers were inexperienced and ill equipped, but first ascents were nevertheless made on peaks that today are still considered difficult. In 1893, Walter Wilcox and Samuel Allen, two Yale schoolmates, spent the summer climbing in the Lake Louise area, making two unsuccessful attempts to reach the north peak of Mount Victoria. The following summer they made first ascents of Mount Temple and Mount Aberdeen, extraordinary achievements considering their lack of experience and proper equipment. Accidents were sure to happen, and they did. During the summer of 1896, P. S. Abbot slipped and plunged to his death attempting to climb Mount Lefroy. In doing so, he became North America's first mountaineering fatality. Following this incident, Swiss mountain guides were employed by the CPR to satisfy the climbing needs of wealthy patrons of the railway and make the sport safer. During the period of their employment, successful climbs were made of Mount Victoria, Mount Lefroy, and Mount Balfour.

In 1906, Arthur O. Wheeler organized the Alpine Club of Canada, which was instrumental in the construction of many trails and backcountry huts still in use today. In 1913, Swiss guide Conrad Kain led a group of the club's members on the successful first ascent of Mount Robson, the highest peak in the Canadian Rockies. By 1915, most of the other major peaks in the range had been climbed as well.

Changing Times

One major change that occurred early on was the shift from railroad-based to automobile-based tourism. Until 1913, motorized vehicles were banned from the mountain parks, allowing the CPR a monopoly on tourists. Wealthy visitors to the mountains came in on the train and generally stayed in the CPR's own hotels for weeks on end and often for the entire summer. The burgeoning popularity of the automobile changed all this; the motor vehicle ban was lifted, and road building went ahead full steam. Many of the trails that had been built for horseback travel were widened to accommodate autos, and new roads were built: from Banff to Lake Louise in 1920, to Radium Hot Springs in 1922, and to Golden in 1930. The Icefields Parkway was finally completed in 1940. Visitor numbers increased, and facilities expanded to keep pace. Dozens of bungalow camps were built specially for those arriving by automobile. Many were built by the CPR, far from their rail line, including in Kootenay National Park and at Radium Hot Springs. Lodges were also built deep in the backcountry, including at Mount Assiniboine and Lake O'Hara.

Another major change is in the way the complex human-wildlife relationship in the parks has been managed. Should the relationship be managed to provide the visiting public the best viewing experience, or rather to provide the wildlife with the most wild and natural environment possible? Today the trend favors the wildlife, but early in the history of the Canadian Rockies' parks, the operating strategy clearly favored the visitor. The Victorian concept of wildlife was that it was either good or evil. Although an early park directive instructed park superintendents to leave nature alone, it also told them to "endeavor to exterminate all those animals which prey upon others." A dusty century-old philosophy, perhaps, but as recently as the 1960s a predator-control program led to the slaughter of nearly every wolf in the park. Seventy years ago, you could view a polar bear on display behind the Banff Park Museum. In the 1970s, hotels were taking guests to local dumps to watch bears feeding on garbage. Creating a balance between growth and its impact on wildlife is today's most critical issue in the Canadian Rockies. Many high-traffic areas are fenced, with passes built over and under the highway for animal movement. Development in the national park towns of Banff and Jasper is strictly regulated, unlike areas outside the parks, such as Canmore and the Columbia River Valley, where development continues unabated.

Amazingly enough, throughout unsavory sagas of the 20th century and ever-increasing human usage, the Canadian Rockies have remained a prime area for wildlife viewing—and, it is hoped, will long continue to be so.

Essentials

Getting There

For international travelers, Vancouver and Calgary are the main gateways to the Banff National Park. From these two cities, as well as points across Canada, scheduled train and bus services pass through the region year-round.

AIR

The closest city to Banff National Park is **Calgary,** Alberta, 128 kilometers (80 miles) east of Banff. **Vancouver,** British Columbia's largest city, is a major gateway to the mountains for international travelers.

Air Taxes

The Canadian government collects a variety of "departure taxes" on all flights originating from Canada. These taxes are generally not in the advertised fare, but they will all be included in the ticket purchase price. First up is the **Air Travellers Security Charge,** $7-15 each way for flights within North America and $25 round-trip for international flights. **NAV Canada** also dips its hand in your pocket, collecting $10-25 per flight for maintaining the country's navigational systems. All major Canadian airports charge an **Airport Improvement Fee** to all departing passengers, with Vancouver and Calgary charging $25 and $30, respectively, per passenger. You'll also need to pay this fee from your original departure point, and if connecting through Toronto, another $5 is collected. And, of course, the above taxes are taxable, with the Canadian government collecting the 5 percent goods and services tax. While there is no bright side to paying these extras, it is made easy for consumers, with airlines lumping all the charges together and into the ticket price.

It lies on Canada's West Coast, 830 kilometers (515 miles) west of Banff. Even though Vancouver is a lot farther from Banff than Calgary, it is a popular starting point, as the trip across British Columbia by rail, bus, or car is spectacular.

Air Canada

Canada's national airline, **Air Canada** (604/688-5515 or 888/247-2262, www.air-canada.com), is one of the world's largest airlines. It offers direct flights to Calgary and Vancouver from all major Canadian cities, as well as from Portland, Los Angeles, San Francisco, Las Vegas, Denver, Phoenix, Houston, Chicago, and New York.

From Europe, Air Canada flies directly from London and Frankfurt to Vancouver and Calgary, and from other major European cities via Toronto. From the South Pacific, Air Canada operates flights from Sydney and in alliance with Air New Zealand from Auckland and other South Pacific islands to Vancouver. Asian cities served by direct Air Canada flights to Vancouver include Beijing, Nagoya, Osaka, Seoul, Shanghai, Taipei, and Tokyo. Air Canada's flights originating in the South American cities of Buenos Aires, São Paulo, Lima, and Bogotá are routed through Toronto, where you'll need to change planes for either Calgary or Vancouver.

WestJet

Canada's other major carrier is **WestJet** (604/606-5525 or 800/538-5696, www.westjet.com), which has daily flights to its Calgary hub, as well as to Vancouver and Edmonton from across Canada as far east as St. John's, Newfoundland.

From the United States

Air Canada offers the most flights into Calgary and Vancouver from the United States, but one or both of the cities are also served by the following U.S. carriers: **Alaska Airlines** (800/252-7522, www.alaskaair.com) from Anchorage and Los Angeles; **American Airlines** (800/433-7300, www.aa.com) from Chicago and Dallas; **Delta** (800/221-1212, www.delta.com), with summer-only flights from Atlanta and Salt Lake City; and finally **United Airlines** (800/241-6522, www.united.com) from Chicago, Denver, Houston, San Francisco, and Seattle.

From Europe

In addition to Air Canada's flights from London to Calgary and Vancouver, **British Airlines** (800/247-9297, www.britishairlines.com) also flies this route daily. Air Canada flights between Vancouver and Continental Europe are routed through Toronto. **Lufthansa** (800/563-5954, www.lufthansa.

Previous: skating on Lake Minnewanka.

com) has a daily flight between Frankfurt and Vancouver.

From Australia and New Zealand

Qantas (604/279-6611, www.qantas.com.au) flies to Vancouver from Sydney; flights originating in Melbourne and Brisbane are routed through Los Angeles. **Air New Zealand** (800/663-5494, www.airnewzealand.com) operates in alliance with Air Canada to either Calgary or Vancouver, with a variety of interesting options, including stops in South Pacific destinations like Nandi (Fiji).

From Asia

Vancouver is the closest West Coast gateway to Asia, being more than 1,200 kilometers (746 miles) closer to Tokyo than Los Angeles. This and Vancouver's large Asian population mean that it is well served by carriers from across the Pacific. In addition to Air Canada's multiple Asian destinations, Vancouver is served by **Air China** (800/882-8122, www.airchina.com) from Beijing; **ANA** (844/728-0647, www.ana.co.jp) from Osaka and Tokyo in affiliation with Air Canada; **Cathay Pacific** (800/268-6868, www.cathaypacific.com) twice daily from Hong Kong; **Japan Airlines** (800/525-3663, www.jal.co.jp) from Tokyo; **Korean Air** (866/584-2303, www.koreanair.com) from Seoul; **Philippine Airlines** (604/ 276-6015, www.philippineairlines.com) from Manila; and **Singapore Airlines** (800/663-3046, www.singaporeair.com) from Singapore via Seoul. For the short hop between Vancouver and Calgary on Air Canada, expect to pay around $200 extra each way.

Rocky Mountaineer

Rocky Mountaineer (604/606-7245 or 877/460-3200, www.rockymountaineer.com) runs a luxurious rail trip between Vancouver and Banff, through the spectacular interior mountain ranges of British Columbia. Travel is during daylight hours only so you don't miss anything. Trains depart in either direction in the morning (every second or third day),

overnighting at Kamloops. One-way travel in RedLeaf Service, which includes light meals, nonalcoholic drinks, and Kamloops accommodations, costs $1,399 per person d from Vancouver to either Banff or Jasper and $1,549 from Vancouver to Calgary. SilverLeaf is a step up in quality, with a glass-domed car allowing a wide range of viewing opportunities. Prices in SilverLeaf are $1,899 per person d from Vancouver to either Banff or Jasper and $2,059 from Vancouver to Calgary. GoldLeaf Service is the ultimate in luxury. Passengers ride in a two-story glass-domed car, eat in a separate dining area, and stay in Kamloops's most luxurious accommodations. GoldLeaf costs $2,499 per person d from Vancouver to Banff and $2,549 to Calgary. Outside of high season (mid-Apr.-May and the first two weeks of Oct.), all fares are reduced a few hundred dollars. Trains terminate in Vancouver off Terminal Avenue at 1755 Cottrell Street (behind Pacific Central Station).

BUS
From Calgary International Airport

This airport, 128 kilometers (80 miles) east of Banff, is the main gateway to the national park. In addition to car rental desks, shuttle bus companies are represented opposite the baggage carousels. Companies that offer service out to Banff National Park are **Brewster Express** (403/762-6700 or 866/606-6700, www.banffjaspercollection.com) and **Banff Airporter** (403/762-3396 or 888/449-2901, www.banffairporter.com). Brewster is the only one of these two services that continues beyond Lake Louise to Jasper. Expect to pay $72 each way to Canmore or Banff and around $90 to Lake Louise.

Backpacker Bus

For young travelers on a budget, **Moose Bus Adventures** (604/297-0255 or 888/244-6673, www.moosebus.travel) is an excellent way to travel to and around the Banff National Park and beyond. It runs along a number of different routes, including a seven-day loop originating in Vancouver and traveling to Jasper and Banff via Whistler ($1,729 per person), a three-day Banff-Jasper-Banff trip ($729), and a two-day Banff-Vancouver shuttle ($549) with an overnight stop in Kamloops. On any of these trips, you can get on and off wherever you please (and jump aboard the next bus as it passes through) or bond with the crowd and stay on the fixed itinerary. Nights are spent at hostels en route. Food is extra, but often all travelers pitch in a token amount to purchase dinner at a grocery store along the way. Tours run three to seven times a week through an April-to-October season.

CAR

Driving to Banff National Park is possible from anywhere in North America but is most convenient if you live in western Canada or the Pacific Northwest. Driving saves money on transportation costs and allows you to bring along camping equipment and sporting gear such as mountain bikes and canoes.

Driver's licenses from all countries are valid in Canada for up to three months. You should also obtain a one-year **International Driving Permit** before leaving home (U.S.-licensed drivers do not require an IDP to drive in Canada) if your license is in a language other than English. Inexpensive and available from most motoring organizations, an IDP allows you to drive in Canada (in conjunction with your regular license), without taking a test, for up to three months. You should also carry vehicle registration papers or rental contracts. Proof of insurance must also be carried, and you must wear seat belts. All highway signs in Canada give distances in **kilometers** and speeds in **kilometers per hour** (kph). The speed limit on most major highways is 100 kph (62 mph).

Insurance

If entering Canada from the United States in your own vehicle, check that your insurance covers travel in Canada and be sure to carry proof of insurance from your insurer. To save any hassles, request that your insurer issue you a Canadian Non-resident Inter-provincial Motor Vehicle Liability Insurance Card.

When renting a vehicle in Canada, you have the option of purchasing a Loss Damage Waiver, along with other types of insurance, such as for your personal effects. Before leaving home, find out if you're already covered. Many people are—through gold credit cards, higher levels of motoring association membership, or home insurance (in the case of personal effects)—and additional coverage may be unnecessary.

Routes in Canada

The Trans-Canada Highway (Highway 1) stretches from one end of Canada to the other and is the world's longest national highway (7,821 km/4,860 mi from end to end). It passes through the Canadian Rockies towns of Canmore, Banff, and Golden. The first major city east of the mountains is Calgary, 128 kilometers (80 miles) from Banff along the Trans-Canada. The northern route across western Canada is the Yellowhead Highway, which passes through the town of Jasper, in Jasper National Park, 364 kilometers (226 miles) east of Edmonton. From Vancouver, on the west coast of British Columbia and the major air gateway from Asia, it's 836 kilometers (519 miles) west to Banff along the Trans-Canada Highway and 781 kilometers (486 miles) northwest to Jasper along Highway 5. The Trans-Canada and Yellowhead Highways are linked within the Canadian Rockies by the Icefields Parkway, which runs parallel to the Continental Divide between Lake Louise and Jasper, a distance of 230 kilometers (143 miles).

Routes from the United States

Reaching Banff National Park from the United States is possible via a number of routes. From Seattle, the shortest approach is to follow I-5 north to Vancouver and jump on the Trans-Canada Highway. If you're traveling north from the Rocky Mountain states, U.S. Highway 93 will provide a warm-up for the mountain scenery north of the border. This route crosses into Canada north of Kalispell, Montana, merging with U.S. Highway 95 from Coeur d'Alene, Idaho, at Cranbrook, then continuing up the west side of the Canadian Rockies to Radium Hot Springs, where you can cut through Kootenay National Park to Banff. Much quicker is I-15, which begins in Los Angeles and loops through Las Vegas and Salt Lake City on its way north to Montana. I-15 enters Canada at the 24-hour Coutts/Sweetgrass border crossing south of Lethbridge, Alberta. From Lethbridge, it's a three-hour drive to Banff. Total distance from Los Angeles to Banff via I-15 is 2,600 kilometers (1,617 miles). From the Midwest and eastern states, there are innumerable options, including I-94 through Minneapolis or crossing into Canada east of the Great Lakes and driving the entire way within Canada.

Getting Around

BUS

Getting around Banff National Park is easiest with your own vehicle because public transportation is limited. **Pursuit** (403/762-6700 or 866/606-6700, www.banffjaspercollection.com) is primarily a tour company but also runs a scheduled bus service linking Calgary International Airport, Canmore, Banff, and Lake Louise with a summer-only service between Lake Louise and Jasper. You can use **Moose Bus Adventures** (604/297-0255 or 888/244-6673, www.moosebus.travel) to travel between Banff and Jasper.

CAR
Driving in Canada

U.S. and international driver's licenses are valid in Canada. All highway signs give distances in kilometers and speeds in kilometers per hour. Unless otherwise posted, the maximum speed limit on the highways is 100 kph (62 mph).

Use of safety belts is mandatory, and motorcyclists must wear helmets. Infants and toddlers weighing up to nine kilograms (20 pounds) must be strapped into an appropriate children's car seat. Use of a child car seat for larger children weighing 9-18 kilograms (20-40 pounds) is required of British Columbia residents and recommended to nonresidents. Before venturing north of the 49th parallel, U.S. residents should ask their vehicle insurance company for a Canadian Non-resident Inter-provincial Motor Vehicle Liability Insurance Card. You may also be asked to prove vehicle ownership, so carry your vehicle registration form.

If you're a member in good standing of an automobile association, take your membership card—the Canadian AA provides members of related associations full services, including free maps, itineraries, excellent tour books, road- and weather-condition information, accommodations reservations, travel agency services, and emergency road services. For more information, contact the **Alberta Motor Association** (www.ama.ab.ca) or the **British Columbia Automobile Association** (www.bcaa.com).

Note: Drinking and driving (with a blood-alcohol level of 0.05 percent or higher) in Canada can get you imprisoned on a first offense and will cost you your license for up to 12 months.

Car Rental

All major car rental agencies have outlets at Calgary and Vancouver International Airports. Car rentals are also available in Banff and Canmore, but it is strongly recommended to rent a vehicle *before* arriving in the Canadian Rockies for two reasons: cost and mileage charges (the now-standard unlimited mileage with major car rentals doesn't apply in Banff). Generally, vehicles can be booked through parent companies in the United

States. Rates start at $80 per day for a small economy car, $95 for a midsize car, and $105 for a full-size car, although you can expect to pay more if renting from an airport.

Major rental companies with outlets in Calgary, Edmonton, and Vancouver are **Avis** (800/974-0808, www.avis.ca), **Budget** (800/268-8900, www.budget.com), **Dollar** (800/800-5252, www.dollarcanada.ca), **Enterprise** (800/325-8007, www.enterprise.com), **Hertz** (800/263-0600, www.hertz.ca), and **National** (800/962-7070, www.nationalcar.com).

RV Rental

Camper vans, recreational vehicles, and travel trailers are a great way to get around the Canadian Rockies without having to worry about accommodations each night. The downside is cost. The smallest vans, capable of sleeping two people, start at $260 per day with 100 free kilometers (62 miles) per day. Standard extra charges include insurance, a preparation fee (usually around $100 per rental), a linen/cutlery charge (around $100 per person per trip), and taxes. Major agencies, with rental outlets in both Calgary and Vancouver, include **Cruise Canada** (403/291-4963, 800/671-8042, www.cruiseamerica.com) and **Canadream** (403/259-5447 or 800/347-7126, www.canadream.com). In most cases, a drop-off fee of $500 applies to drop-offs made in Vancouver from rentals originating in Calgary, or vice versa. At the end of the summer season (September and October), look for some great online bargains.

Gas Stations

Gas stations are located in Banff, Lake Louise, and Canmore. There are also gas stations off the main highways, including along the Icefields Parkway (summer only), but expect to pay significantly more for a fill. Outside of summer, don't rely on these more remote stations to be open. Gas station hours vary greatly, but at least one in Banff opens at 6am, and most are closed by 10pm. To avoid summer lines at Banff and Jasper gas stations, plan on filling up earlier in the morning—waiting vehicles often spill onto surrounding streets during the middle of the day. Also note that all gas purchases in the Canadian Rockies are pre-pay, meaning you must pay at the pump prior to filling up or, in the case of those with non-Canadian credit cards, go inside and leave your credit card with the clerk.

Gasoline is sold in liters (3.78 liters equals one U.S. gallon) and is generally $1.20-1.50 per liter for regular unleaded, rising to $1.70 along the Icefields Parkway. If you're driving in from Calgary, plan on filling up in Dead Man's Flats, which generally has the least expensive gas anywhere in the Canadian Rockies.

TOURS

For those with limited time, an organized tour is the best way to see the Canadian Rockies. **Pursuit** (403/762-6700 or 866/606-6700, www.banffjaspercollection.com) offers day tours and overnight tours throughout the mountains, as well as car rental and accommodation packages. **Rocky Mountaineer** (604/606-7245 or 877/460-3200, www.rockymountaineer.com) offers a wide variety of longer tours in conjunction with rail travel between Vancouver and Banff or Jasper. At the opposite end of the price spectrum, by joining a **Moose Bus Adventures** (604/297-0255 or 888/244-6673, www.moosebus.travel) tour, you get to see the region with budget travelers.

Recreation

Banff National Park is a four-season playground, their great outdoors offering something for everyone. Hiking grabs first place in the popularity stakes; many thousands of kilometers of trails crisscross the entire region. But you can also enjoy canoeing and kayaking, mountain climbing, golfing, horseback riding, photography, skiing and snowboarding, scuba diving, and everything in between. An overview of available outdoor-recreation opportunities is provided in the following sections, and you'll find more detail in the individual destination chapters.

HIKING

Banff National Park is a hiker's paradise. Hiking is free, and the mountains offer some of the world's most spectacular scenery. With exceptions made for the most popular overnight hikes, all trails detailed in this book are day hikes. Anyone of moderate fitness could complete them in the time allotted. Strong hikers will need less time, and if you stop for lunch, it will take you a little longer. Remember, all distances and times are one-way (unless otherwise noted), so allow yourself time at the destination and time to return to the trailhead. Basic trail descriptions are available through local information centers, but anyone planning on focusing their trip around hiking should pick up a copy of the *Canadian Rockies Trail Guide,* authored by Brian Patton and Bart Robinson; check www.canadianrockiestrailguide.com for more information.

Banff National Park holds the greatest variety of trails. Here you can find anything from short interpretive trails with little elevation gain to strenuous slogs up high alpine passes. Trailheads for some of the best hikes are accessible on foot from the town of Banff. Those farther north begin at higher elevations, from which access to the tree line is less arduous.

Scrambling

Banff has many peaks that can be reached without ropes or climbing skills, provided you have a good level of fitness and, more important, common sense. Obviously, this type of activity has more inherent dangers than hiking, but these can be minimized by planning ahead. Check weather forecasts; take food, water, and warm clothing; and be aware of the terrain. Routes to the top of the most popular peaks are flagged with tape or marked with rock cairns showing the way, but you should always check with information centers or locals before attempting any ascent. The Bow Valley offers a good selection of well-traveled scrambles.

Backpacking

Most hikers are just out for the day or a few hours, but staying overnight in the backcountry offers many rewards. Some effort is involved in a backcountry trip—you'll need a backpack, lightweight stove, and tent, among other things—but you'll be traveling through country inaccessible to the casual day hiker, well away from the crowds and far from any road. **Lake O'Hara,** in Yoho National Park, is the trailhead for what is generally considered to be Canada's finest backcountry hiking area. The lake is easily accessible; a shuttle bus runs from the highway up an old fire road to this alpine gem. Unlike at other backcountry destinations, visitors to Lake O'Hara not equipped for camping have the option of visiting for just a day. The Egypt Lakes region of Banff National Park and **Mount Assiniboine Provincial Park** are other popular spots far from civilization. As at Lake O'Hara, there's a lodge for hikers not equipped to camp out. Banff and Jasper National Parks also have backcountry lodges. Another option for backcountry accommodations is offered by the **Alpine Club of Canada** (403/678-3200, www.alpineclubofcanada.ca). The club

Safe Hiking

When venturing out on the trails, using a little common sense will help keep you from getting into trouble. First, don't underestimate the forces of nature; weather can change dramatically anywhere in the mountains at any time. That clear, sunny sky that looked so inviting during breakfast can turn into a driving snowstorm within hours. Go prepared for all climatic conditions (always carry food, a sweater, a waterproof jacket, and matches) and take plenty of water—open slopes can get very hot on sunny days.

At the beginning of hiking trail descriptions throughout this book, I have included some very important information that you should read before heading out. Length is of course important (most people walk between 3-4 km/1.9-2.5 miles per hour on flat ground), but so is Elevation Gain, which can slow down even the fittest of hikers. I've combined these two elements to give one of three difficulty Ratings: Easy, Moderate, and Difficult. It is very important that you assess your own level of fitness combined with the three elements discussed above to decide if a trail is suited to you—a three-kilometer (2.1-mile) hike with 400 meters (1,310 feet) of elevation gain is much harder than an eight-kilometer (5.3-mile) trail with no elevation gain.

All national park visitors centers, as well as those in Kananaskis Country, post daily trail reports and weather forecasts. Check trail conditions before heading out; lingering snow, wildlife closures, or a washed-out trail could ruin your best-laid plans. Also, hikers must register at park information centers for all overnight hikes in national parks.

Topographic maps aren't required for the hikes detailed in this book, but they provide an interesting way to identify natural features. For extended hiking in the backcountry, topo maps are vital. For most hikes, the waterproof hiking maps produced by **Gem Trek Maps** (www.gemtrek.com) are sufficient. You can purchase them from park information centers, bookstores, and other outlets throughout the region.

maintains a series of huts, each generally a full-day hike from the nearest road, throughout the Canadian Rockies.

CLIMBING AND MOUNTAINEERING

The Canadian Rockies are a mecca for those experienced in climbing and mountaineering, but for those who aren't, instruction is available. **Canmore,** in the Bow Valley, is the self-proclaimed capital of mountain sports. Surrounded by towering peaks of limestone, Canmore has routes to challenge all levels of ability on the immediate outskirts of town and along narrow canyons that open to the valley. The distinctive south face of Yamnuska, easily recognized to the north of the Trans-Canada Highway as you enter the Bow Valley from the east, is the most popular climbing spot in the mountains, with dozens of routes up its sheer 350-meter-high (1,150-foot-high) walls. *Bow Valley Rock* (Rocky Mountain Books, www.rmbooks.

com) is an indispensable book for Yamnuska-bound climbers. Experienced climbers should also gather as much information as possible before attempting any unfamiliar routes; quiz locals, hang out at climbing stores, and contact park information centers.

Learning the Ropes

For the inexperienced, the Canadian Rockies are the perfect place to learn to climb. Climbers and mountaineers can't live on past accomplishments alone, so to finance their lifestyle, some turn to teaching others the skills of their sport. Canmore is home to many qualified mountain guides who operate both in and outside of Banff National Park. One of these—and one of North America's most respected climbing schools—is **Yamnuska** (403/678-4164, www.yamnuska.com). Learn basic climbing skills over an Outdoor Rock Intro weekend ($435 per person), with the option to make a full climb (from an extra $300). The school also offers guided climbs of peaks throughout Banff National Park, wilderness first-aid classes, and ice-climbing instruction.

ROAD CYCLING AND MOUNTAIN BIKING

Banff National Park is perfect for both road biking and mountain biking. On-road cyclists will appreciate the wide shoulders on all main highways, while those on mountain bikes will enjoy the many designated trails. One of the most popular paved routes is the **Legacy Trail** between Banff and Canmore, which links up with the Bow Valley Parkway to Lake Louise. The most challenging and scenic on-road route is the 230-kilometer (143-mile) **Icefields Parkway** between Lake Louise and Jasper (*Outside* magazine rates it as one of North America's 10 best). Most cyclists allow 4-5 days, but it's easy to spend a lot longer on the parkway. With 11 campgrounds, four hostels, and four lodges along the way, you'll have plenty of accommodation options. An extension of the Icefields Parkway is the **Bow Valley Parkway,** the original route between Banff and Lake Louise, which can easily be cycled in one day.

Backroads (510/527-1555 or 800/462-2848, www.backroads.com) offers biking trips through the Canadian Rockies, as well as trips that include hiking and touring. These trips are designed to suit all levels of fitness and all budgets. On the biking trips, around six hours are spent cycling each day. The per-week cost, inclusive of luxury accommodations, is US$3,498, which includes all meals.

Mountain biking is allowed on designated trails throughout the national parks. Park information centers hand out brochures detailing these trails and giving them ratings.

HORSEBACK RIDING

Horses were used for transportation in the mountains by the earliest explorers. Even after the completion of the railway, horses remained the most practical way to get deep into the backcountry because crossing unbridged rivers and carrying large amounts of supplies were impossible on foot. The names of early outfitters—Tom Wilson, Jim and Bill Brewster, Bill Peyto, Jimmy Simpson, and Curly Phillips were the best known—crop up again and again through the mountains. Another legacy of their trade is that many of the main hiking trails began as horse trails.

The tradition of travel by horseback continues today in the Canadian Rockies; some companies have been operating since before the parks were established. Trail riding is available in Banff and Lake Louise, as well as in Canmore. Expect to pay around $55-70 for a one-hour ride (usually covering around 3 km/1.9 mi), $80-90 for a two-hour ride, and $140-180 for a ride that includes a meal.

GOLFING

Banff National Park holds special appeal for golfers because it's home to the Fairmont Banff Springs Golf Course, a 27-hole layout that graces the grounds of the Fairmont Banff Springs and is rated one of the world's most scenic courses. Stanley Thompson, generally regarded as one of the preeminent golf course architects of the early 1900s, designed this and the Jasper course, both typified by holes aligned with distant mountains, elevated tee boxes, and fairways following natural contours of the land. (As most of Thompson's work was in Canada, he is little known in the United States.)

The golfing season is fairly short, May-early October, depending on snow cover. But with the long days of summer, there's plenty of time for golfing.

PADDLESPORTS

Canoeing, kayaking, and stand-up paddleboarding are great ways to explore the waterways of the mountains that are otherwise inaccessible—places such as **Vermilion Lakes**, where beavers, elk, and a great variety of birds can be appreciated from water level. Canoes and paddleboards can be rented on the **Bow River** (in the town of Banff), while canoes are available for rent at **Lake Louise** and **Moraine Lake** and **Emerald.** Expect to pay around $45-120 per hour.

FISHING

The Canadian Rockies are an angler's delight. Fish are abundant in many lakes and rivers (the exceptions to good fishing are the lakes and rivers fed by glacial runoff, such as Lake Louise), and outfitters provide guiding services throughout the mountains. Many lakes are stocked annually with a variety of trout—most often rainbows—and although stocking was discontinued in the national parks in 1988, populations have been maintained. In Banff National Park, **Lake Minnewanka** is home to the mountains' largest fish—lake trout—as well a variety of other trout and whitefish.

Fish Species

Rainbow trout are the fighting fish of the Canadian Rockies. Although not native, through stocking they are found in lakes and streams throughout the mountains. The Bow River is considered one of the world's great trout rivers, but most of the action happens downstream of Calgary. Wet flies and small spinners are preferred methods of catching these fish. The largest fish found in the region is the **lake trout,** which grows to 18 kilograms (40 pounds). It feeds near the surface after winter breakup and then moves to deeper, colder water in summer. Long lines and heavy lures are needed to hook these giants. **Brown trout,** introduced from Europe, are found in the Upper Bow River (downstream from Banff). They are most often caught on dry flies, but they are finicky feeders and therefore difficult to hook. **Brook trout** are widespread throughout lower-elevation lakes and streams. **Cutthroat trout** inhabit the cold and clear waters of the highest lakes, which generally require a hike to access. Fishing for cutthroat requires using the lightest of tackle because the water is generally very clear; fly casting is most productive on the still water of lakes, while spinning is the preferred river-fishing method.

Note: The **bull trout** is an endangered species and is a catch-and-release fish.

Possession of bull trout—a dark-colored fish with light spots—is illegal. The defining difference between the bull trout and the brook trout, with which it is often confused, is that the bull trout has *no black spots on its dorsal fin;* due to its status, correct identification of this species is especially important.

Regulations and Licenses

Licenses are available from visitor centers and some sport shops; $10 for a one-day license, $35 for an annual license. The brochure *Fishing Regulations Summary,* available from all park information centers and online at pc.gc.ca, details limits and closures.

WINTER RECREATION
Downhill Skiing and Snowboarding

Three world-class winter resorts are perched among the high peaks of the region. The largest, and Canada's second largest (only Whistler/Blackcomb is larger), is **Lake Louise,** overlooking the lake of the same name in Banff National Park. The resort boasts 1,700 hectares (4,200 acres) of skiing and boarding on four distinct faces, with wide-open bowls and runs for all abilities. Banff's other two resorts are **Sunshine Village,** sitting on the Continental Divide and accessible only by gondola, and **Ski Norquay,** a resort with heart-pounding runs overlooking the town of Banff.

Winter is low season in the mountains, so many accommodations reduce their rates drastically. Lift-and-lodging package deals at many resorts start around $100 per person per night.

Heli-Skiing

Helicopters are banned in the national parks of the Canadian Rockies, but two regional heli-ski operators provide transfers from Banff. **R.K. Heli-Ski** (250/342-3889 or 800/661-6060, www.rkheliski.com) is based on the west side of the mountains at Panorama but provides daily transfers from Banff and Lake Louise for a day's heli-skiing or boarding high in the Purcell Mountains. The cost is $960-1,000 per person.

The town of Banff is headquarters for the world's largest heli-skiing operation, **CMH** (403/762-7100 or 800/661-0252, www.cmh-heli.com), although the skiing and boarding terrain is accessed from 12 upscale lodges scattered throughout eastern British Columbia. Seven-day packages begin at around $8,200 per person, rising to more than $9,000 in the high season.

Other Winter Activities

Many hiking trails provide ideal routes for **cross-country skiing,** and some are groomed for that purpose, including around Banff. Anywhere you can cross-country ski you can **snowshoe,** a traditional form of winter transportation that is making a comeback. **Sleigh rides** are offered in Banff and Lake Louise.

Winter travel brings its own set of potential hazards, such as hypothermia, avalanches, frostbite, and sunburn. Necessary precautions should be taken. Park information centers can provide information on hazards and advise on current weather conditions.

Accommodations and Camping

Following is a summary of the types of accommodations you can expect to find throughout the region. Individual properties are detailed in each destination chapter, along with prices and contact information. Nearly all accommodations now have toll-free numbers and websites, through which you can find out more information about each property and make bookings.

Accommodation Taxes

Except for campgrounds and bed-and-breakfasts with fewer than four guest rooms, accommodations collect tax on behalf of various levels of government. In Alberta, a 4 percent Tourism Levy is added. Banff also has a 2 percent Tourism Improvement Fee. These taxes are in addition to the Canada-wide 5 percent goods and services tax. As a general rule, quoted rates don't include any of these taxes.

HOTELS AND MOTELS

Hotels and motels throughout Banff National Park range from overpriced motels to sublime resorts such as the famous Fairmont Banff Springs. Bookings should be made as far in advance as possible. Finding inexpensive lodging in the mountain national parks is difficult in summer. By late afternoon, the only rooms left will be in the more expensive categories, and by nightfall all of these will go.

Hotel rooms in Banff begin at $400 in peak season. Accommodation prices are slashed by as much as 50 percent outside summer. Always ask for the best rate available and check local tourist literature for discount coupons. All rates quoted in this handbook are for the cheapest category of rooms during the most expensive time period (summer).

OTHER LODGING OPTIONS
Bed-and-Breakfasts

Bed-and-breakfasts are a good option if you don't mind sacrificing some privacy to meet locals and to mingle with like-minded travelers. Bed-and-breakfasts are usually private residences, with up to four guest rooms, although bylaws are different throughout the region. Amenities can vary greatly—the "bed-and-breakfast" may be a single spare room in an otherwise regular family home or a full-time business in a beautifully restored heritage home. If having a bathroom to yourself is important to you, clarify with the bed-and-breakfast operator when reserving. Also, as bed-and-breakfasts also function as private

Getting the Best Lodging Deal

Rates quoted in this book are for a standard double room throughout the high season, which generally extends late June-mid-September. Almost all accommodations are less expensive outside of these busy months. As a general rule of thumb, the more expensive the property, the steeper the discount. For example (and at different ends of the spectrum), the cost of a dorm bed at the Banff Alpine Centre drops $5 per night on September 15, while in downtown Banff, already reasonably priced Brewster's Mountain Lodge cuts its rates from $400 to under $200 in winter, with graduated discounts in spring and fall. Plan on traveling a few weeks on either side of the peak season, then use hotel websites to check when individual properties are offering discounts. Most accommodations post seasonal specials on their websites well in advance.

While you have no influence over seasonal pricing fluctuations, *how* you reserve a room *can* make a difference in how much you pay. Book through a central reservations agency or travel agent, or pay for accommodations as part of a tour package, and you'll pay the full published price.

In some years, getting a room in July and August without advance reservations is almost impossible. Leaving reservations until the last minute is a risky proposition if you're not prepared to be flexible. As a general rule, hotels raise their rates as demand dictates, while lodges don't, so you'll know with the latter what you'll be paying with advance reservations, or booking the day of your arrival.

residences, book in advance—don't just turn up. Rates fluctuate greatly, with the least expensive rooms costing $80 s, $90 d and the most expensive upwards of $400.

Backcountry Huts and Lodges

Throughout the backcountry of the region is an extensive system of 18 rustic huts managed by the **Alpine Club of Canada** (403/678-3200, www.alpineclubofcanada.ca). Due to their locations around favorite climbing areas, they are most often used by mountaineers as an overnight stop before assaulting some of the park's highest peaks, but they are available to anyone who wishes to take advantage of their remote location. Their accessibility ranges from the Elizabeth Parker Hut (Yoho National Park), which can be reached by bus, to the Neil Colgan Hut, Canada's highest habitable structure, 2,960 meters (9,700 feet) above sea level on a windswept ledge above Moraine Lake. Often of historical significance, each of the huts has a stove, lantern, kitchen utensils, and foam mattresses. Rates range $18-32 per person per night.

Privately operated backcountry lodges are found in Banff and Yoho National Parks, as

well as Mount Assiniboine Provincial Park. The most luxurious is **Lake O'Hara Lodge** in Yoho National Park. It lies 11 kilometers (6.8 miles) from the nearest public road—access is by shuttle bus—and is surrounded by some of the finest hiking in the area. Banff National Park has four backcountry lodges: **Sundance** and **Halfway Lodges** in the Brewster Creek Valley, **Shadow Lake Lodge,** northwest of Banff, and **Skoki Lodge,** northeast of Lake Louise. All require some degree of effort to reach—either on foot or on horseback in summer, or on cross-country skis or snowshoes in winter. Rates at these lodges begin at $260 per person (a single room at Skoki is the least expensive option), including three meals. None have television or Internet, but all provide a unique and memorable wilderness experience.

BACKPACKER ACCOMMODATIONS

Throughout the region, traditional hostels operated by Hostelling International are still the most common form of accommodation for budget travelers, but other options do exist. Banff has privately run backpacker lodges, and a YWCA with dormitory accommodations for

Quintessential Mountain Lodgings

You could stay in a basic, boring motel room, but don't. Instead, make reservations at one of the following lodgings, each offering a distinctive mountain experience.

- **Baker Creek Mountain Resort** (403/522-3761, www.bakercreek.com)

- **Paradise Lodge and Bungalows** (105 Lake Louise Dr., 403/522-3595, www.paradiselodge.com)

- **Num-ti-jah Lodge** (403/522-2167, www.num-ti-jah.com)

- **Paintbox Lodge** (629 10th St., 403/609-0482 or 888/678-6100, www.paintboxlodge.com)

- **Emerald Lake Lodge** (250/343-6321 or 800/663-6336, www.crmr.com)

- **Lake O'Hara Lodge** (250/343-6418, www.lakeohara.com)

men and women. Generally, you need to supply your own sleeping bag or linens, but most places supply extra bedding at a minimal cost.

Hostelling International

Hostelling International operates four hostels in Banff National Park. Canmore also has one. Whenever you can, make reservations in advance, especially in summer. Bookings can be made online at www.hihostels.ca.

All of the hostels are equipped with a kitchen and lounge room, and some have laundries and private rooms. Those in Banff and Lake Louise are world-class, with hundreds of beds as well as libraries and cafés. The five rustic hostels along the Icefields Parkway are evenly spaced, perfect for a bike trip along one of the world's great mountain highways. A sheet or sleeping bag is required at more remote locations, although these can usually be rented. Rates for members are $36-57 per night, nonmembers $40-64. Staying in hostels is an especially good bargain for skiers and snowboarders; packages including accommodation and a day pass at a local resort start at $150.

You don't *have* to be a member to stay in an affiliated hostel of Hostelling International, but membership pays for itself after only a few nights of discounted lodging. Aside from lower rates, benefits of membership vary from country to country but often include

discounted air, rail, and bus travel; discounts on car rental; and discounts on some attractions and commercial activities. For Canadians, the membership charge is $25 annually, or $175 for a lifetime membership. For more information, contact **HI-Canada** (613/237-7884, www.hihostels.ca). Joining the Hostelling International affiliate of your home country entitles you to reciprocal rights in Canada, as well as around the world; click through the links on the Hostelling International website (www.hihostels.com) to your country of choice.

CAMPING

Camping is the way to stay cheaply in the region. Many of the campgrounds consist of nothing more than picnic tables, drinking water, pit toilets, and firewood ($9 per site per night), but at least one campground in each park has hot showers and full hookups.

Sites at the most popular national park campgrounds can be reserved through the **Parks Canada Reservation Service** (877/737-3783, www.reservation.pc.gc.ca) for a nonrefundable $12 reservation fee. If you're traveling between June and September, this booking system is highly recommended. Reservations begin in January for the upcoming summer (check exact date online), and in some cases campgrounds will fill for the entire summer within an hour of the system opening. Only a few campgrounds in the national parks operate on a first-come, first-served basis (mostly along the Icefields Parkway) and often fill by midday in July and August.

Backcountry Camping
A **backcountry permit** is required for anyone planning an overnight trip into the backcountry of any national park. The nightly rate is $10 per person and the reservation fee is $12

per booking. Sites at most popular backcountry campgrounds should be reserved through the **Parks Canada Reservation Service** (877/737-3783, www.reservation.pc.gc.ca) beginning in January each year for the upcoming summer season. The less-popular or more remote campgrounds are first come, first served. Most campgrounds in the backcountry have pit toilets, and some have bearproof lockers or poles for secure food storage. Fires are discouraged, so bring a stove.

Travel Tips

WHAT TO PACK
You'll find little use for a suit and tie in Banff National Park. Instead, pack for the outdoors. At the top of your must-bring list should be walking or **hiking boots.** Even in summer, you should be geared up for a variety of weather conditions, especially at the change of seasons. Do this by preparing to **dress in layers,** including at least one pair of fleece pants and a heavy long-sleeved top. For dining out, **casual dress** is accepted at all but the most upscale restaurants.

Electrical appliances from the United States work in Canada, but those from other parts of the world will require a current **converter** (transformer) to bring the voltage down. Many travel-size shavers, hair dryers, and irons have built-in converters.

EMPLOYMENT AND STUDY
Banff is especially popular with young workers from across Canada and beyond. Aside from Careers pages on company websites, a good place to start looking for work is the **Job Resource Centre** (304 Caribou St., Banff, 403/760-3311, www.jobresourcecentre.com).

International visitors wishing to work or study in Canada must obtain authorization *before* entering the country. Authorization to work will only be granted if no qualified Canadians are available for the work in

question. Applications for work and study are available from all Canadian embassies and must be submitted with a nonrefundable processing fee. The Canadian government has a reciprocal agreement with Australia for a limited number of **holiday work visas** to be issued each year. Australian citizens age 30 and under are eligible; contact your nearest Canadian embassy or consulate. For general information on immigrating to Canada, contact **Citizenship and Immigration Canada** (604/666-2171, www.cic.gc.ca).

VISITORS WITH DISABILITIES
A lack of mobility should not deter you from traveling to Banff National Park, but you should definitely do some research before leaving home.

Government of Canada has a section of its website for those with disabilities planning travel within and between Canadian cities (https://travel.gc.ca). The website also has a lot of general travel information for those with disabilities.

The **Society for Accessible Travel and Hospitality** (212/447-7284, www.sath.org) supplies information on tour operators, vehicle rentals, specific destinations, and companion services. For frequent travelers, the annual membership fee (adult US$49, senior US$29) is well worthwhile. *Emerging Horizons* (www.emerginghorizons.com) is a U.S. online quarterly magazine dedicated to travelers with special needs.

The **Canadian National Institute for the Blind** (800/563-2642, www.cnib.ca) offers a wide range of services across the country. Finally, **Spinal Cord Injury Alberta** (780/424-6312, www.sci-ab.ca) is another good source of information on local resources.

LGBTQ+ TRAVELERS

The Canadian Rockies are very inclusive and accepting. The first week of October is **Banff Pride** (www.banffpride.ca). The **IGLTA** (954-776-2626, www.iglta.org) is the trade association for the LGBTQ+ travel industry, and offers an online directory of LGBTQ-friendly travel businesses.

TRAVELING WITH CHILDREN

The natural wonders of Banff National Park are a marvelous place to bring children on a vacation, and luckily for you, many of the best things to do—walking, watching wildlife, and more—don't cost a cent.

Admission and tour prices for children are included throughout the destination chapters of this guide. As a general rule, these reduced prices are for children ages 6-16 years. For two adults and two or more children, always ask about family tickets. Children under six nearly always get in free. Most hotels and motels will happily accommodate children, but always try to reserve your room in advance and let the reservations desk know the ages of your kids. Generally, bed-and-breakfasts aren't suitable for children and in some cases don't accept kids at all. Ask ahead.

As a general rule when it comes to traveling with children, let them help you plan the trip, looking at websites and reading up on the region together. To make your vacation more enjoyable if you'll be spending a lot of time on the road, rent a minivan (all major rental agencies have a supply). Don't forget to bring along favorite toys and games from home—whatever you think will keep your kids entertained when the joys of sightseeing wear off.

The website of **Travel Alberta** (www.travelalberta.com) has a section devoted to children's activities within the two provinces. The website **Family Fun Canada** (www.familyfuncanada.com) is a Calgary-based operation with lots of tips and stories about travel to Banff National Park.

Health and Safety

Compared to other parts of the world, Canada is a relatively safe place to visit. That said, wherever you are traveling, carry a medical kit that includes bandages, insect repellent, sunscreen, antiseptic, antibiotics, and water-purification tablets. Good first-aid kits are available through most outdoor shops.

It's a good idea to get health insurance or some form of coverage before heading to Canada if you're going to be there for a while, but check that your plan covers foreign services. Hospital charges vary from place to place but can start at around $1,000 a day, and some facilities impose a surcharge for nonresidents. Some Canadian companies offer coverage specifically aimed at visitors.

If you're on medication, take adequate supplies with you and get a prescription from your doctor to cover the time you will be away. You may not be able to get a prescription filled at Canadian pharmacies without visiting a Canadian doctor, so don't wait till you've almost run out. If you wear glasses or contact lenses, ask your optometrist for a spare prescription in case you break or lose your lenses, and stock up on your usual cleaning supplies.

Giardia

Giardiasis, also known as beaver fever, is a

Coronavirus in the Canadian Rockies

At the time of writing in April 2022, Canada had mostly stabilized from the effects of the coronavirus, but the situation was constantly evolving.

Now more than ever, Moon encourages its readers to be courteous and ethical in their travel. Be respectful to residents and mindful of the evolving situation when planning your trip.

TRAVEL CHECKLIST

- Check websites (listed below) for **local restrictions** and the **overall health status** of the Canadian Rockies and your point of origin. If you're traveling to or from an area that is currently a COVID-19 hotspot, you may want to reconsider your trip.

- **Only fully vaccinated travelers are permitted entry into Canada** and you must provide proof of a negative COVID-19 test by an accepted agency (rapid antigen tests are not accepted). Use **ArriveCAN** (www.travel.gc.ca/travel-covid) to submit proof of vaccination and your negative test up to 72 hours in advance of your arrival. If traveling by air, you may also be required to be tested upon arrival in Canada. Use ArriveCAN to register for this test and when doing so you are required to submit a proposed quarantine plan in the event you test positive.

- If you plan to fly into Canada, check with your airline for updated **travel requirements.** Some airlines may be taking more steps than others to help you travel safely, such as limited occupancy; check their websites for more information before buying your ticket, and consider a very early or very late flight, to limit exposure. Flights may be more infrequent, with increased cancellations.

- Pack **hand sanitizer,** a **thermometer,** and plenty of **face masks.** Consider packing **snacks, bottled water,** a **cooler,** or anything else you might need to limit the number of stops along your route, and to be prepared for possible closures and reduced services over the course of your travels.

- **Assess the risk** of entering crowded spaces, joining tours, and taking public transit.

- Expect **general disruptions.** Events may be postponed or cancelled, and some tours and venues may require reservations, enforce limits on the number of guests, be operating during different hours than the ones listed, or be closed entirely.

RESOURCES

- Government of Canada: www.travel.gc.ca/travel-covid

- Alberta Health Resources: www.albertahealthservices.ca

- BC Centre for Disease Control: www.bccdc.ca

- Town of Banff: www.banff.ca

- Town of Jasper: www.jasper-alberta.com

- City of Calgary: www.calgary.ca

real concern for those who drink water from backcountry water sources. It's caused by an intestinal parasite, *Giardia lamblia,* that lives in lakes, rivers, and streams. Once the parasite is ingested, its effects, although not instantaneous, can be dramatic; severe diarrhea, cramps, and nausea are the most common. Preventive measures should always be taken. **Pristine** (www.pristine.ca) is a Canadian company that has developed water bottles with built-in filters; the alternative is boiling water for at least 10 minutes or treating with iodine.

Winter Travel

Travel through Banff National Park during winter months should not be undertaken lightly. Before setting out in a vehicle, check antifreeze levels, and always carry a spare tire and blankets or sleeping bags. **Frostbite** is a potential hazard, especially when cold temperatures are combined with high winds (a combination known as **windchill**). Most often it leaves a numbing, bruised sensation, and the skin turns white. Exposed areas of skin, especially the nose and ears, are most susceptible.

Hypothermia occurs when the body fails to produce heat as fast as it loses it. It can strike at any time of year but is more common during cooler months. Cold weather, combined with hunger, fatigue, and dampness, creates a recipe for disaster. Symptoms are not always apparent to the victim. The early signs are numbness, shivering, slurring of words, and dizziness, and, in extreme cases, violent behavior, unconsciousness, and even death. The best way to dress for the cold is in layers, including a waterproof outer layer. Most important, wear headgear. The best treatment for hypothermia is to get the patient out of the cold, replace wet clothing with dry, slowly give hot liquids and sugary foods, and place the victim in a sleeping bag. Warming too quickly can lead to heart attacks.

Information and Services

All prices quoted in this guide are in Canadian dollars and cents unless otherwise noted.

Canadian currency is based on dollars and cents, with 100 cents equal to one dollar. Coins come in denominations of 5, 10, and 25 cents, and one and two dollars. The 11-sided, gold-colored, one-dollar coin is known as a "loonie" for the bird featured on it. The unique two-dollar coin is silver with a gold-colored insert. The most common notes are $5, $10, $20, and $50. A $100 bill does exist but is uncommon.

Visa and MasterCard credit and debit cards are also readily accepted in the Canadian Rockies; American Express charge cards are less widely accepted. By using these cards, you eliminate the necessity of thinking about the exchange rate—the transaction and rate of exchange on the day of the transaction will automatically be reflected in the bill from your credit-card company. On the downside, you'll always get a better exchange rate when dealing directly with a bank.

It's also handy to carry small amounts of Canadian cash. Banks offer the best exchange rates, but other foreign-currency exchange outlets are available.

Costs

The cost of living in the region is generally higher than in other parts of Canada, especially when it comes to accommodations. Provincially, the cost of living is lower in Alberta than in British Columbia but higher than in the United States. By planning ahead, having a tent or joining Hostelling International, and being prepared to cook your own meals, it is possible to get by on $100 per person per day.

Tipping charges are not usually added

Currency Exchange

At the time of writing, exchange rates (into CDN$) for major currencies are:

- US$1 = $1.25
- AUS$1 = $0.92
- €1 = $1.45
- HK$10 = $1.61
- NZ$1 = $0.88
- UK£1 = $1.68
- ¥100 = $1.11

On the Internet, check current exchange rates at www.xe.com/currencyconverter.

All major currencies can be exchanged at banks in Canmore, Banff, and Jasper, or at airports in the gateway cities of Calgary, Edmonton, and Vancouver. Many Canadian businesses will accept U.S. currency, but you will get a better exchange rate from the banks.

to your bill. You are expected to add a tip of 15-20 percent to the total amount for waiters and waitresses, barbers and hairdressers, taxi drivers, and other such service providers. Bellhops, doormen, and porters generally receive $1 per item of baggage.

Taxes

Canada imposes a 5 percent **goods and services tax (GST)** on most consumer purchases. Alberta has no provincial tax.

MAPS AND TOURIST INFORMATION
Maps

The best maps of Banff National Park are produced by **Gem Trek Maps** (www.gemtrek.com). They cover all of the region, using computer-generated 3-D imagery to clearly define changes in elevation and GPS to plot hiking trails. The backs of the maps are filled with trail information as well as tidbits of history.

Park Information

Park information centers are located in downtown Banff and in the village of Lake Louise. These are the places to head for interpretive displays, all park-related information, trail reports, weather forecasts, and backcountry permits. The national parks are managed by **Parks Canada** (www.pc.gc.ca).

Tourism Information

Begin planning your trip by scanning the website of the official government tourist office of Alberta: **Travel Alberta** (780/427-4321 or 800/252-3782, www.travelalberta.com).

In Calgary, you'll find an information booth on the Arrivals level of the airport. The **Vancouver Visitor Centre** (604/683-2000) is at 200 Burrard Street, although information on Banff National Park is limited.

COMMUNICATIONS
Postal Services

Canada Post (www.canadapost.ca) issues postage stamps that must be used on all mail posted in Canada. First-class letters and postcards sent within Canada are $1.07, to the United States $1.30, to other international destinations $2.71. Prices increase along with the weight of the mailing.

Phones and Cell Reception

The **area code** for southern Alberta, including Banff and Canmore, is **403.** Unless otherwise noted, all numbers must be dialed with this prefix, including local calls made from within Alberta. The country code for Canada is 1, the same as the United States.

Cell phone reception is good in populated areas, but you will lose reception quickly beyond town boundaries. For example, there is no reception along the Icefields Parkway between Lake Louise and Jasper, and on the Trans-Canada Highway between Lake Louise and Golden. Even busy thoroughfares such as the Trans-Canada Highway between Banff and Lake Louise have spotty coverage.

Heading Farther Afield

If your travels take you beyond Banff, you may find the following resources helpful for pre-trip planning:

- **Travel Alberta:** www.travelalberta.com

- **Tourism British Columbia:** www.hellobc.com

- **Yukon Department of Tourism and Culture:** www.travelyukon.com

- **State of Alaska Tourism:** www.travelalaska.com

- **NWT Tourism:** www.spectacularnwt.com

- **Tourism Saskatchewan:** www.tourismsaskatchewan.com

- **Travel Manitoba:** www.travelmanitoba.com

Internet Access

Public Internet access is available throughout Banff National Park. Most lodgings have wireless Internet access (the exceptions are lodges in remote locations), and it's usually free (the exceptions are larger hotels like the Fairmont chain).

WEIGHTS AND MEASURES
The Metric System

Canada officially adopted the metric system back in 1975, though you still hear grocers talking in ounces and pounds, golfers talking in yards, and sailors talking in nautical miles. Metric is the primary unit used in this guide, but we've added imperial conversions for readers from the United States, Liberia, and Myanmar, the only three countries that have not adopted the metric system.

Time Zones

Alberta is in the **mountain time zone,** one hour later than Pacific standard time, two hours earlier than Eastern standard time. The mountain time zone extends west into southern British Columbia, which includes Yoho National Park. The rest of British Columbia is in the **Pacific time zone.**

Daylight saving time is in effect from the second Sunday of March to the first Sunday in November. This corresponds with the United States (except Arizona and Hawaii) and all other Canadian provinces (except Saskatchewan).

Resources

Suggested Reading

NATURAL HISTORY

The Atlas of Breeding Birds of Alberta. Edmonton: Federation of Alberta Naturalists, 1992. Comprehensive study of all birds that breed in Alberta with easy-to-read distribution maps, details on nesting and other behavioral patterns, and color plates.

Dettling, Peter. *The Will of the Land.* Victoria: Rocky Mountain Books, 2010. Filled with stunning images, this book includes thoughtful dialogue on the often controversial relationship between man and wolf.

Gadd, Ben. *Canadian Rockies Geology Road Tours.* Canmore: Corax Press, 2009. The best reference for those interested in the geology of the Canadian Rockies. Includes information on almost 300 roadside stops.

Gadd, Ben. *Handbook of the Canadian Rockies.* Canmore: Corax Press, 2009. At over 800 pages and one kilogram (2.2 pounds), this is the classic field guide to the Canadian Rockies. It is in full color, and although bulky for backpackers, it's a must-read for anyone interested in the natural history of the region.

Hallworth, Beryl, and C. C. Chinnappa. *Plants of Kananaskis Country.* Calgary: University of Calgary Press, 1997. An incredibly detailed book, encompassing more than 400 species of flora, complete with detailed black-and-white illustrations. It could be used in the field anywhere in the Canadian Rockies.

Herrero, Stephen. *Bear Attacks: Their Causes and Avoidances.* New York: The Lyons Press, 2018. Through a series of gruesome stories, this book catalogs the stormy relationship between people and bruins, provides hints on avoiding attacks, and tells what to do in case you're attacked.

Leckie, Dale. *Rocks, Ridges, and Rivers.* Calgary: self-published, 2017. Explores the geology of Banff, Yoho, and Jasper National Parks through detailed descriptions of the best-known natural attractions, including Lake Louise and Mount Edith Cavell.

Marty, Sid. *The Black Grizzly of Whiskey Creek.* Toronto: McClelland & Stewart, 2008. True story of a grizzly bear that went on a terrifying rampage near the town of Banff.

Musiani, Marco. *A New Era for Wolves and People.* Calgary: University of Calgary Press, 2009. A detailed analysis of the relationship between wolves and people in both North America and Europe. All contributors are wolf experts; includes stunning images.

Rezendes, Paul. *Tracking and the Art of Seeing.* Charlottesville, VA: Camden House Publishing, 1992. This is one of the best of many books dedicated to tracking North American mammals. It begins with a short essay on the relationship of humans with nature.

Scotter, George. *Wildflowers of the Rocky Mountains.* Vancouver: Whitecap Books, 2007. Simplified descriptions, color-coded chapters, and the delicate photography of Halle Flygare combine to create the region's best wildflower field guide.

Slinger, Joey. *Down & Dirty Birding.* Toronto: Key Porter Books, 1996. A hilarious but practical look at the art of bird-watching, with sections of text such as "How to steer clear of people who think bird-watching is better than sex."

Whitaker, John. *National Audubon Society Field Guide to Mammals.* New York: Alfred A. Knopf, 1996. One of a series of field guides produced by the National Audubon Society, this one details mammals through color plates and detailed descriptions of characteristics, habitat, and range.

Wilkinson, Kathleen. *Wildflowers of Alberta.* Edmonton: University of Alberta Press, 1999. Color plates of all flowers found in the mountain national parks and beyond. The detailed color plates and line drawings are indispensable for identification.

HUMAN HISTORY

Barnes, Christine. *Great Lodges of the Canadian Rockies.* Seattle: Sasquatch Books, 1999. This book delves into the history of the many famous mountain lodges—such as the Fairmont properties and Emerald Lake Lodge—and lesser known but equally interesting historic accommodations like Num-ti-jah and Skoki.

Hart, E. J. (Ted). *Ain't it Hell.* Banff: Summerthought Publishing, 2008. "Wild" Bill Peyto was one of the most interesting and colorful characters in the history of the Canadian Rockies. This book tells his story through fictional diary entries.

Hart, E. J. (Ted). *Banff: A History of the Park and Town.* Banff: Summerthought

Publishing, 2015. The complete history of Banff in one hardcover book. Hart is arguably the most knowledgeable person alive when it comes to the history of the park, making this limited edition an obvious choice for those looking to learn about local history.

Hart, E. J. (Ted). *Cave and Basin.* Banff: Summerthought Publishing, 2017. The region's preeminent historian tells the story of the discovery of Banff's Cave and Basin and its importance to the creation of Canada's national park system.

Hart, E. J. (Ted). *Jimmy Simpson: Legend of the Rockies.* Victoria: Rocky Mountain Books, 2009. Details the life of one of the most colorful of the pioneer outfitters in the Canadian Rockies.

Hempstead, Andrew. *A Guide to the History of Banff National Park.* Banff: Summerthought Publishing, 2020. A guidebook to 88 historic sites and heritage properties in and around the town of Banff, in Lake Louise, and along the Icefields Parkway.

Lavallee, Omer. *Van Horne's Road.* Montreal: Railfare Enterprises, 1974. William Van Horne was instrumental in the construction of Canada's first transcontinental railway. This is the story of his dream and the boomtowns that sprang up along the route. Lavallee devotes an entire chapter to telling the story of the railway's push over the Canadian Rockies.

Marty, Sid. *Switchbacks: True Stories from the Canadian Rockies.* Toronto: McClelland & Stewart, 1999. This book tells of Marty's experiences in the mountains and of the people he came in contact with in his role as a park warden. Along the way, he describes how his experiences with both nature and fellow humans have shaped his views on conservation today.

McMillan, Alan D. *Native Peoples and Cultures of Canada.* Vancouver: Douglas & McIntyre, 1995. A comprehensive look at the archaeology, anthropology, and ethnography of the native peoples of Canada. The last chapters delve into the problems facing these people today.

Robinson, Bart. *A Castle in the Wilderness.* Banff: Summerthought Publishing, 2019. This detailed history of one of the world's best-known hotels includes up-to-date changes, rare black-and-white photographs, and interviews with longtime employees.

Schäffer, Mary T. S. *A Hunter of Peace.* Banff: Whyte Museum of the Canadian Rockies, 2014. This book was first published in 1911 by G. P. Putnam & Sons, New York, under the name *Old Indian Trails of the Canadian Rockies.* Tales of Schäffer's adventures recount the exploration of the Rockies during the turn of the 20th century. Many of the author's photographs appear throughout.

Scott, Chic. *Pushing the Limits.* Victoria: Rocky Mountain Books, 2000. A chronological history of mountaineering in Canada, with special emphasis on many largely unknown climbers and their feats, as well as the story of Swiss guides in Canada and a short section on ice climbing.

RECREATION

Butcher, Marlis. *Park Bagger.* Victoria: Rocky Mountain Books, 2021. A collection of inspirational adventure stories that the author has put together over decades of exploring the Canadian Rockies and beyond.

Corbett, Bill. *The 11,000ers.* Victoria: Rocky Mountain Books, 2004. A reference to all 54 mountain peaks in the Canadian Rockies that are higher than 11,000 feet. The author discusses the human history of each, as well as access and popular routes.

Correy, Ryan. *Bikepacking in the Canadian Rockies.* Victoria: Rocky Mountain Books, 2021. Renowned long-distance rider Correy researched and wrote about 10 long-distance bike routes before his untimely death in 2018. The book includes maps, detailed directions, and color photos.

Gadd, Ben. *The Canadian Hiker's and Backpacker's Handbook.* Vancouver: Whitecap Books, 2008. Whether you're interested in learning the basics or a seasoned traveler, this is the best book for reading up on your backcountry and hiking skills.

Kane, Alan. *Scrambles in the Canadian Rockies.* Victoria: Rocky Mountain Books, 2015. Routes detailed in this regularly revised guide lead to summits without the use of ropes or mountaineering equipment.

Martin, John, and Jon Jones. *Sport Climbs in the Canadian Rockies.* Victoria: Rocky Mountain Books, 2011. Details 2,000 routes through the Bow Valley and Banff National Park. Includes maps and photographs.

Patton, Brian. *The Best Day Hikes in Banff National Park.* Banff: Summerthought Publishing, 2018. The coauthor of the *Canadian Rockies Trail Guide* details his favorite day hikes in this full-color guidebook.

Patton, Brian, and Bart Robinson. *Canadian Rockies Trail Guide.* Banff: Summerthought Publishing, 2022. First published in 1971 and now in its tenth edition, this book covers 230 hiking trails and 3,400 kilometers (2,100 miles) in the mountain national parks as well as in surrounding provincial parks. At least one full page is devoted to each trail, making it the most comprehensive hiking book available.

Potter, Mike. *Fire Lookouts in the Canadian Rockies.* Calgary: Luminous Compositions, 1998. This book specializes in hikes to fire lookouts. Trail descriptions are detailed, and each is accompanied by the history of the lookout.

Scott, Chic, and Darren Farley. *Ski Trails of the Canadian Rockies*. Victoria: Rocky Mountain Books, 2016. After reading this book, it quickly becomes apparent that there is a lot more to wintertime than the downhill alpine resorts. You'll find yourself spoiled for options with this book covering both groomed and backcountry trails.

GUIDEBOOKS AND MAPS

Gem Trek Maps. Banff. This company produces waterproof and tearproof hiking maps for all regions of the Canadian Rockies. Relief shading clearly and concisely shows elevation, and all hiking trails have been plotted using a global positioning system. On the backs of the maps are descriptions of attractions and hikes, along with general, practical, and educational information. Highly recommended. Website: www.gemtrek.com.

Hempstead, Andrew. *Moon British Columbia*. Berkeley, CA: Avalon Travel. Regularly updated guide that comprehensively covers Canada's westernmost province.

MapArt. Driving maps for all of Canada, including provinces and cities. Maps are published as old-fashioned foldout versions, as well as laminated and in atlas form. Website: www.mapart.com.

The Milepost. Bellevue, WA: Vernon Publications. This annual publication is a must-have for those traveling through western Canada and Alaska. The maps and logged highway descriptions are incredibly detailed. Most northern bookstores stock *The Milepost*, or call 800/726-4707 or go to www.milepost.com.

Patton, Brian. *Parkways of the Canadian Rockies*. Banff: Summerthought Publishing, 2008. A comprehensive map and driving guide to all major highways. Includes color photography and details of many short hikes.

PERIODICALS

The Canadian Alpine Journal. Canmore. The annual magazine of the Alpine Club of Canada, with mountaineering articles from its members and climbers from around the world. Website: www.alpineclubofcanada.ca.

Canadian Geographic. Ottawa: Royal Canadian Geographical Society. Bimonthly publication pertaining to Canada's natural and human histories and resources. Website: www.canadiangeographic.ca.

Explore. Vancouver. Bimonthly publication of adventure travel throughout Canada. Website: www.explore-mag.com.

Nature Canada. Ottawa. Quarterly magazine of the Canadian Nature Federation. Website: www.cnf.ca.

Western Living. Vancouver. Lifestyle magazine for western Canada. Includes travel, history, homes, and cooking. Website: www.westernliving.ca.

REFERENCE

Daffern, Tony. *Avalanche Safety for Skiers & Climbers*. Victoria: Rocky Mountain Books, 1992. Covers all aspects of avalanches, including their causes, practical information on how to avoid them, and a section on rescue techniques and first aid.

Guide to Manuscripts: The Fonds and Collections of the Archives, Whyte Museum of the Canadian Rockies. Banff: Whyte Museum of the Canadian Rockies, 1988. This book makes finding items in the museum easy by providing alphabetical lists of all parts of the collection.

Karamitsanis, Aphrodite. *Place Names of Alberta*. Calgary: University of Alberta Press, 1991. Volume 1 alphabetically lists all geographic features of the mountains and foothills, with explanations of each name's origin. Volume 2 does the same for southern Alberta.

Internet Resources

TRAVEL PLANNING

Destination Canada
www.canada.travel
Official tourism website for all of Canada.

Indigenous Tourism Association of Canada
www.indigenoustourism.ca
The website includes a database of Indigenous travel experiences.

Thecanadianrockies.com
www.thecanadianrockies.com
Extensive travel planning website for all of the Canadian Rockies; includes a blog that addresses local tourism issues.

Tourism British Columbia
www.hellobc.com
Learn more about the province, plan your travels, and download tourism literature.

Travel Alberta
www.travelalberta.com
Similar to the British Columbia tourism website, but includes information on Banff and Jasper National Parks.

PARKS

Alberta Parks
www.albertaparks.ca
BC Parks
www.env.gov.bc.ca
These departments oversee management of the provincial parks in Alberta and British Columbia. The websites detail facilities, fees, and seasonal openings of the parks.

Parks Canada
www.pc.gc.ca
Official website of the agency that manages Canada's national parks and national historic sites. The website has information on each park and historic site, including fees, camping, and wildlife.

Parks Canada Reservation Service
www.reservation.pc.gc.ca
Online reservation service for national park campgrounds.

GOVERNMENT

Citizenship and Immigration Canada
www.cic.gc.ca
Check this government website for anything related to entry into Canada.

Environment Canada
www.weather.gc.ca
Seven-day forecasts from across Canada, including dozens of locations throughout the Canadian Rockies. Includes weather archives such as seasonal trends and snowfall history.

Government of Canada
www.gc.ca
The official website of the Canadian government.

ACCOMMODATIONS

Banff Lodging Co.
www.bestofbanff.com
Operates 10 hotels in Banff and 2 in Canmore.

Canadian Rocky Mountain Resorts
www.crmr.com
Small chain of upscale Canadian Rockies resorts.

Fairmont Hotels and Resorts
www.fairmont.com
Lodging chain that owns famous mountain resorts such as the Banff Springs, Chateau Lake Louise, and Jasper Park Lodge.

Hostelling International-Canada
www.hihostels.ca
Canadian arm of the worldwide organization.

Mountain Park Lodges
www.banffjaspercollection.com
Hotels in Banff and Jasper owned by the Pursuit company.

CONSERVATION

Biosphere Institute of the Bow Valley
www.biosphereinstitute.org
Canmore-based organization mandated to gather and circulate information on management of the Bow River watershed. Online references include studies, publications, and human-use guidelines for the region.

Bow Valley Wildsmart
www.wildsmart.ca
Operating under the banner of the Biosphere Institute, this website is a wealth of information on how to stay safe in the Bow Valley, including reported wildlife sightings.

Canadian Parks and Wilderness Society
www.cpaws.org
Nonprofit organization that is instrumental in highlighting conservation issues throughout Canada. The link to the Alberta-Southern chapter provides local information and a schedule of guided walks.

Yellowstone to Yukon Conservation Initiative
www.y2y.net
Network of 800 groups working on conservation issues in the Canadian Rockies and beyond.

TRANSPORTATION AND TOURS

Air Canada
www.aircanada.ca
Canada's national airline.

Pursuit
www.banffjaspercollection.com
Banff-based operator offering attractions, tours, airport shuttles, and accommodations.

Rocky Mountaineer
www.rockymountaineer.com
Luxurious rail service from Vancouver to Banff and Jasper.

VIA Rail
www.viarail.ca
Passenger rail service across Canada.

Westjet
www.westjet.com
Calgary-based airline with flights throughout Canada and beyond.

PUBLISHERS

Gem Trek Maps
www.gemtrek.com
This Banff-based company produces award-winning topo maps covering all the most popular regions of the Canadian Rockies, including a series of waterproof and tearproof hiking maps.

Lone Pine
www.lonepinepublishing.com
Respected for its field guides, this company has books on almost every natural history subject pertinent to the Canadian Rockies.

Rocky Mountain Books
www.rmbooks.com
Check out this publisher's catalog, and you'll surely be impressed by the list of local history and outdoor recreation guides.

Summerthought Publishing
www.summerthought.com
The world's only publisher devoted solely to publishing books about the Canadian Rockies. If you plan on doing lots of hiking, you'll want a copy of their authoritative *Canadian Rockies Trail Guide*. Index

Index

List of Maps

Photo Credits

All photos © Andrew Hempstead except: page 6 © (top right) Parks Canada / Scott Munn; page 8 © Stevengaertner | Dreamstime.com; page 77 © (bottom) Justin Roy | Unsplash.com; page 97 © (top) Andy Holmes | Unsplash.com; (bottom) Riekefoto | Dreamstime.com; page 102 © (bottom) Skylightpictures | Dreamstime.com; page 107 © (top left) Accolade Creative | Unsplash.com; page 117 © (bottom left) Hanasladeckova | Dreamstime.com

DOMINICAN REPUBLIC

JAMAICA

PUERTO RICO

AMALFI COAST

AMSTERDAM
BRUSSELS & BRUGES

EGYPT

Greek Islands
& ATHENS

ICELAND

WITH A ROAD TRIP ON THE RING ROAD

MOROCCO

NORMANDY
& BRITTANY

WITH MONT-SAINT MICHEL

PORTUGAL

PRAGUE, VIENNA
& BUDAPEST

ROME,
FLORENCE
& VENICE

Scotland

SOUTHERN
ITALY

SICILY, PUGLIA, NAPLES & THE AMALFI COAST

BAHAMAS

Provinces & Regions

ATLANTIC CANADA
Nova Scotia, New Brunswick, Prince Edward Island, Newfoundland & Labrador
ANDREW HEMPSTEAD

BRITISH COLUMBIA
Including the Alaska Highway
ANDREW HEMPSTEAD

MOON
CANADIAN ROCKIES
WITH BANFF & JASPER NATIONAL PARKS
SCENIC DRIVES · WILDLIFE
HIKING & SKIING
ANDREW HEMPSTEAD

NEWFOUNDLAND & LABRADOR
ANDREW HEMPSTEAD

NOVA SCOTIA
NEW BRUNSWICK & PRINCE EDWARD ISLAND
ANDREW HEMPSTEAD

VANCOUVER
Including Victoria, Vancouver Island & Whistler
CAROLYN B. HELLER

VICTORIA & VANCOUVER ISLAND
ANDREW HEMPSTEAD

Best Ofs & Road Trips

MOON
- BEST OF -
GLACIER, BANFF, & JASPER
MAKE THE MOST OF ONE TO THREE DAYS IN THE PARKS
TOP SIGHTS, TOP HIKES, TOP SCENIC DRIVES
BECKY LOMAX & ANDREW HEMPSTEAD

MOON
PACIFIC NORTHWEST
Road Trip
OUTDOOR ADVENTURES AND CREATIVE CITIES FROM THE COAST TO THE MOUNTAINS
ALLISON WILLIAMS

MOON
U.S. & CANADIAN ROCKY MOUNTAINS
Road Trip
DRIVE THE CONTINENTAL DIVIDE AND EXPLORE 9 NATIONAL PARKS
BECKY LOMAX

MOON
VANCOUVER & CANADIAN ROCKIES
Road Trip
VICTORIA, BANFF, JASPER, CALGARY, THE OKANAGAN, WHISTLER & THE SEA-TO-SKY HIGHWAY
CAROLYN B. HELLER

MAP SYMBOLS

══════	Highway	○	City/Town	✈	International Airport	🇹	Trailhead
═════	Primary Road	◉	State Capital	✈	Airfield	🇧	Bike Trailhead
────	Other Road	⊛	National Capital	▲	Mountain	🇵	Parking Area
═ ═ ═ ═	Unpaved Road	★	Point of Interest	✦	Unique Natural Feature	⚲	Golf Course
----------	Trail	•	Accommodation	✦	Unique Natural Feature Hydro	⛷	Ski Area
·············	Ferry	▾	Restaurant/Bar	🗮	Waterfall	⬥	Place of Worship
━ ━ ▸	Railroad	■	Other Site			⛽	Gas Station
════	Pedestrian Walkway	♠	Park	▲	Campground	⬭	Glacier
⫘⫘⫘	Stairs						

CONVERSION TABLES

°C = (°F − 32) / 1.8
°F = (°C x 1.8) + 32
1 inch = 2.54 centimeters (cm)
1 foot = 0.304 meters (m)
1 yard = 0.914 meters
1 mile = 1.6093 kilometers (km)
1 km = 0.6214 miles
1 fathom = 1.8288 m
1 chain = 20.1168 m
1 furlong = 201.168 m
1 acre = 0.4047 hectares
1 sq km = 100 hectares
1 sq mile = 2.59 square km
1 ounce = 28.35 grams
1 pound = 0.4536 kilograms
1 short ton = 0.90718 metric ton
1 short ton = 2,000 pounds
1 long ton = 1.016 metric tons
1 long ton = 2,240 pounds
1 metric ton = 1,000 kilograms
1 quart = 0.94635 liters
1 US gallon = 3.7854 liters
1 Imperial gallon = 4.5459 liters
1 nautical mile = 1.852 km

MOON BANFF NATIONAL PARK

Avalon Travel
Hachette Book Group
1700 Fourth Street
Berkeley, CA 94710, USA
www.moon.com

Editor: Kimberly Ehart
Acquiring Editor: Nikki Ioakimedes
Series Manager: Kathryn Ettinger
Copy Editor: Brett Keener
Graphics and Production Coordinator: Ravina Schneider
Cover Design: Kimberly Glyder
Map Editor: Albert Angulo
Cartographers: Brian Shotwell, Karin Dahl, and John Culp
Indexer: Greg Jewett

ISBN-13: 978-1-64049-700-9

Printing History
1st Edition — 2016
4th Edition — December 2022
5 4 3 2 1

Front cover photo: Moraine Lake © Kaedeenari | Alamy Stock Photo
Back cover photo: bighorn sheep © Izanbar | Dreamstime.com

Printed in Malaysia for Imago